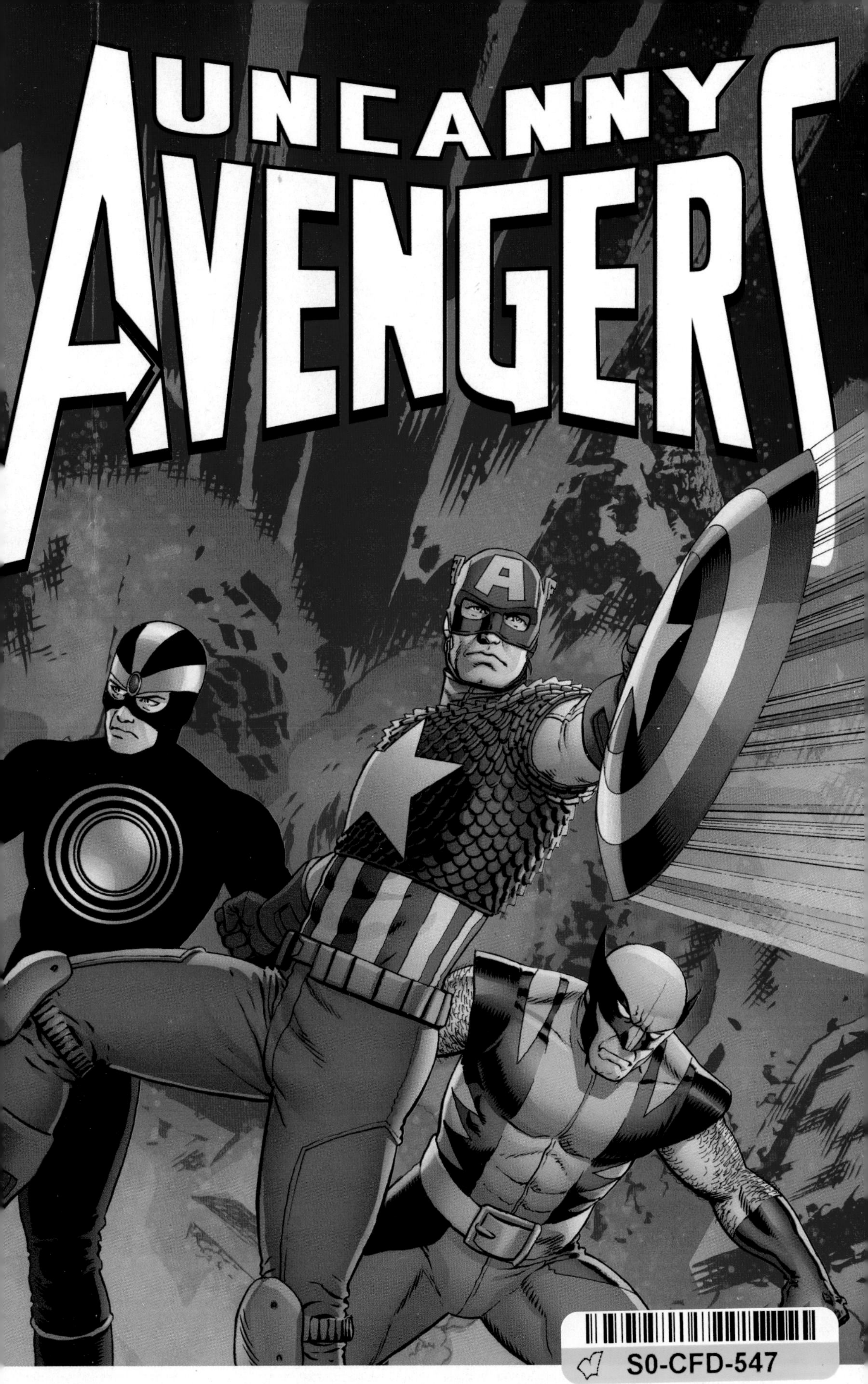
UNCANNY
AVENGERS

THE RED SHADOW

UNCANNY AVENGERS VOL. 1: THE RED SHADOW. Contains material originally published in magazine form as UNCANNY AVENGERS #1-5. First printing 2014. ISBN# 978-0-7851-6603-0. Published by MA WORLDWIDE, INC., a subsidiary of MARVEL ENTERTAINMENT, LLC. OFFICE OF PUBLICATION: 135 West 50th Street, New York, NY 10020. Copyright © 2013 and 2014 Marvel Characters, Inc. All rights reserve characters featured in this issue and the distinctive names and likenesses thereof, and all related indicia are trademarks of Marvel Characters, Inc. No similarity between any of the names, characters, persons, a institutions in this magazine with those of any living or dead person or institution is intended, and any such similarity which may exist is purely coincidental. **Printed in the U.S.A.** ALAN FINE, EVP - Office of the Pres Marvel Worldwide, Inc. and EVP & CMO Marvel Characters B.V.; DAN BUCKLEY, Publisher & President - Print, Animation & Digital Divisions; JOE QUESADA, Chief Creative Officer; TOM BREVOORT, SVP of Publishing; BOGART, SVP of Operations & Procurement, Publishing; C.B. CEBULSKI, SVP of Creator & Content Development; DAVID GABRIEL, SVP of Print & Digital Publishing Sales; JIM O'KEEFE, VP of Operations & Logistics CARR, Executive Director of Publishing Technology; SUSAN CRESPI, Editorial Operations Manager; ALEX MORALES, Publishing Operations Manager; STAN LEE, Chairman Emeritus. For information regarding adve in Marvel Comics or on Marvel.com, please contact Niza Disla, Director of Marvel Partnerships, at ndisla@marvel.com. For Marvel subscription inquiries, please call 800-217-9158. **Manufactured between 1/3.** **and 2/10/2014 by R.R. DONNELLEY, INC., SALEM, VA, USA.**

10 9 8 7 6 5 4 3 2 1

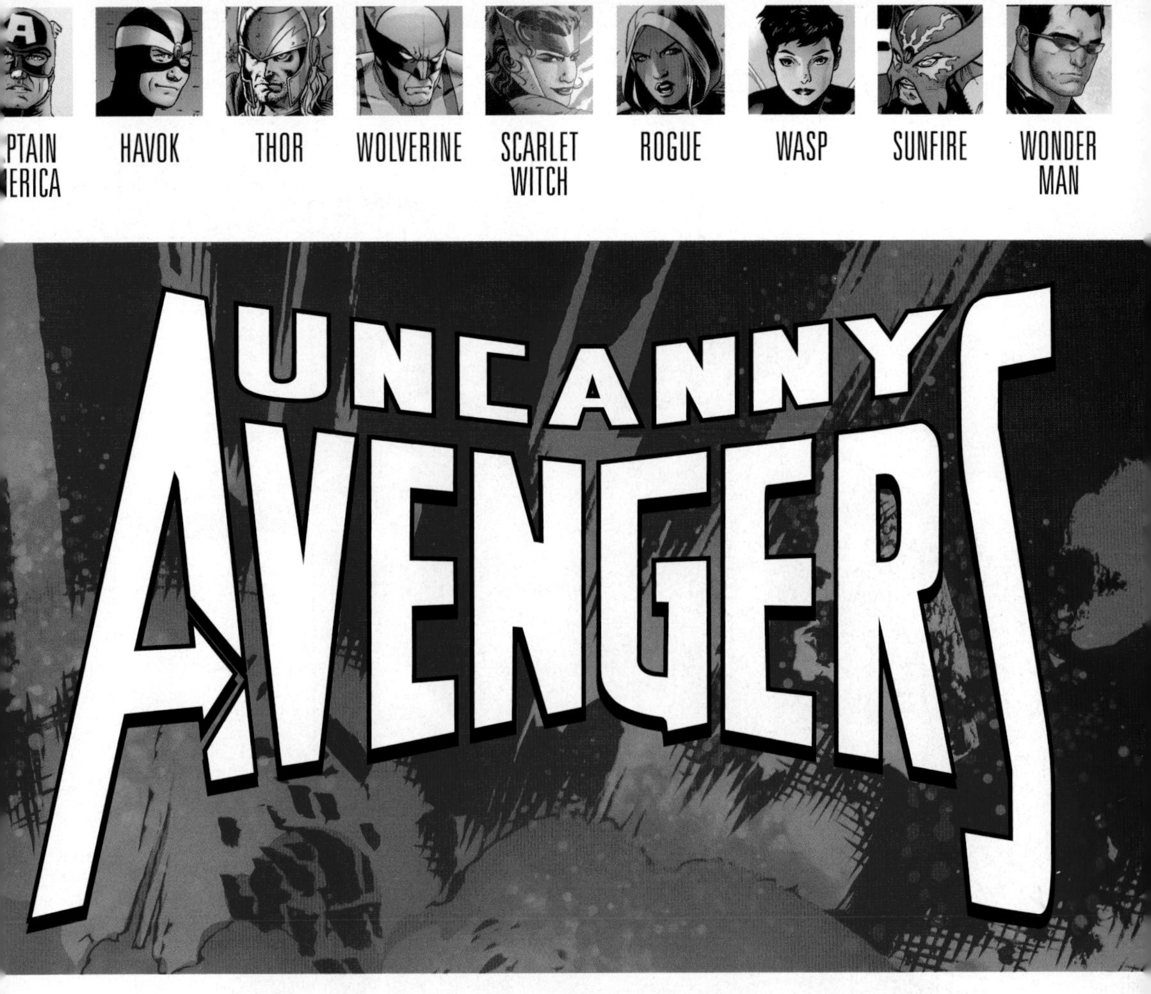

PTAIN ERICA | HAVOK | THOR | WOLVERINE | SCARLET WITCH | ROGUE | WASP | SUNFIRE | WONDER MAN

UNCANNY AVENGERS

THE RED SHADOW

WRITER
RICK REMENDER

ARTIST, #1–4
JOHN CASSADAY

PENCILER, #5
OLIVIER COIPEL

INKER, #5
MARK MORALES

COLOR ARTISTS
LAURA MARTIN
WITH
LARRY MOLINAR (#4)

LETTERER
VC'S CHRIS ELIOPOULOS

COVER ART
JOHN CASSADAY
& LAURA MARTIN

EDITORS
TOM BREVOORT
WITH DANIEL KETCHUM

COLLECTION EDITOR: JENNIFER GRÜNWALD
ASSOCIATE MANAGING EDITOR: ALEX STARBUCK
EDITOR, SPECIAL PROJECTS: MARK D. BEAZLEY
SENIOR EDITOR, SPECIAL PROJECTS: JEFF YOUNGQUIST
SVP PRINT, SALES & MARKETING: DAVID GABRIEL
BOOK DESIGN: JEFF POWELL AND RODOLFO MURAGUCHI

EDITOR IN CHIEF: AXEL ALONSO
CHIEF CREATIVE OFFICER: JOE QUESADA
PUBLISHER: DAN BUCKLEY
EXECUTIVE PRODUCER: ALAN FINE

UNCANNY AVENGERS #1

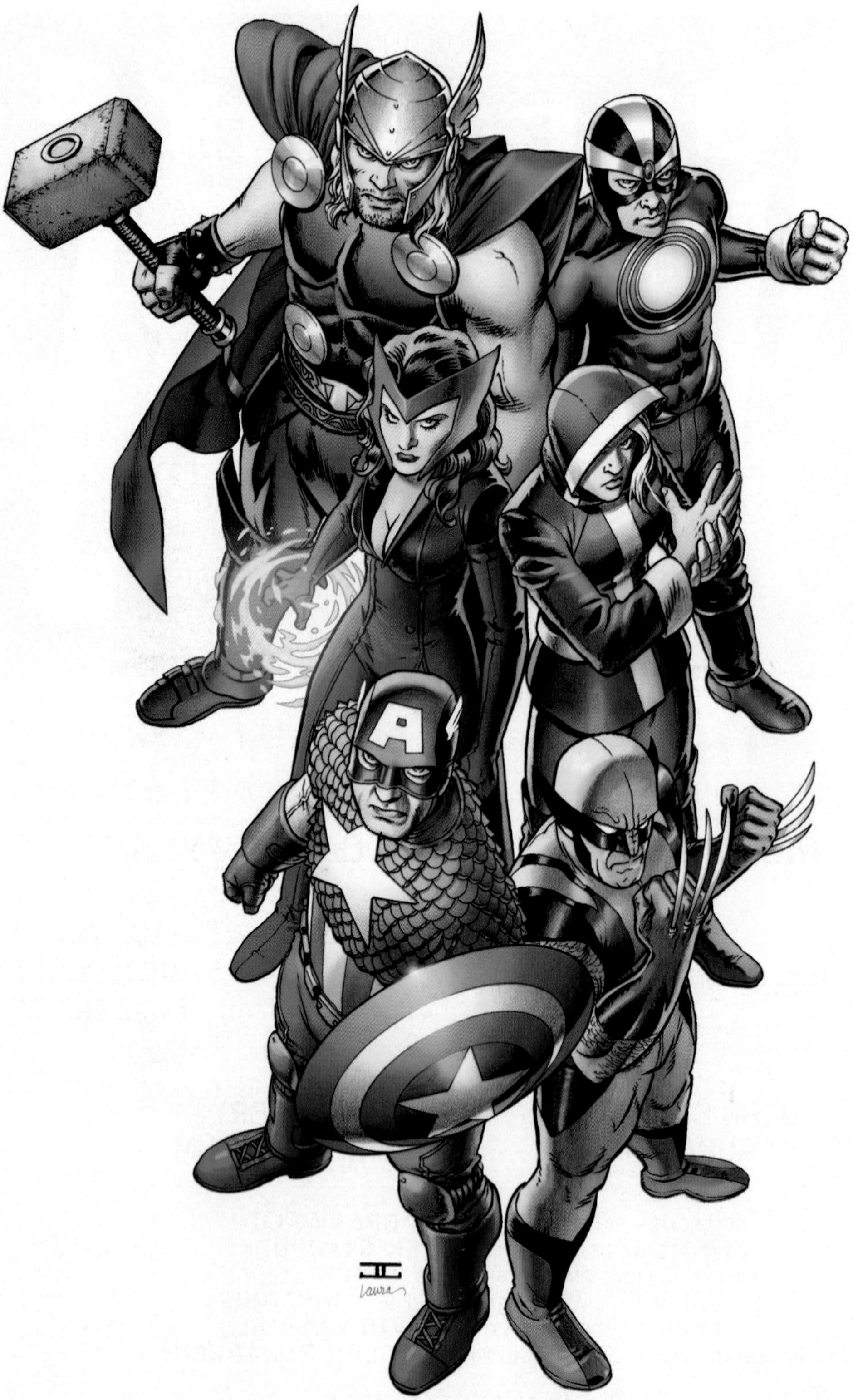

Laura

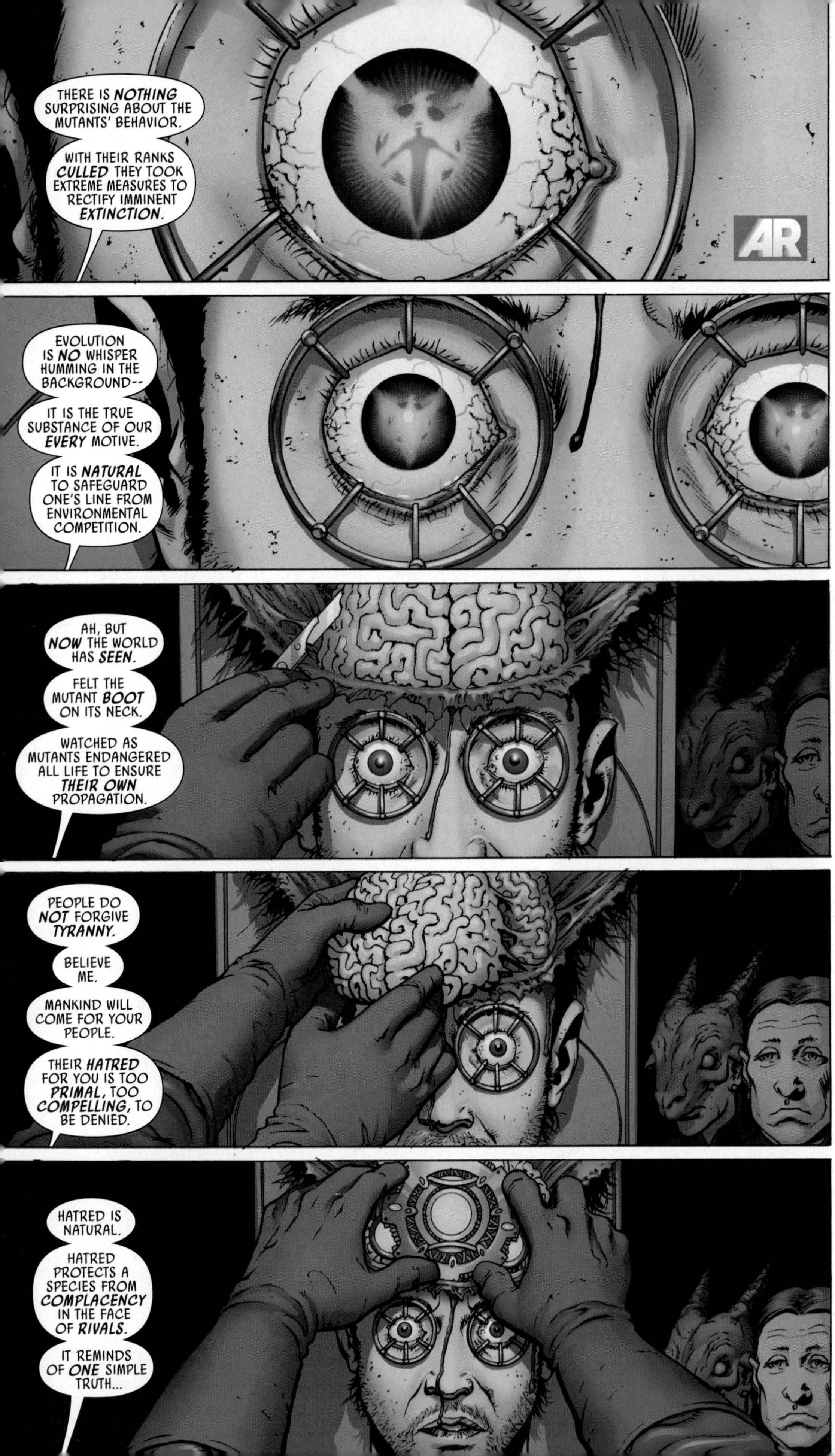

THERE IS NOTHING SURPRISING ABOUT THE MUTANTS' BEHAVIOR.
WITH THEIR RANKS CULLED THEY TOOK EXTREME MEASURES TO RECTIFY IMMINENT EXTINCTION.
AR
EVOLUTION IS NO WHISPER HUMMING IN THE BACKGROUND--
IT IS THE TRUE SUBSTANCE OF OUR EVERY MOTIVE.
IT IS NATURAL TO SAFEGUARD ONE'S LINE FROM ENVIRONMENTAL COMPETITION.
AH, BUT NOW THE WORLD HAS SEEN.
FELT THE MUTANT BOOT ON ITS NECK.
WATCHED AS MUTANTS ENDANGERED ALL LIFE TO ENSURE THEIR OWN PROPAGATION.
PEOPLE DO NOT FORGIVE TYRANNY.
BELIEVE ME.
MANKIND WILL COME FOR YOUR PEOPLE.
THEIR HATRED FOR YOU IS TOO PRIMAL, TOO COMPELLING, TO BE DENIED.
HATRED IS NATURAL.
HATRED PROTECTS A SPECIES FROM COMPLACENCY IN THE FACE OF RIVALS.
IT REMINDS OF ONE SIMPLE TRUTH...

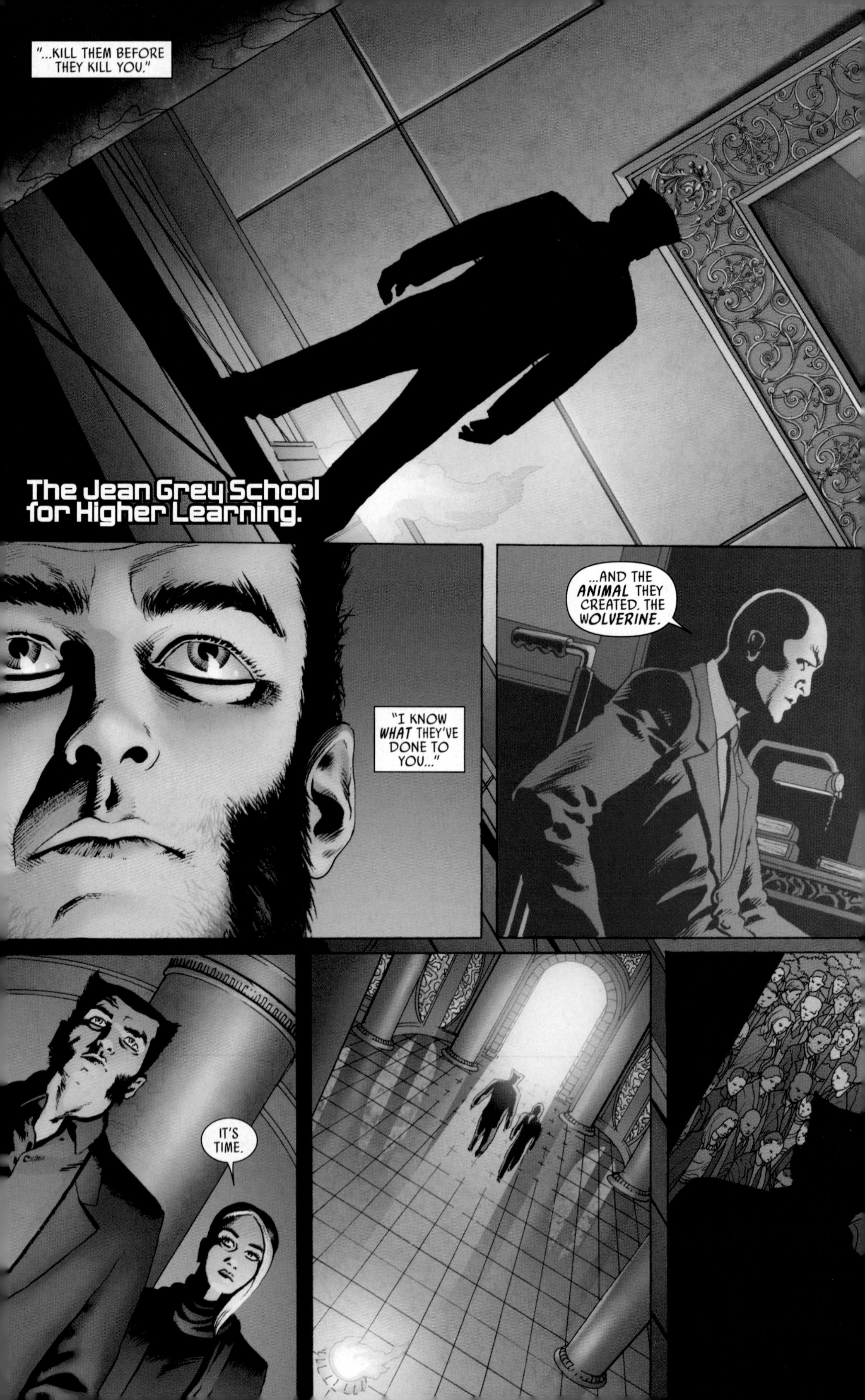
"...KILL THEM BEFORE THEY KILL YOU."
The Jean Grey School for Higher Learning.
"I KNOW WHAT THEY'VE DONE TO YOU..."
...AND THE ANIMAL THEY CREATED. THE WOLVERINE.
IT'S TIME.

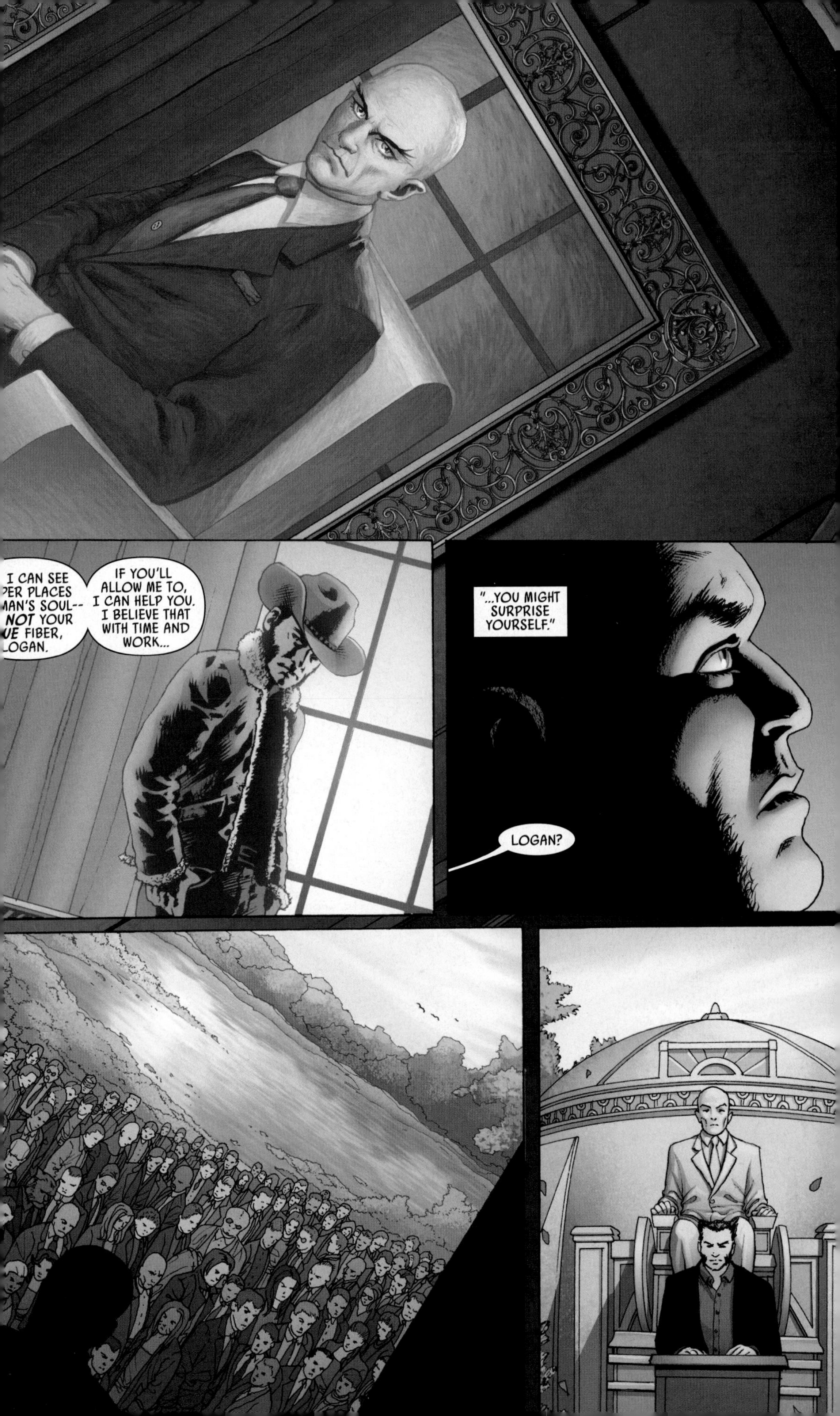
I CAN SEE
PER PLACES
MAN'S SOUL--
NOT YOUR
UE FIBER,
LOGAN.
IF YOU'LL ALLOW ME TO, I CAN HELP YOU. I BELIEVE THAT WITH TIME AND WORK...
"...YOU MIGHT SURPRISE YOURSELF."
LOGAN?

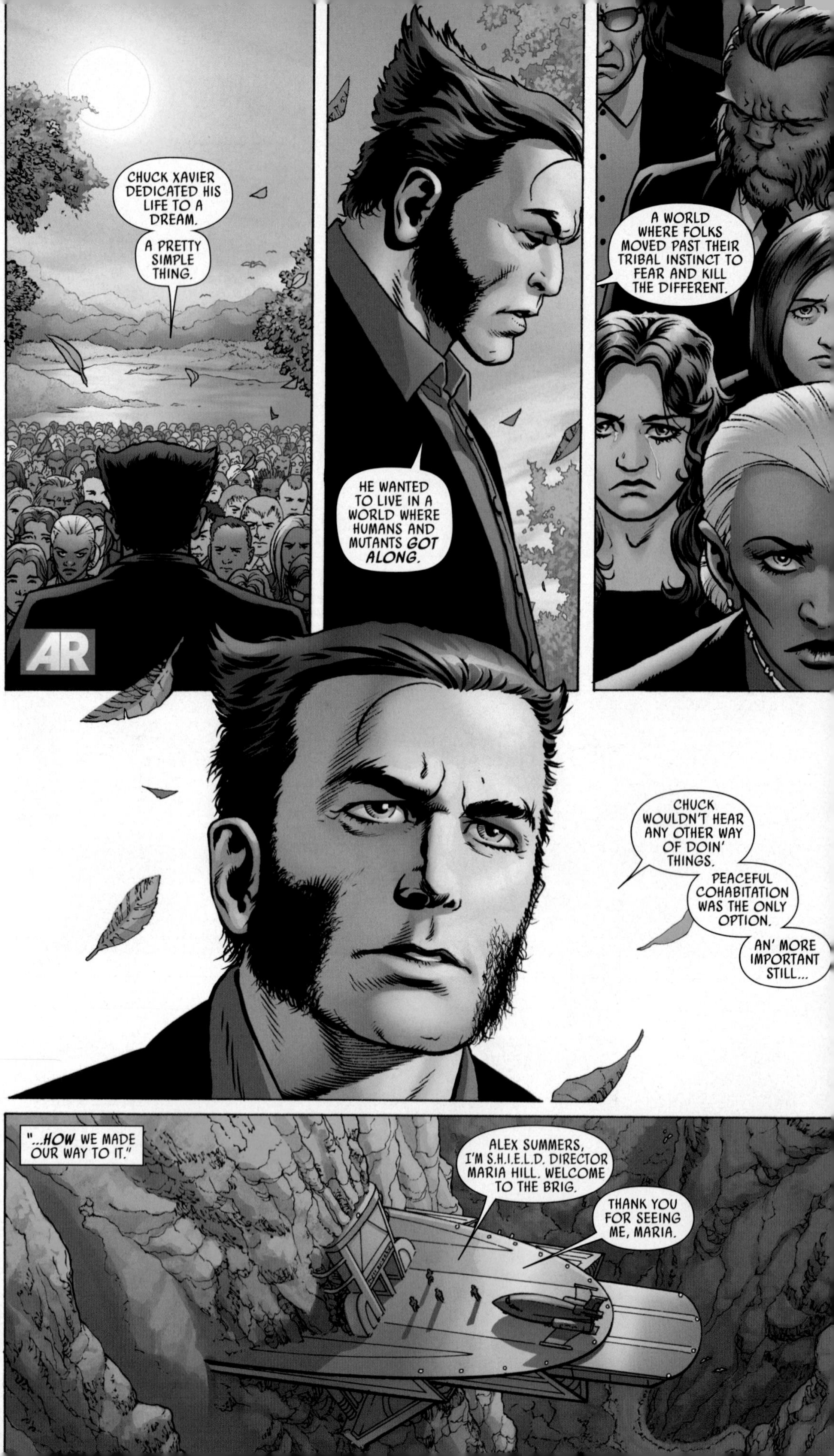
CHUCK XAVIER DEDICATED HIS LIFE TO A DREAM.
A PRETTY SIMPLE THING.
HE WANTED TO LIVE IN A WORLD WHERE HUMANS AND MUTANTS GOT ALONG.
A WORLD WHERE FOLKS MOVED PAST THEIR TRIBAL INSTINCT TO FEAR AND KILL THE DIFFERENT.
CHUCK WOULDN'T HEAR ANY OTHER WAY OF DOIN' THINGS.
PEACEFUL COHABITATION WAS THE ONLY OPTION.
AN' MORE IMPORTANT STILL...
"...HOW WE MADE OUR WAY TO IT."
ALEX SUMMERS, I'M S.H.I.E.L.D. DIRECTOR MARIA HILL. WELCOME TO THE BRIG.
THANK YOU FOR SEEING ME, MARIA.

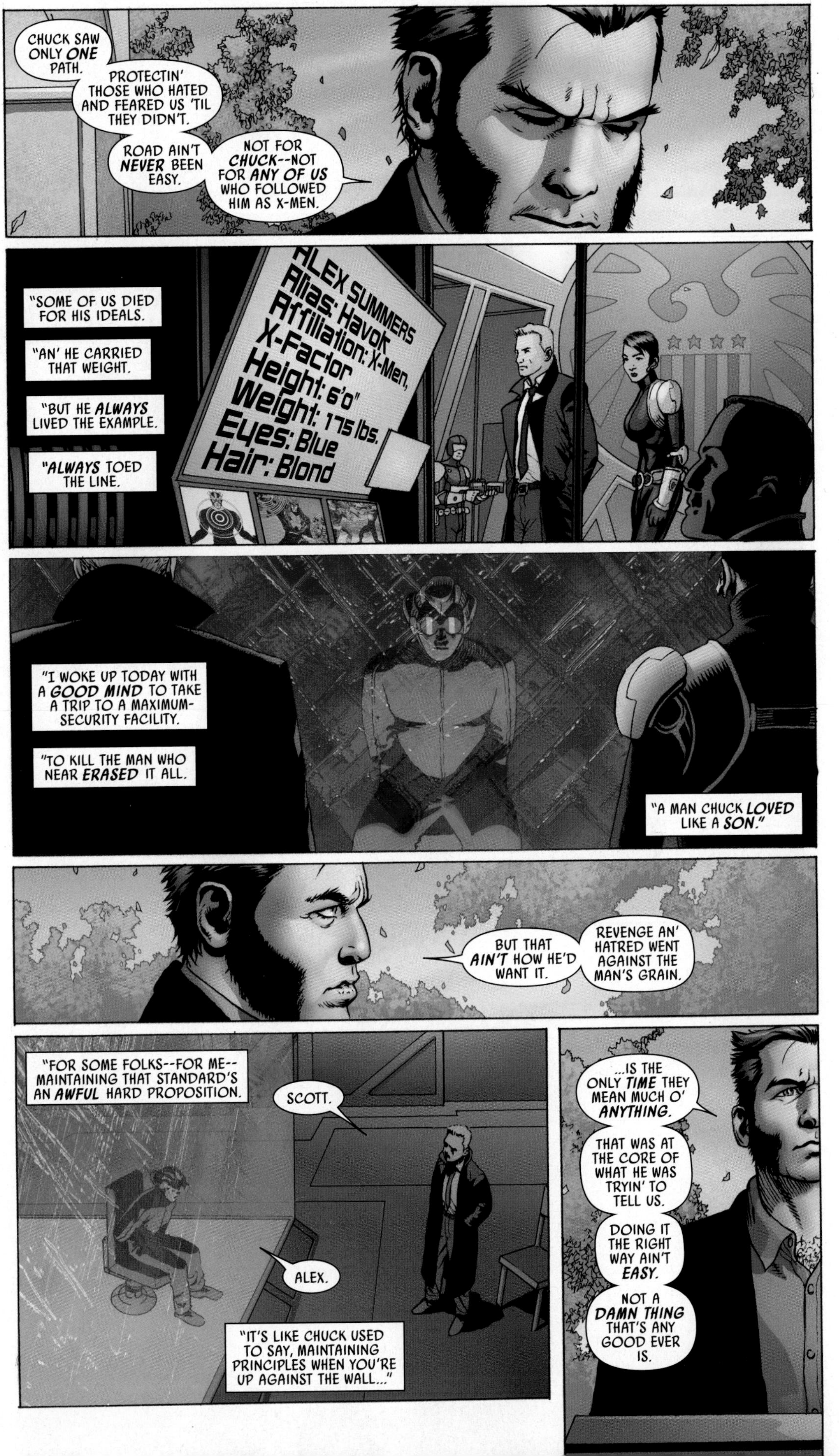

CHUCK SAW ONLY ONE PATH.
PROTECTIN' THOSE WHO HATED AND FEARED US 'TIL THEY DIDN'T.
ROAD AIN'T NEVER BEEN EASY.
NOT FOR CHUCK--NOT FOR ANY OF US WHO FOLLOWED HIM AS X-MEN.
"SOME OF US DIED FOR HIS IDEALS.
"AN' HE CARRIED THAT WEIGHT.
"BUT HE ALWAYS LIVED THE EXAMPLE.
"ALWAYS TOED THE LINE.
ALEX SUMMERS
Alias: Havok
Affiliation: X-Men, X-Factor
Height: 6'0"
Weight: 175 lbs.
Eyes: Blue
Hair: Blond
"I WOKE UP TODAY WITH A GOOD MIND TO TAKE A TRIP TO A MAXIMUM-SECURITY FACILITY.
"TO KILL THE MAN WHO NEAR ERASED IT ALL.
"A MAN CHUCK LOVED LIKE A SON."
BUT THAT AIN'T HOW HE'D WANT IT.
REVENGE AN' HATRED WENT AGAINST THE MAN'S GRAIN.
"FOR SOME FOLKS--FOR ME--MAINTAINING THAT STANDARD'S AN AWFUL HARD PROPOSITION.
SCOTT.
ALEX.
"IT'S LIKE CHUCK USED TO SAY, MAINTAINING PRINCIPLES WHEN YOU'RE UP AGAINST THE WALL..."
...IS THE ONLY TIME THEY MEAN MUCH O' ANYTHING.
THAT WAS AT THE CORE OF WHAT HE WAS TRYIN' TO TELL US.
DOING IT THE RIGHT WAY AIN'T EASY.
NOT A DAMN THING THAT'S ANY GOOD EVER IS.

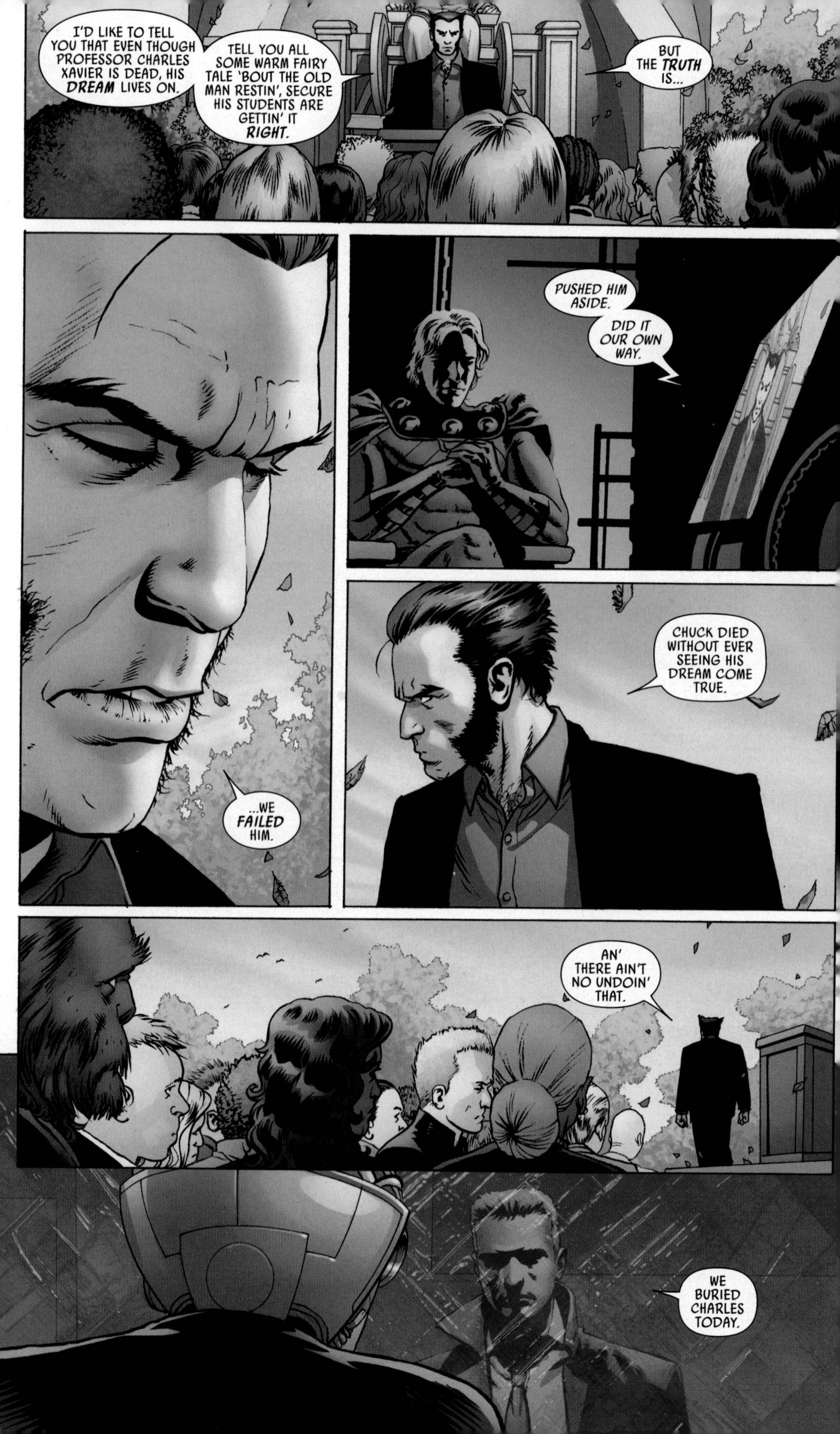
I'D LIKE TO TELL YOU THAT EVEN THOUGH PROFESSOR CHARLES XAVIER IS DEAD, HIS DREAM LIVES ON.
TELL YOU ALL SOME WARM FAIRY TALE 'BOUT THE OLD MAN RESTIN', SECURE HIS STUDENTS ARE GETTIN' IT RIGHT.
BUT THE TRUTH IS...
...WE FAILED HIM.
PUSHED HIM ASIDE.
DID IT OUR OWN WAY.
CHUCK DIED WITHOUT EVER SEEING HIS DREAM COME TRUE.
AN' THERE AIN'T NO UNDOIN' THAT.
WE BURIED CHARLES TODAY.

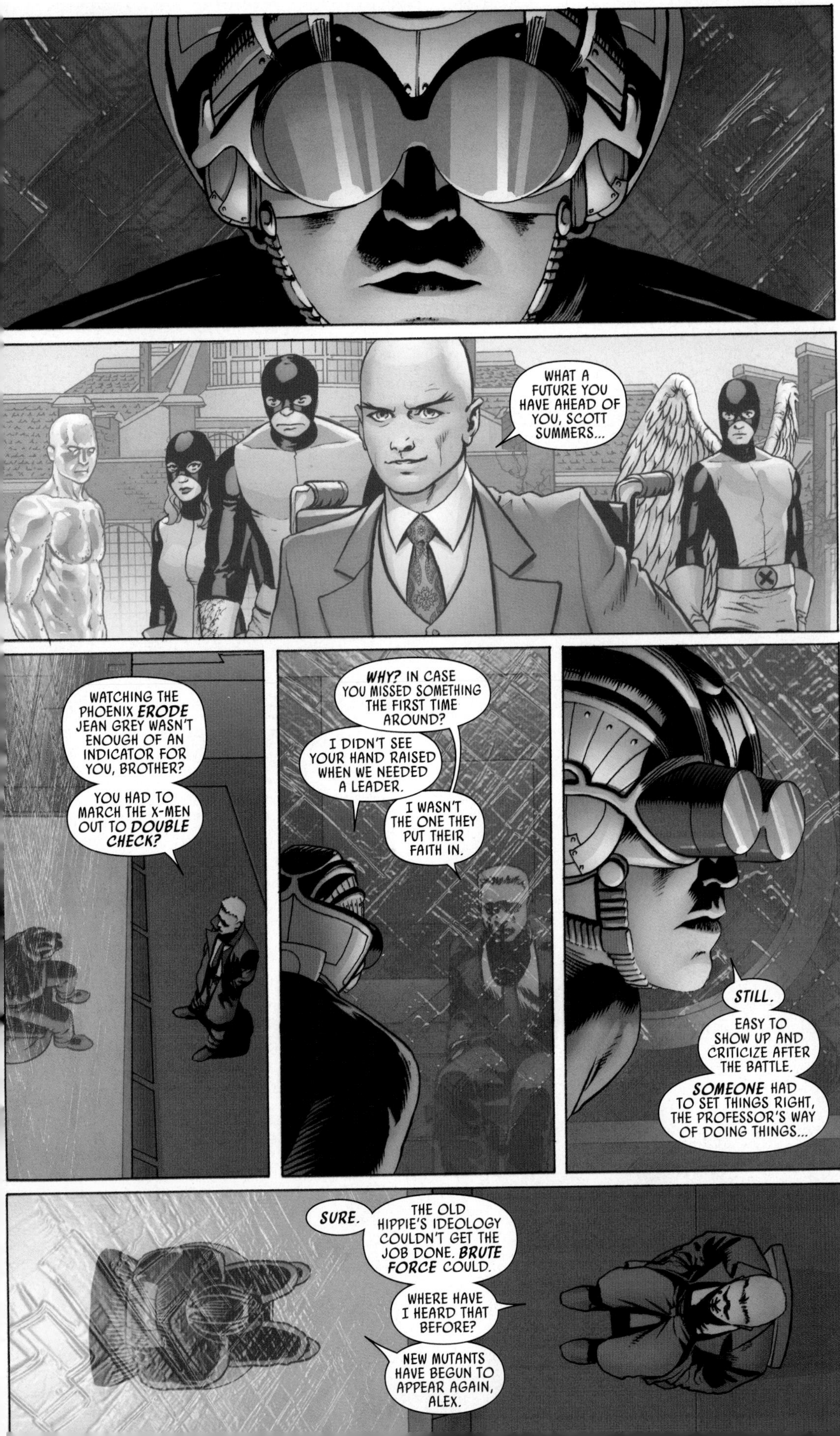

WHAT A FUTURE YOU HAVE AHEAD OF YOU, SCOTT SUMMERS...
WATCHING THE PHOENIX ERODE JEAN GREY WASN'T ENOUGH OF AN INDICATOR FOR YOU, BROTHER?
YOU HAD TO MARCH THE X-MEN OUT TO DOUBLE CHECK?
WHY? IN CASE YOU MISSED SOMETHING THE FIRST TIME AROUND?
I DIDN'T SEE YOUR HAND RAISED WHEN WE NEEDED A LEADER.
I WASN'T THE ONE THEY PUT THEIR FAITH IN.
STILL.
EASY TO SHOW UP AND CRITICIZE AFTER THE BATTLE.
SOMEONE HAD TO SET THINGS RIGHT, THE PROFESSOR'S WAY OF DOING THINGS...
SURE.
THE OLD HIPPIE'S IDEOLOGY COULDN'T GET THE JOB DONE. BRUTE FORCE COULD.
WHERE HAVE I HEARD THAT BEFORE?
NEW MUTANTS HAVE BEGUN TO APPEAR AGAIN, ALEX.

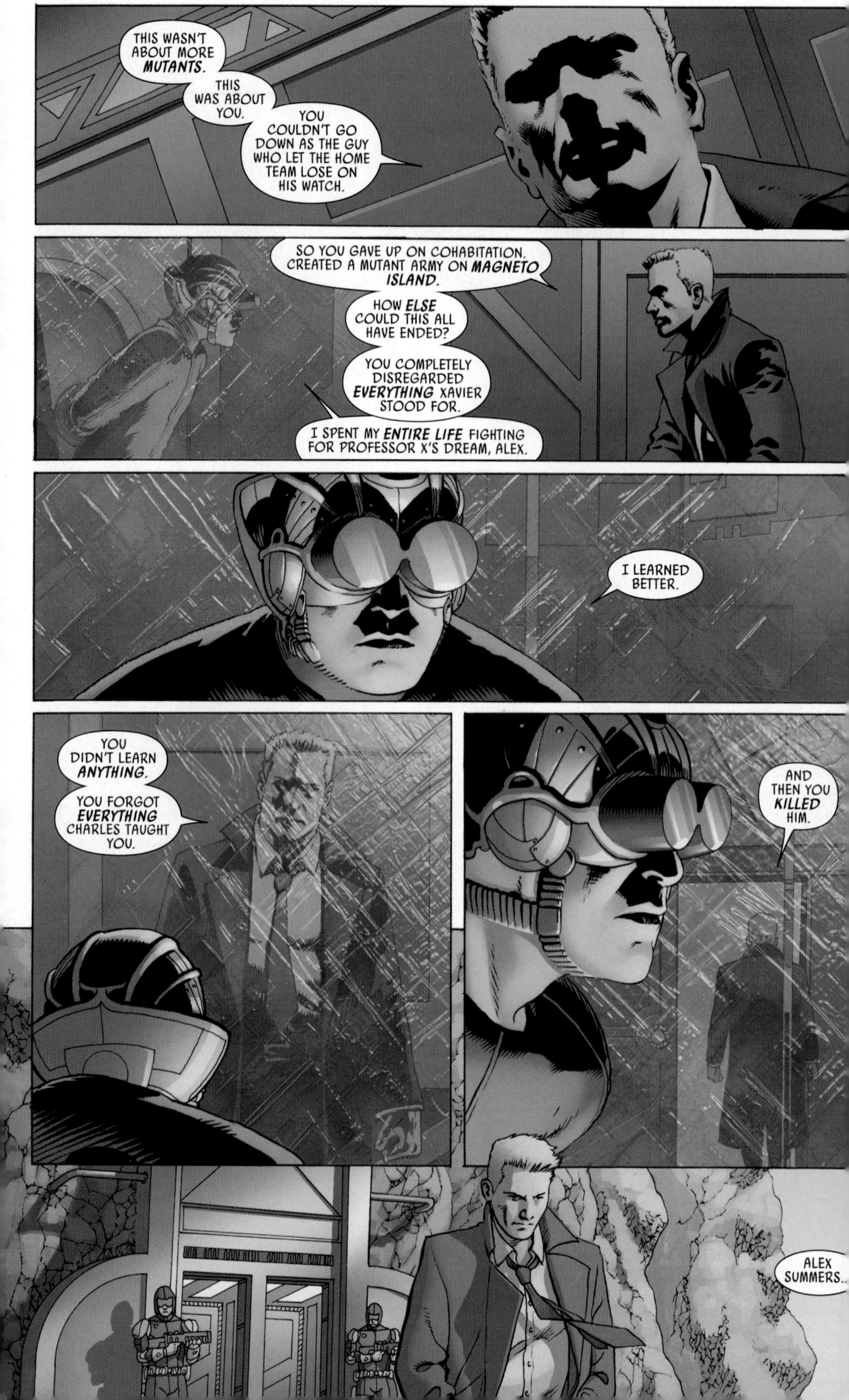
THIS WASN'T ABOUT MORE MUTANTS.
THIS WAS ABOUT YOU.
YOU COULDN'T GO DOWN AS THE GUY WHO LET THE HOME TEAM LOSE ON HIS WATCH.
SO YOU GAVE UP ON COHABITATION. CREATED A MUTANT ARMY ON MAGNETO ISLAND.
HOW ELSE COULD THIS ALL HAVE ENDED?
YOU COMPLETELY DISREGARDED EVERYTHING XAVIER STOOD FOR.
I SPENT MY ENTIRE LIFE FIGHTING FOR PROFESSOR X'S DREAM, ALEX.
I LEARNED BETTER.
YOU DIDN'T LEARN ANYTHING.
YOU FORGOT EVERYTHING CHARLES TAUGHT YOU.
AND THEN YOU KILLED HIM.
ALEX SUMMERS...

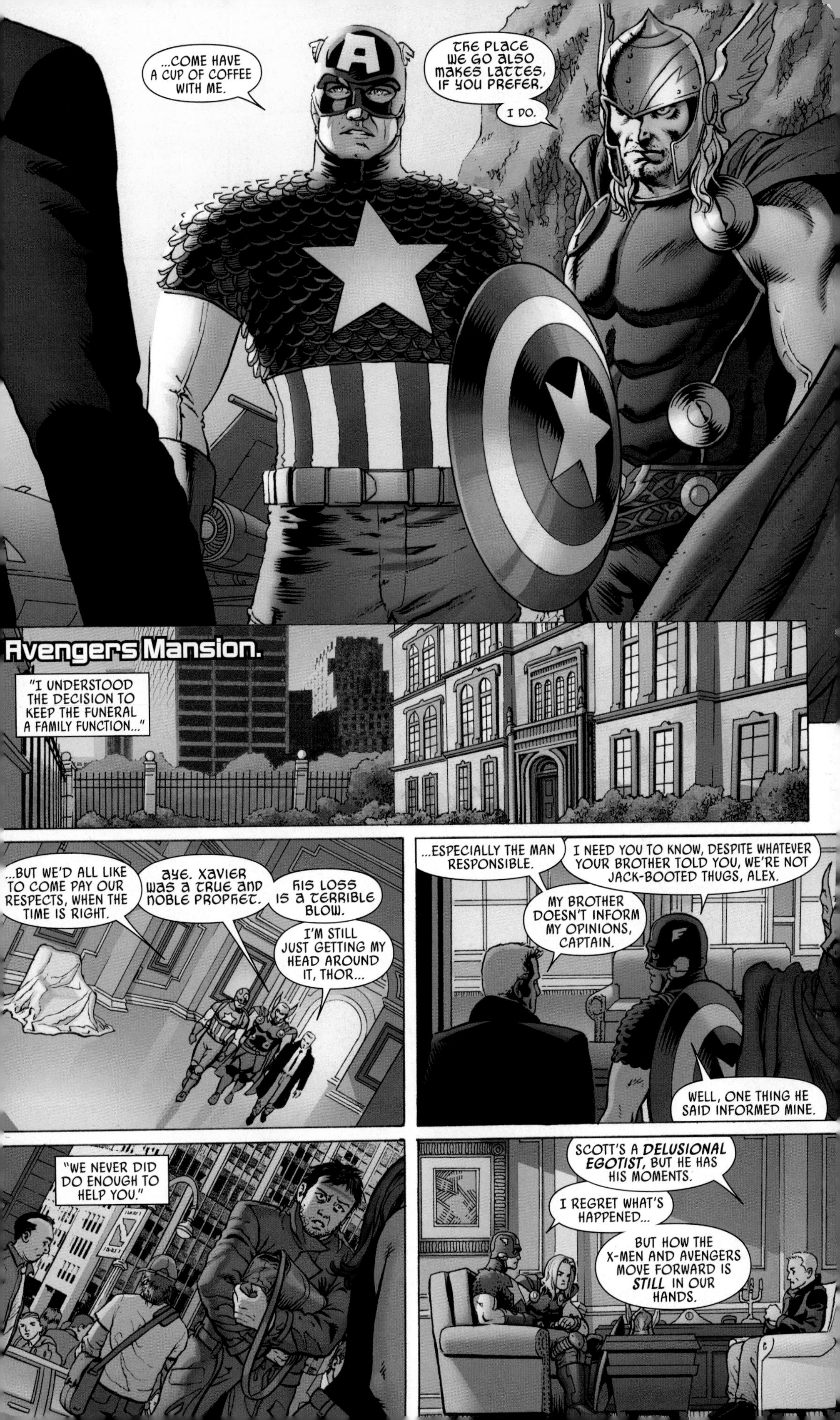

...COME HAVE A CUP OF COFFEE WITH ME.
THE PLACE WE GO ALSO MAKES LATTES, IF YOU PREFER.
I DO.
Avengers Mansion.
"I UNDERSTOOD THE DECISION TO KEEP THE FUNERAL A FAMILY FUNCTION..."
...BUT WE'D ALL LIKE TO COME PAY OUR RESPECTS, WHEN THE TIME IS RIGHT.
AYE. XAVIER WAS A TRUE AND NOBLE PROPHET.
HIS LOSS IS A TERRIBLE BLOW.
I'M STILL JUST GETTING MY HEAD AROUND IT, THOR...
...ESPECIALLY THE MAN RESPONSIBLE.
I NEED YOU TO KNOW, DESPITE WHATEVER YOUR BROTHER TOLD YOU, WE'RE NOT JACK-BOOTED THUGS, ALEX.
MY BROTHER DOESN'T INFORM MY OPINIONS, CAPTAIN.
WELL, ONE THING HE SAID INFORMED MINE.
"WE NEVER DID DO ENOUGH TO HELP YOU."
SCOTT'S A *DELUSIONAL EGOTIST,* BUT HE HAS HIS MOMENTS.
I REGRET WHAT'S HAPPENED...
BUT HOW THE X-MEN AND AVENGERS MOVE FORWARD IS *STILL* IN OUR HANDS.

I'D LIKE YOU TO JOIN US--TO BECOME AN AVENGER.

MORE THAN JOIN, I WANT YOU TO LEAD A SQUAD OF OUR VERY BEST.

X-MEN AND AVENGERS WORKING TOGETHER, SETTING AN EXAMPLE OF COOPERATION.

WITH XAVIER GONE, AND CYCLOPS LOCKED AWAY, SOMEONE HAS TO STAND UP AND REPRESENT THE MUTANTS.

"LOGAN IS TRYING, AND HE'S DOING GOOD WORK AT THE SCHOOL...

"...BUT WITH HIS CHECKERED PAST HE CAN'T BE THE FACE OF THIS.

BEEP-BEEP!

HONK!

HEY! WHADDAYA, ON DRUGS?! MOVE YER ASS!

SOMEBODY CALL THE COPS--

"YOU'RE A GOVERNMENT MAN, DEGREE IN GEOPHYSICS, A STUDENT OF XAVIER'S WITH A CLEAN HISTORY.

"PEOPLE WILL LISTEN TO YOU.

"THEY'LL FOLLOW YOU."

HEY, MAN... Y-YOU ALL RIGHT?

NEVER BETTER.

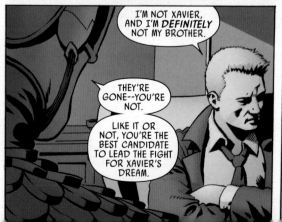

I'M NOT XAVIER, AND I'M DEFINITELY NOT MY BROTHER.

THEY'RE GONE--YOU'RE NOT.

LIKE IT OR NOT, YOU'RE THE BEST CANDIDATE TO LEAD THE FIGHT FOR XAVIER'S DREAM.

NO. NOT ME.

SOMEONE HAS TO STAND UP AND FILL THEIR SHOES, ALEX.

RIGHT...

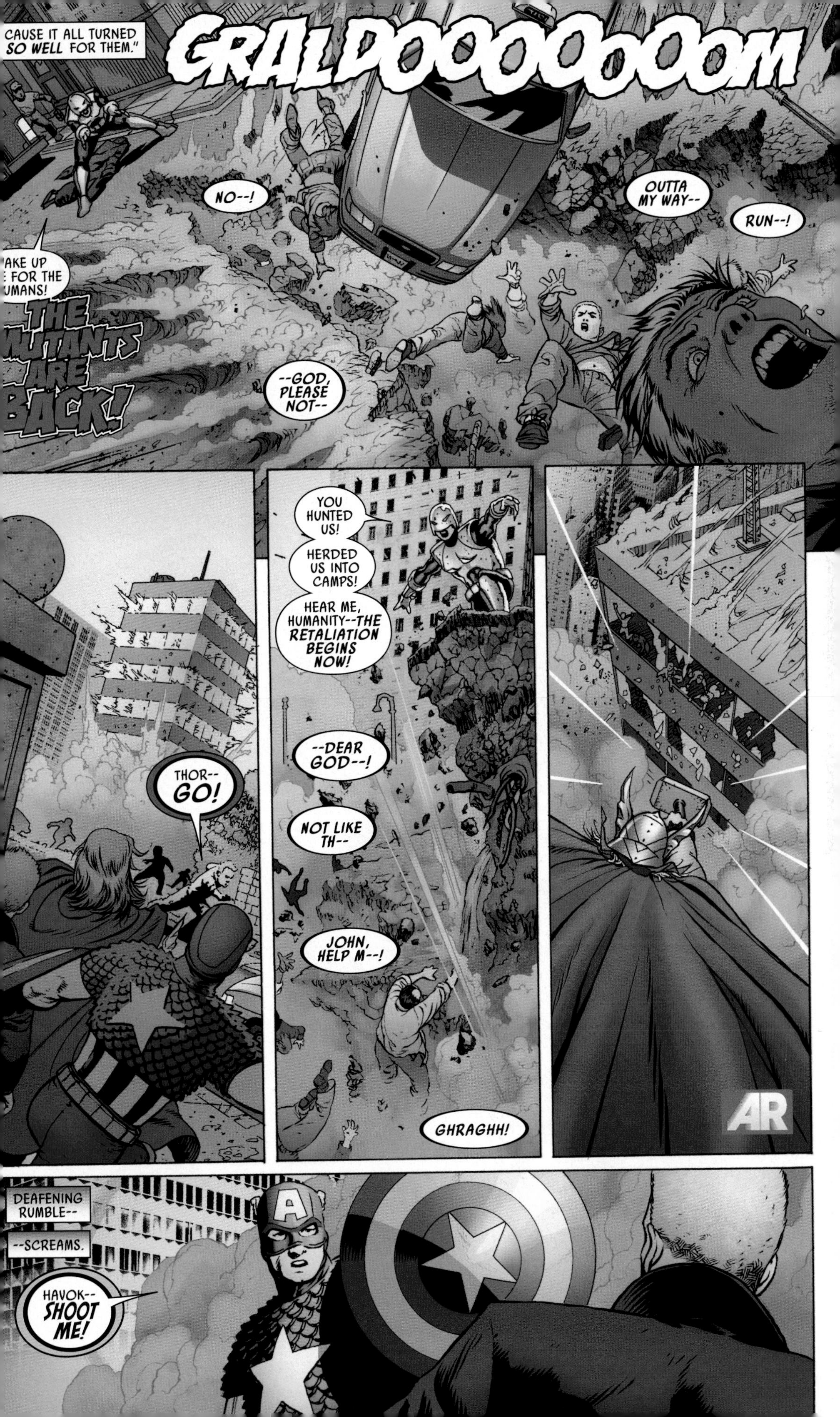
CAUSE IT ALL TURNED SO WELL FOR THEM."
GRALDOOOOOOOOM
NO--!
OUTTA MY WAY--
RUN--!
AKE UP
E FOR THE
UMANS!
THE MUTANTS ARE BACK!
--GOD, PLEASE NOT--
THOR--GO!
YOU HUNTED US!
HERDED US INTO CAMPS!
HEAR ME, HUMANITY--THE RETALIATION BEGINS NOW!
--DEAR GOD--!
NOT LIKE TH--
JOHN, HELP M--!
GHRAGHH!
AR
DEAFENING RUMBLE--
--SCREAMS.
HAVOK--SHOOT ME!

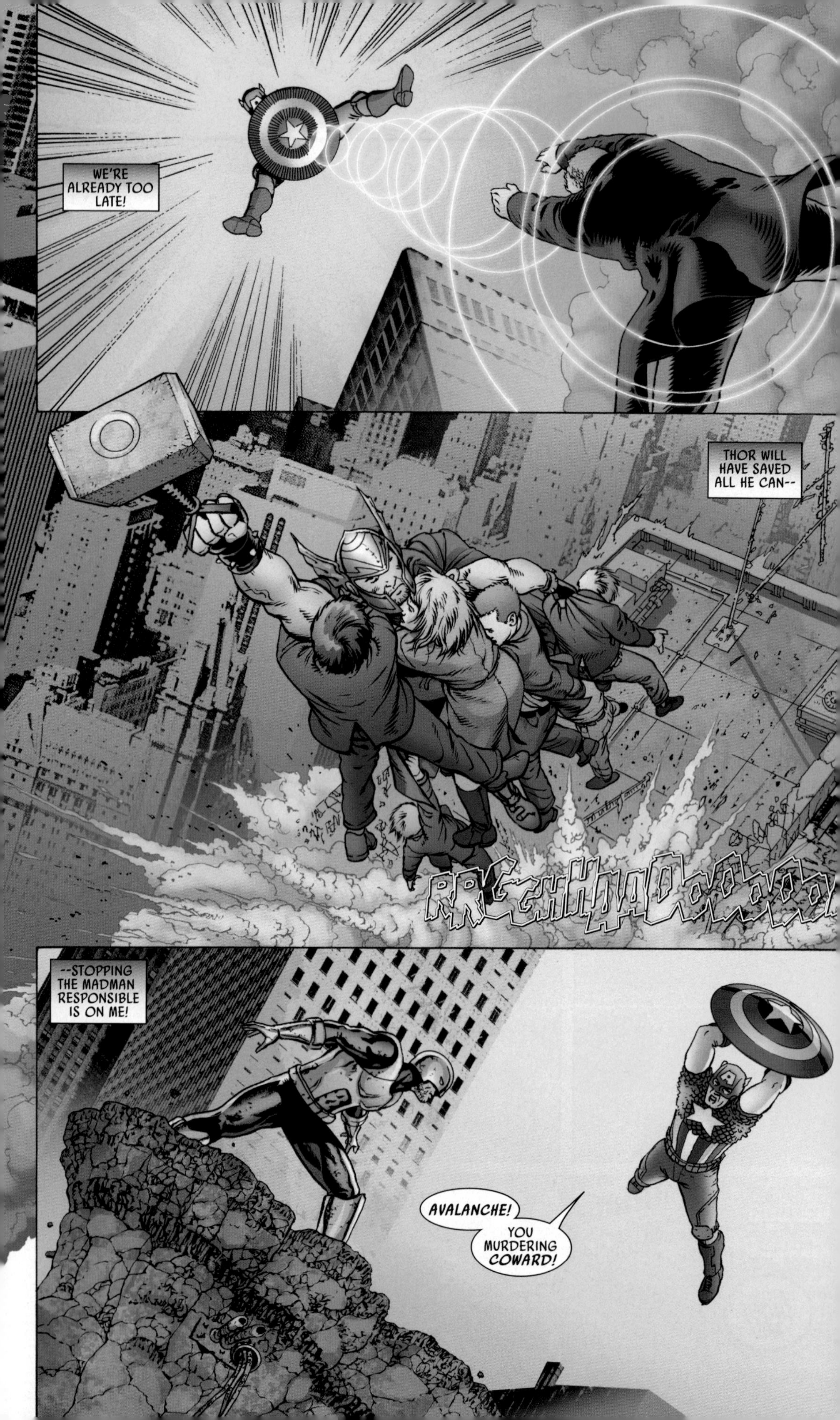
WE'RE ALREADY TOO LATE!
THOR WILL HAVE SAVED ALL HE CAN--
RRKchHHHAOooooo
--STOPPING THE MADMAN RESPONSIBLE IS ON ME!
AVALANCHE!
YOU MURDERING COWARD!

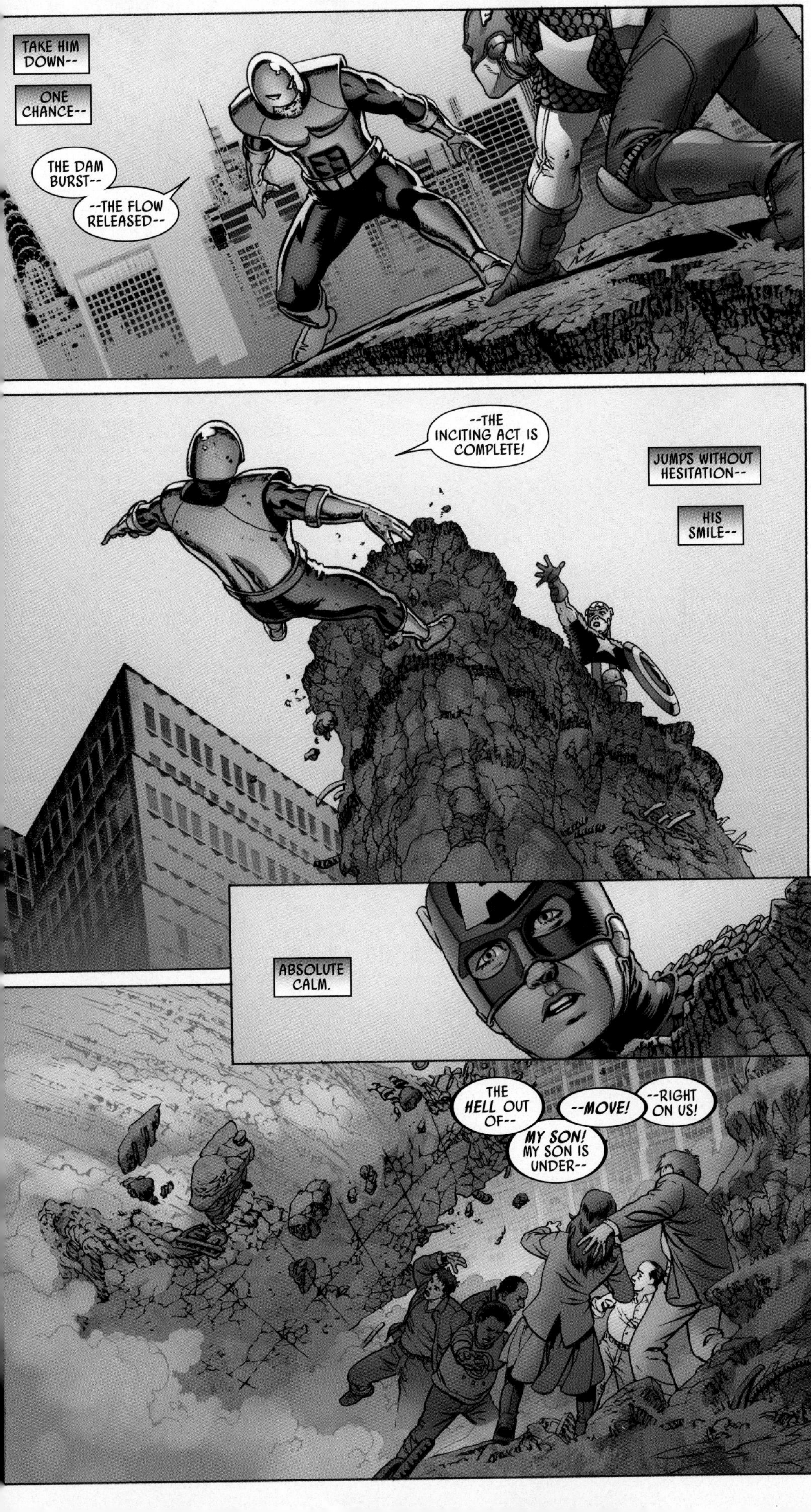
TAKE HIM DOWN--
ONE CHANCE--
THE DAM BURST--
--THE FLOW RELEASED--
--THE INCITING ACT IS COMPLETE!
JUMPS WITHOUT HESITATION--
HIS SMILE--
ABSOLUTE CALM.
THE HELL OUT OF--
--MOVE!
--RIGHT ON US!
MY SON! MY SON IS UNDER--

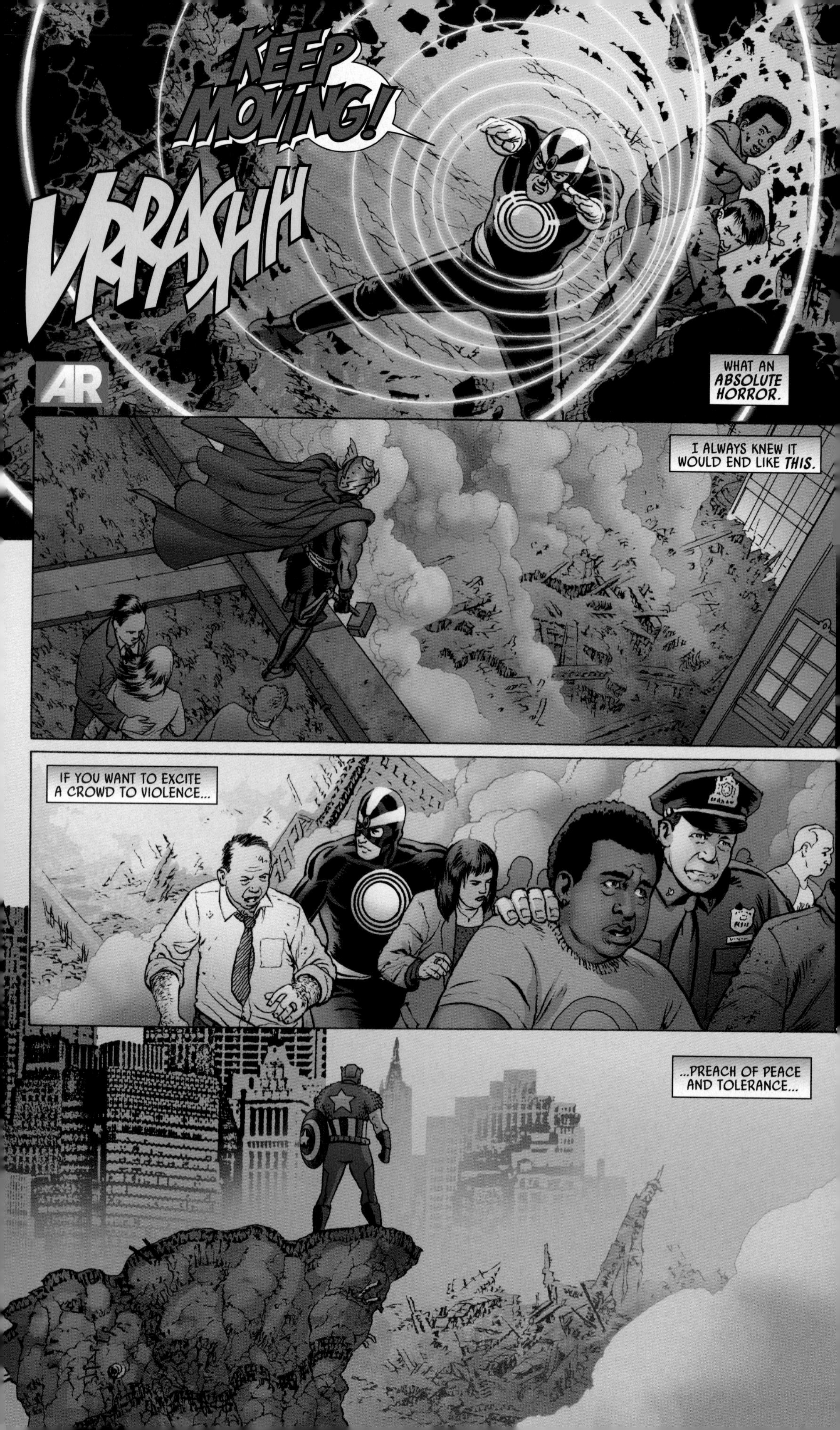
KEEP MOVING!
VRRASHH
WHAT AN ABSOLUTE HORROR.
I ALWAYS KNEW IT WOULD END LIKE THIS.
IF YOU WANT TO EXCITE A CROWD TO VIOLENCE...
...PREACH OF PEACE AND TOLERANCE...

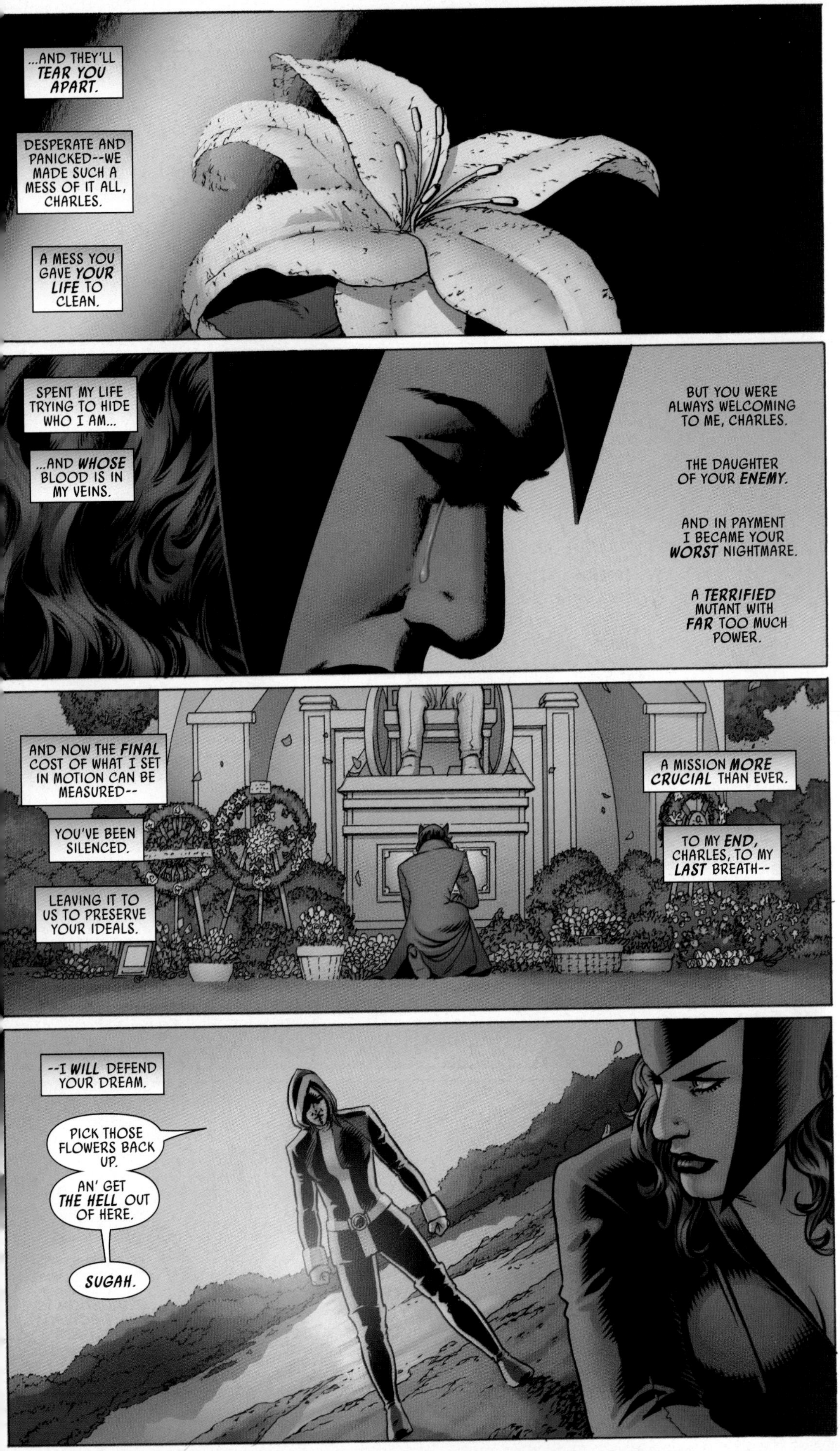

...AND THEY'LL TEAR YOU APART.
DESPERATE AND PANICKED--WE MADE SUCH A MESS OF IT ALL, CHARLES.
A MESS YOU GAVE YOUR LIFE TO CLEAN.
SPENT MY LIFE TRYING TO HIDE WHO I AM...
...AND WHOSE BLOOD IS IN MY VEINS.
BUT YOU WERE ALWAYS WELCOMING TO ME, CHARLES.
THE DAUGHTER OF YOUR ENEMY.
AND IN PAYMENT I BECAME YOUR WORST NIGHTMARE.
A TERRIFIED MUTANT WITH FAR TOO MUCH POWER.
AND NOW THE FINAL COST OF WHAT I SET IN MOTION CAN BE MEASURED--
YOU'VE BEEN SILENCED.
LEAVING IT TO US TO PRESERVE YOUR IDEALS.
A MISSION MORE CRUCIAL THAN EVER.
TO MY END, CHARLES, TO MY LAST BREATH--
--I WILL DEFEND YOUR DREAM.
PICK THOSE FLOWERS BACK UP.
AN' GET THE HELL OUT OF HERE.
SUGAH.

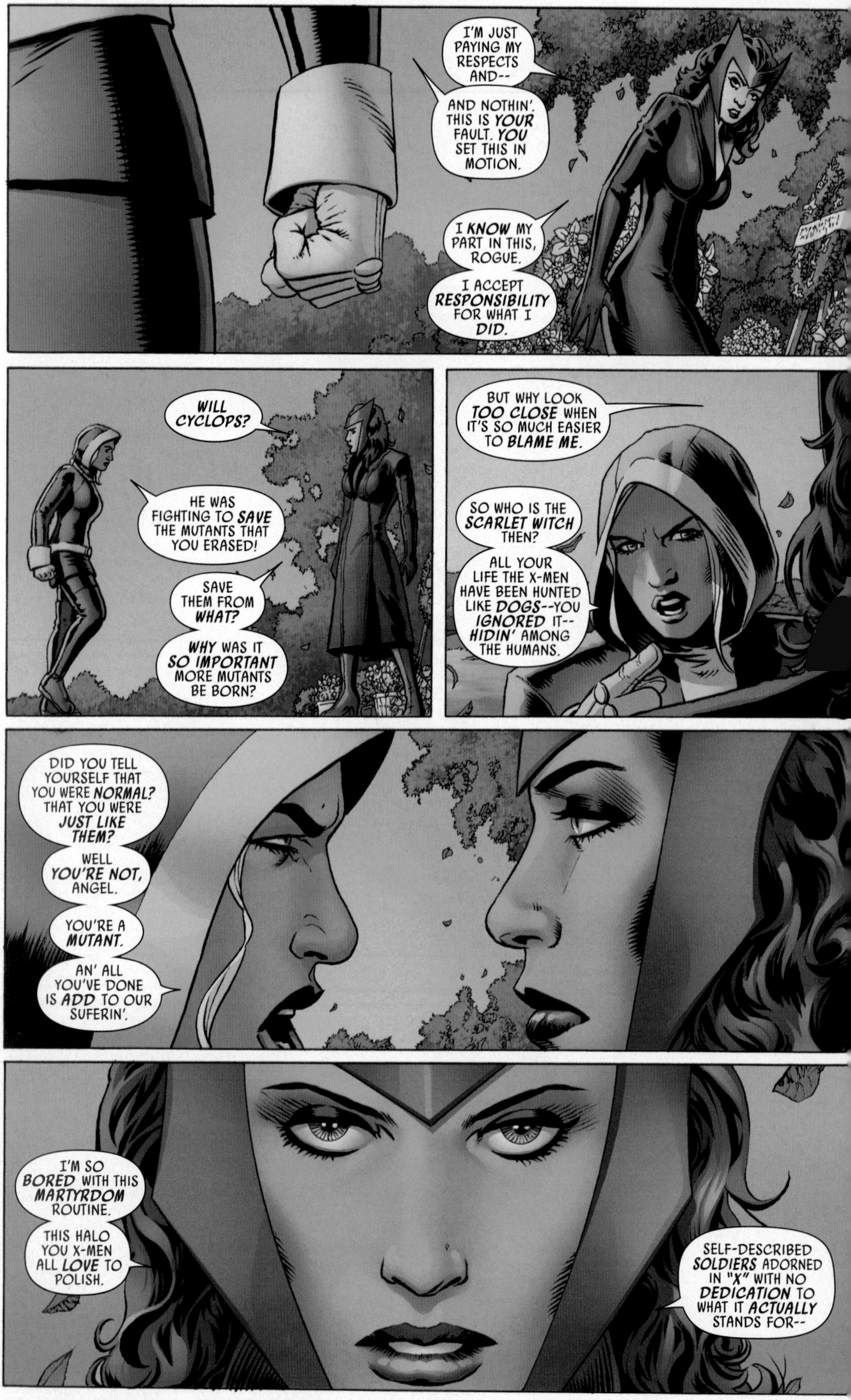
I'M JUST PAYING MY RESPECTS AND--
AND NOTHIN'. THIS IS YOUR FAULT. YOU SET THIS IN MOTION.
I KNOW MY PART IN THIS, ROGUE.
I ACCEPT RESPONSIBILITY FOR WHAT I DID.
WILL CYCLOPS?
HE WAS FIGHTING TO SAVE THE MUTANTS THAT YOU ERASED!
SAVE THEM FROM WHAT?
WHY WAS IT SO IMPORTANT MORE MUTANTS BE BORN?
BUT WHY LOOK TOO CLOSE WHEN IT'S SO MUCH EASIER TO BLAME ME.
SO WHO IS THE SCARLET WITCH THEN?
ALL YOUR LIFE THE X-MEN HAVE BEEN HUNTED LIKE DOGS--YOU IGNORED IT--HIDIN' AMONG THE HUMANS.
DID YOU TELL YOURSELF THAT YOU WERE NORMAL? THAT YOU WERE JUST LIKE THEM?
WELL YOU'RE NOT, ANGEL.
YOU'RE A MUTANT.
AN' ALL YOU'VE DONE IS ADD TO OUR SUFERIN'.
I'M SO BORED WITH THIS MARTYRDOM ROUTINE.
THIS HALO YOU X-MEN ALL LOVE TO POLISH.
SELF-DESCRIBED SOLDIERS ADORNED IN "X" WITH NO DEDICATION TO WHAT IT ACTUALLY STANDS FOR--

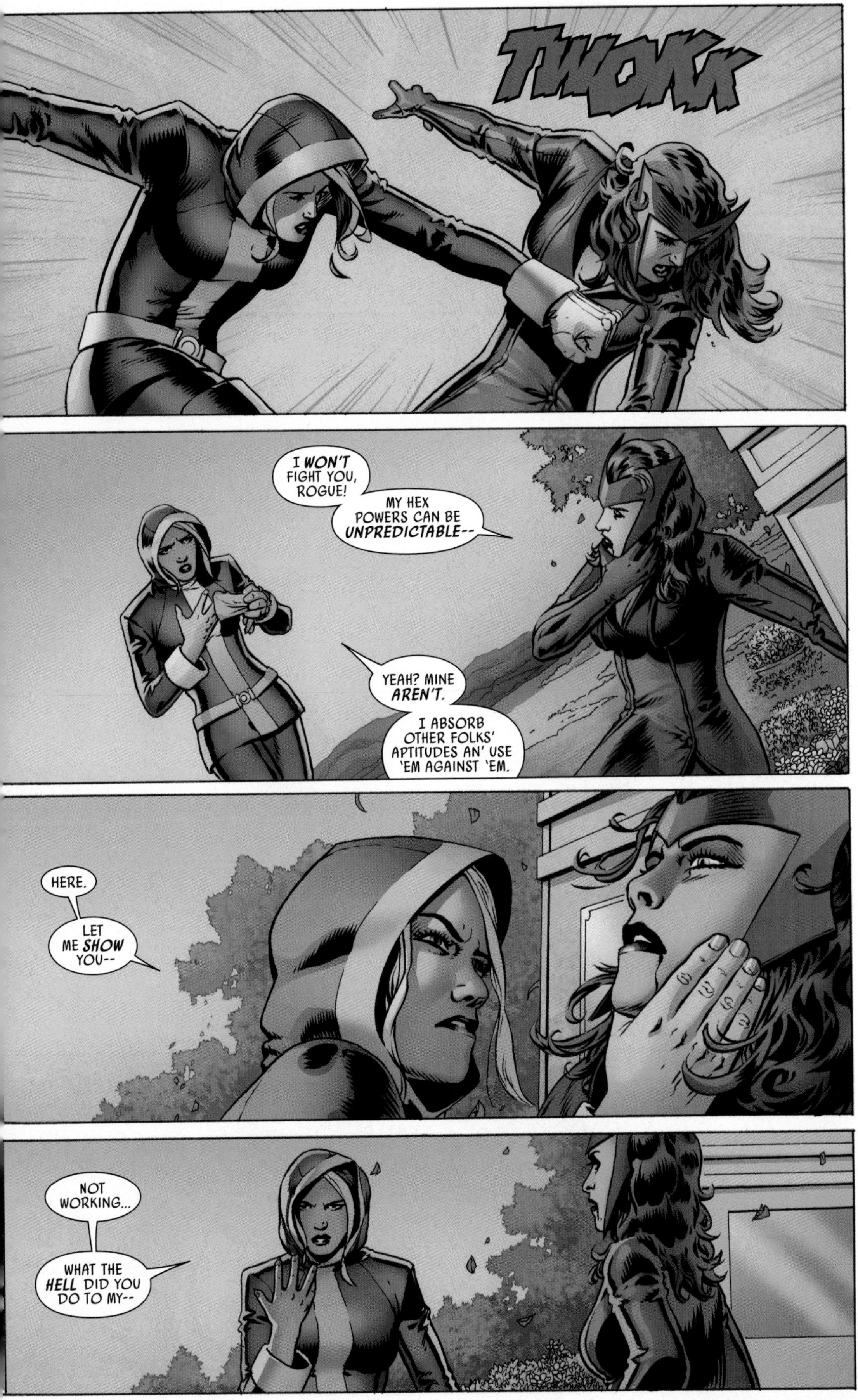
TWOKK
I WON'T FIGHT YOU, ROGUE!
MY HEX POWERS CAN BE UNPREDICTABLE--
YEAH? MINE AREN'T.
I ABSORB OTHER FOLKS' APTITUDES AN' USE 'EM AGAINST 'EM.
HERE.
LET ME SHOW YOU--
NOT WORKING...
WHAT THE HELL DID YOU DO TO MY--

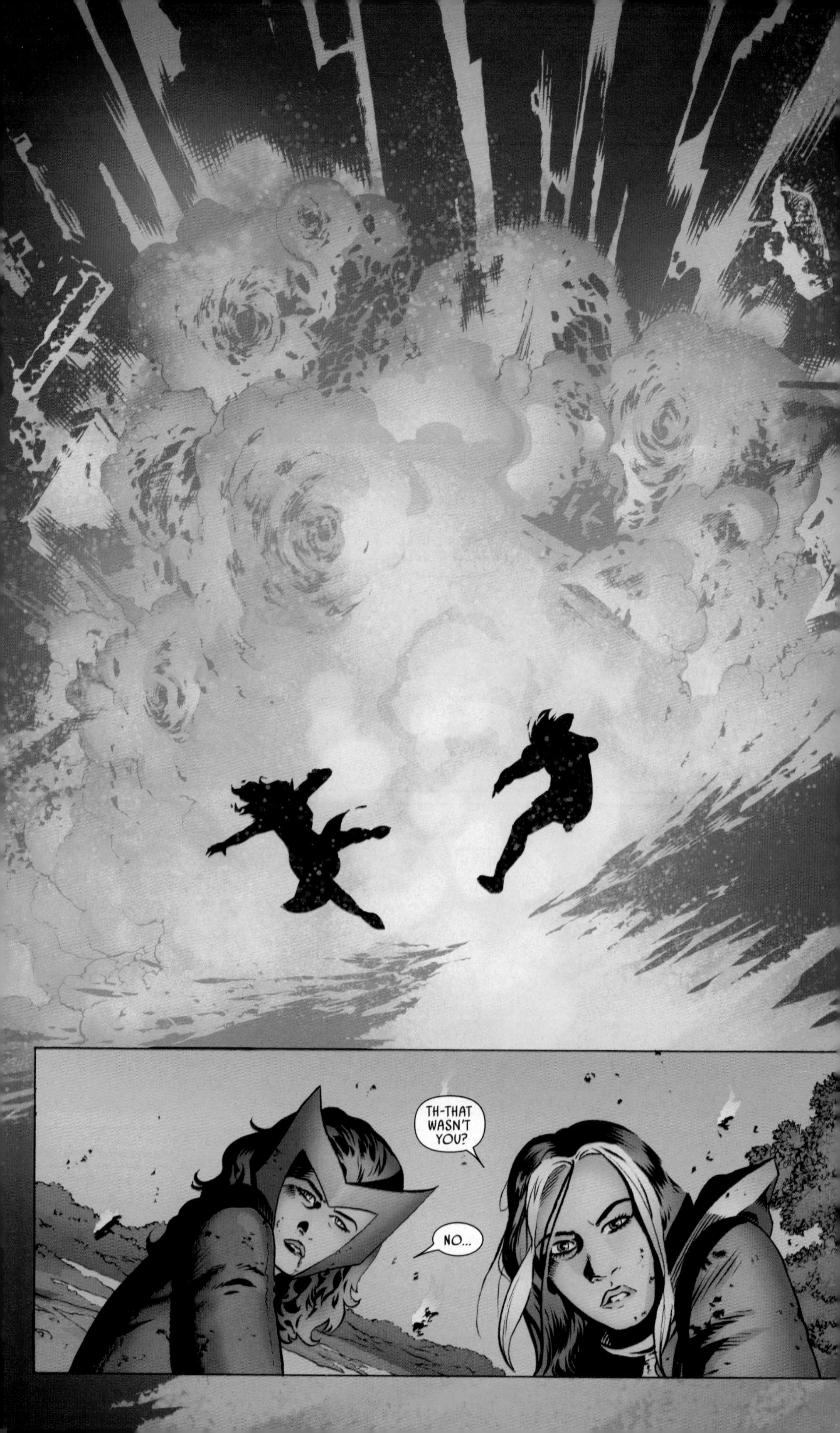
TH-THAT WASN'T YOU?
NO...

"...IT WAS *THEM*."

YOUR FOUL "*GIFTS*" FAIL AS YOU SUFFER THE GAZE OF **THE GOAT-FACED GIRL**!

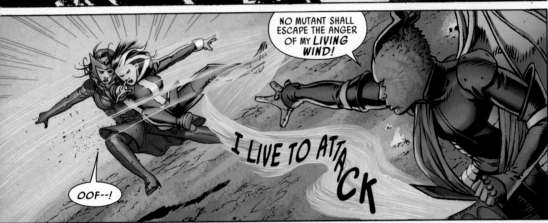

NO MUTANT SHALL ESCAPE THE ANGER OF MY *LIVING WIND*!

I LIVE TO ATTACK

OOF--!

I SUFFER *THE INSECT* UNTO MYSELF--

--FOR THE *GOOD* OF *ALL MAN.*

MY *CASSANDRA TOXIN* WILL END THE THREAT *THEY* REFUSE TO SEE!

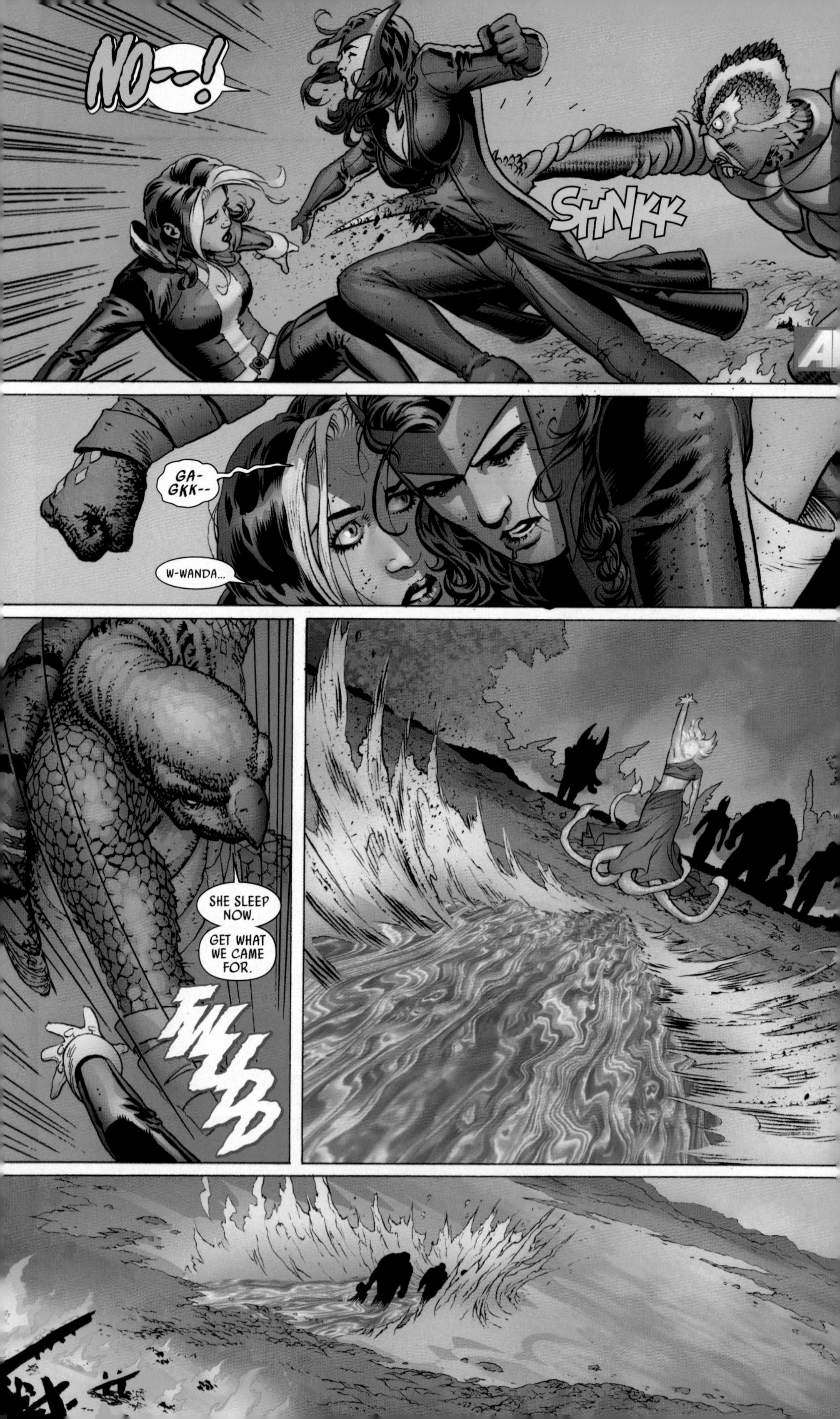
NO--!
SHNKK
GA-GKK--
W-WANDA...
SHE SLEEP NOW.
GET WHAT WE CAME FOR.
FWUDD

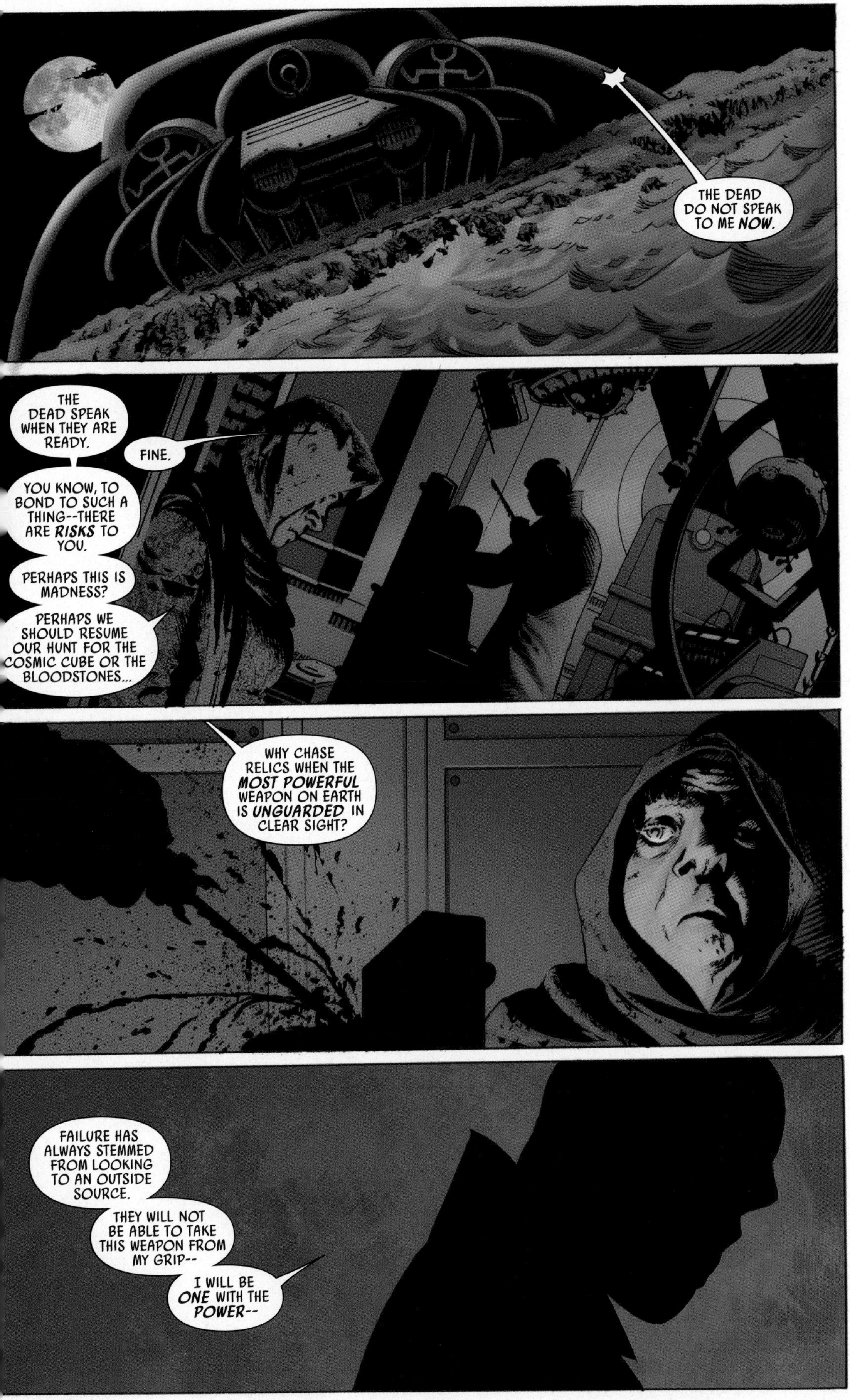
THE DEAD DO NOT SPEAK TO ME NOW.
THE DEAD SPEAK WHEN THEY ARE READY.
FINE.
YOU KNOW, TO BOND TO SUCH A THING--THERE ARE RISKS TO YOU.
PERHAPS THIS IS MADNESS?
PERHAPS WE SHOULD RESUME OUR HUNT FOR THE COSMIC CUBE OR THE BLOODSTONES...
WHY CHASE RELICS WHEN THE MOST POWERFUL WEAPON ON EARTH IS UNGUARDED IN CLEAR SIGHT?
FAILURE HAS ALWAYS STEMMED FROM LOOKING TO AN OUTSIDE SOURCE.
THEY WILL NOT BE ABLE TO TAKE THIS WEAPON FROM MY GRIP--
I WILL BE ONE WITH THE POWER--

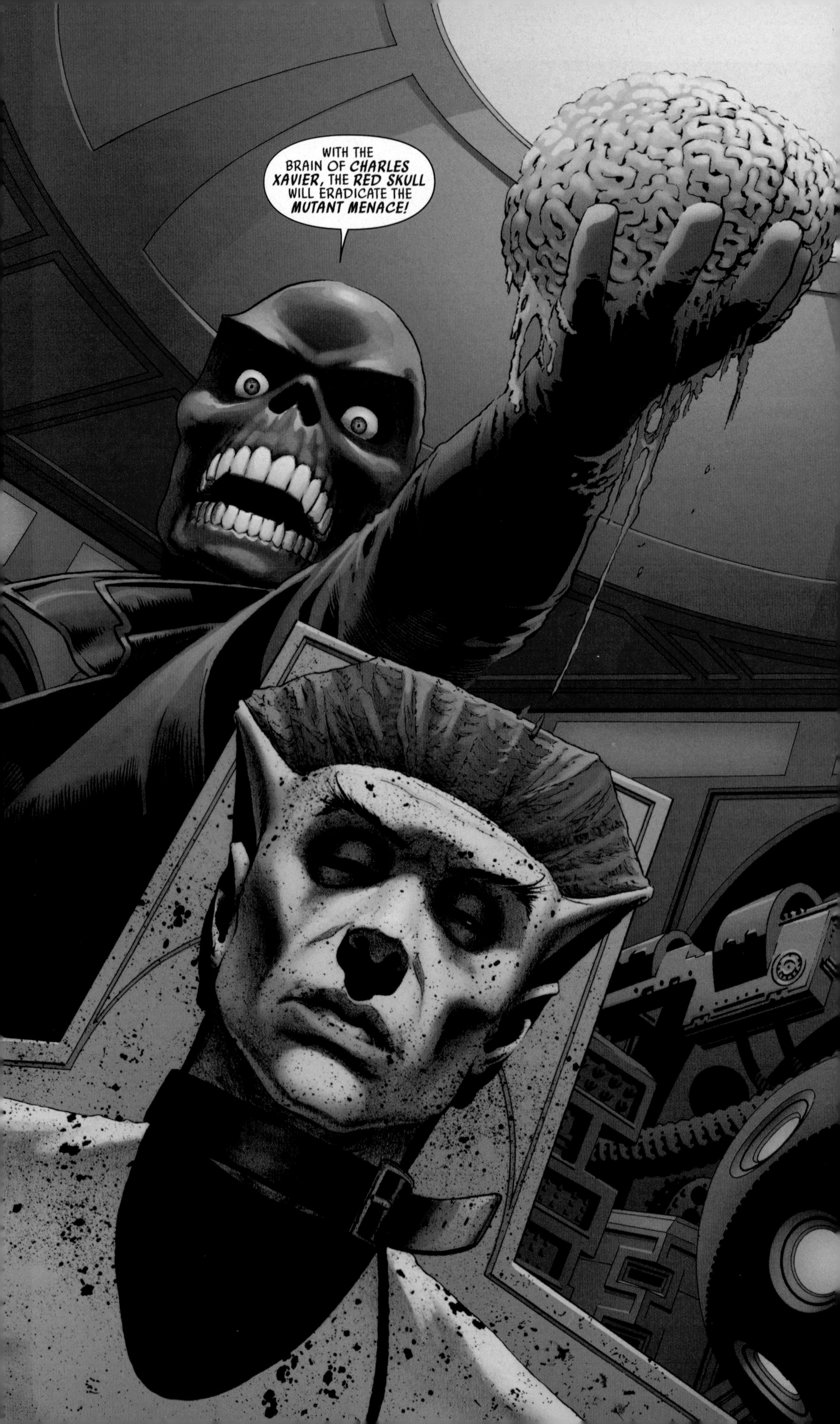
WITH THE BRAIN OF CHARLES XAVIER, THE RED SKULL WILL ERADICATE THE MUTANT MENACE!

UNCANNY AVENGERS #1 VARIANT BY OLIVIER COIPEL & JUSTIN PONSOR

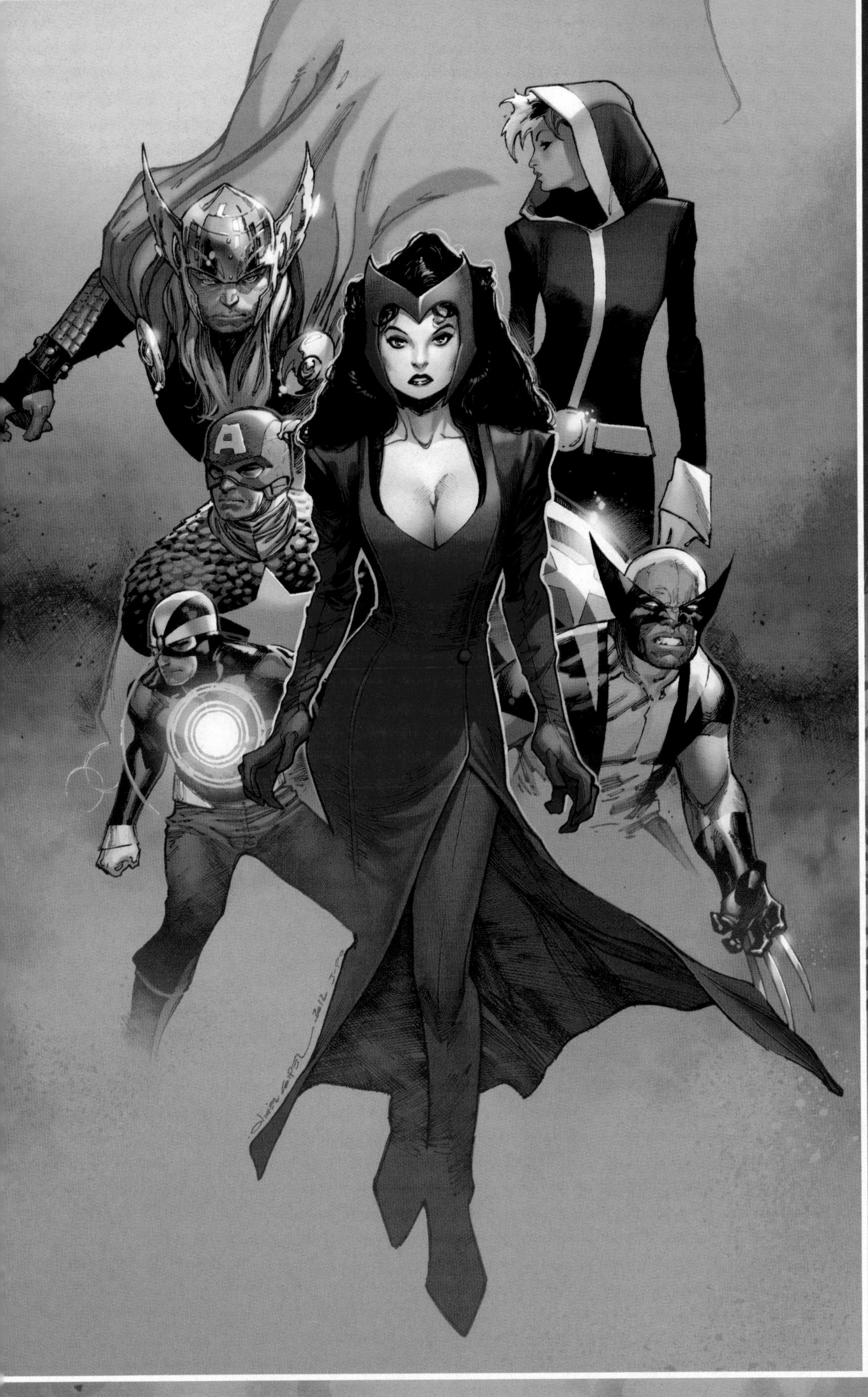

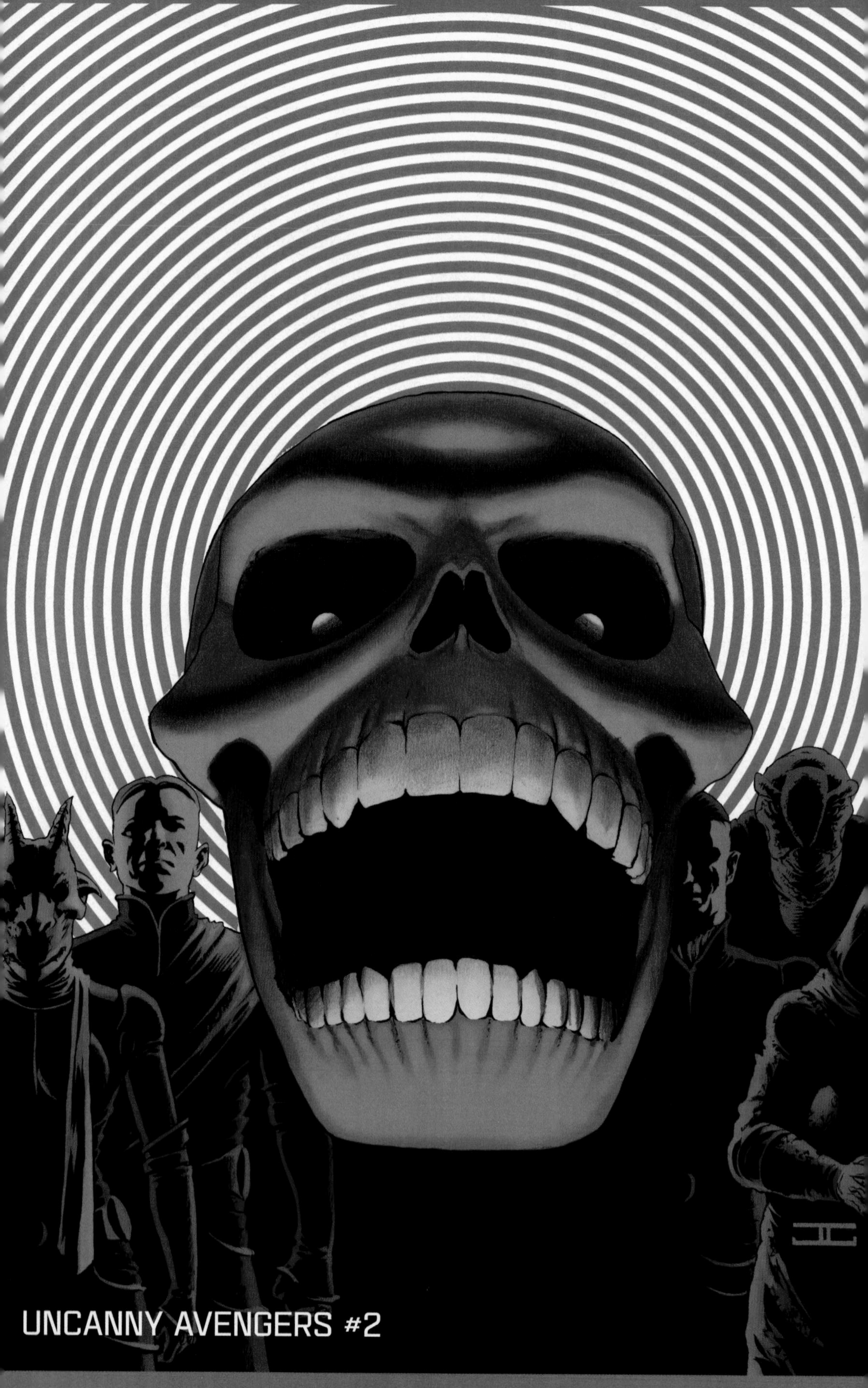
UNCANNY AVENGERS #2

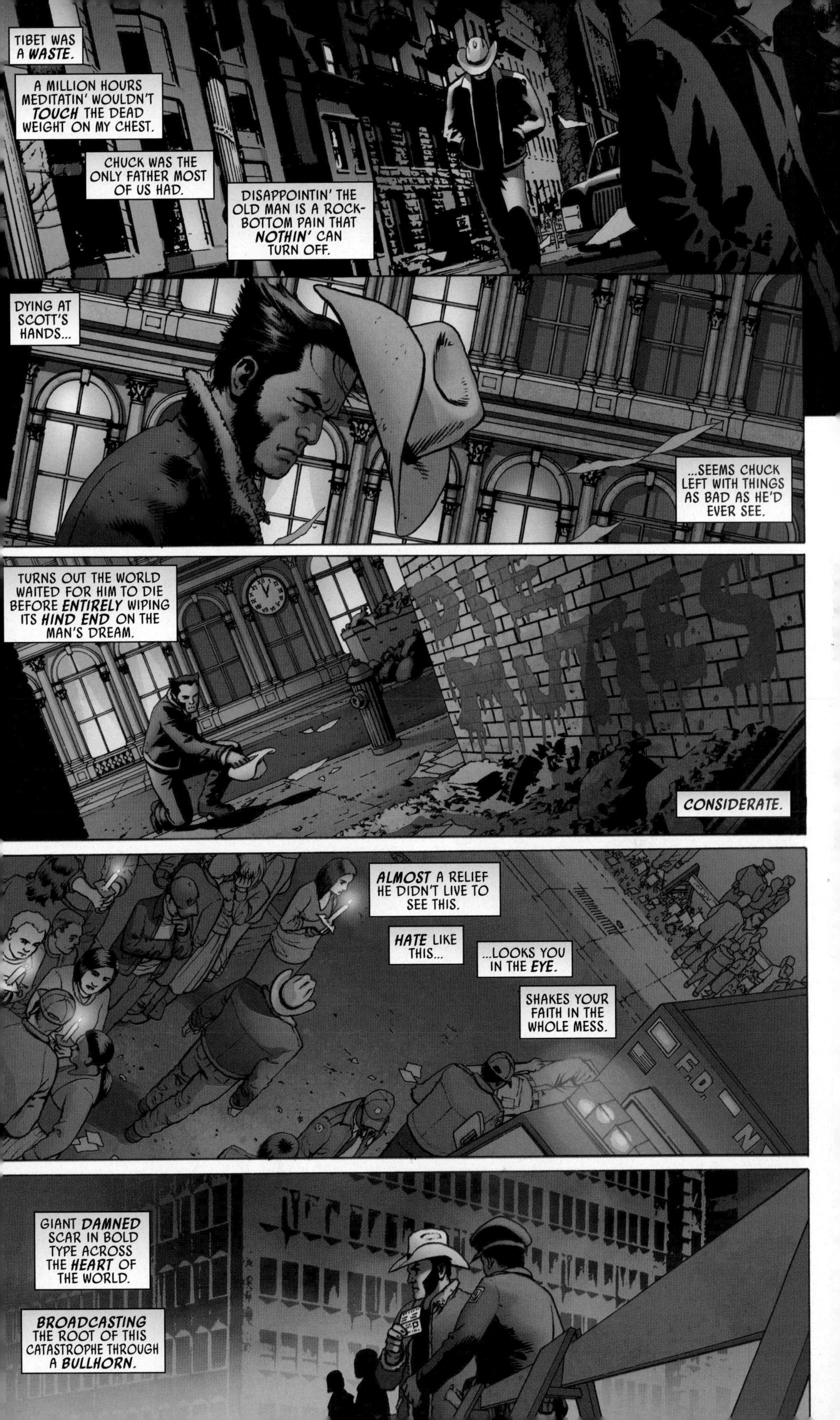
TIBET WAS A WASTE.
A MILLION HOURS MEDITATIN' WOULDN'T TOUCH THE DEAD WEIGHT ON MY CHEST.
CHUCK WAS THE ONLY FATHER MOST OF US HAD.
DISAPPOINTIN' THE OLD MAN IS A ROCK-BOTTOM PAIN THAT NOTHIN' CAN TURN OFF.
DYING AT SCOTT'S HANDS...
...SEEMS CHUCK LEFT WITH THINGS AS BAD AS HE'D EVER SEE.
TURNS OUT THE WORLD WAITED FOR HIM TO DIE BEFORE ENTIRELY WIPING ITS HIND END ON THE MAN'S DREAM.
DIE MUTIES
CONSIDERATE.
ALMOST A RELIEF HE DIDN'T LIVE TO SEE THIS.
HATE LIKE THIS...
...LOOKS YOU IN THE EYE.
SHAKES YOUR FAITH IN THE WHOLE MESS.
F.D.
GIANT DAMNED SCAR IN BOLD TYPE ACROSS THE HEART OF THE WORLD.
BROADCASTING THE ROOT OF THIS CATASTROPHE THROUGH A BULLHORN.

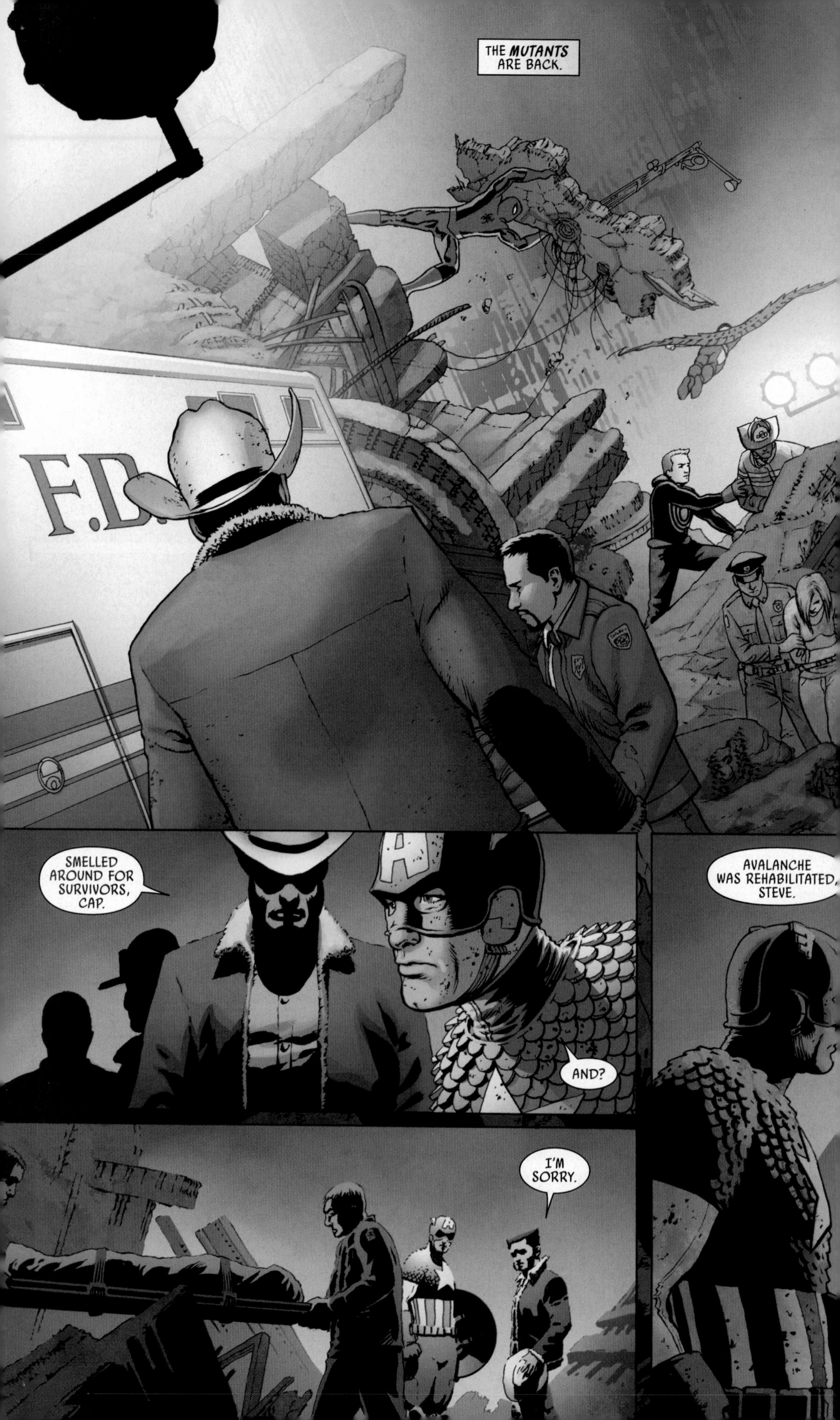
THE MUTANTS ARE BACK.
F.D.
SMELLED AROUND FOR SURVIVORS, CAP.
AND?
AVALANCHE WAS REHABILITATED, STEVE.
I'M SORRY.

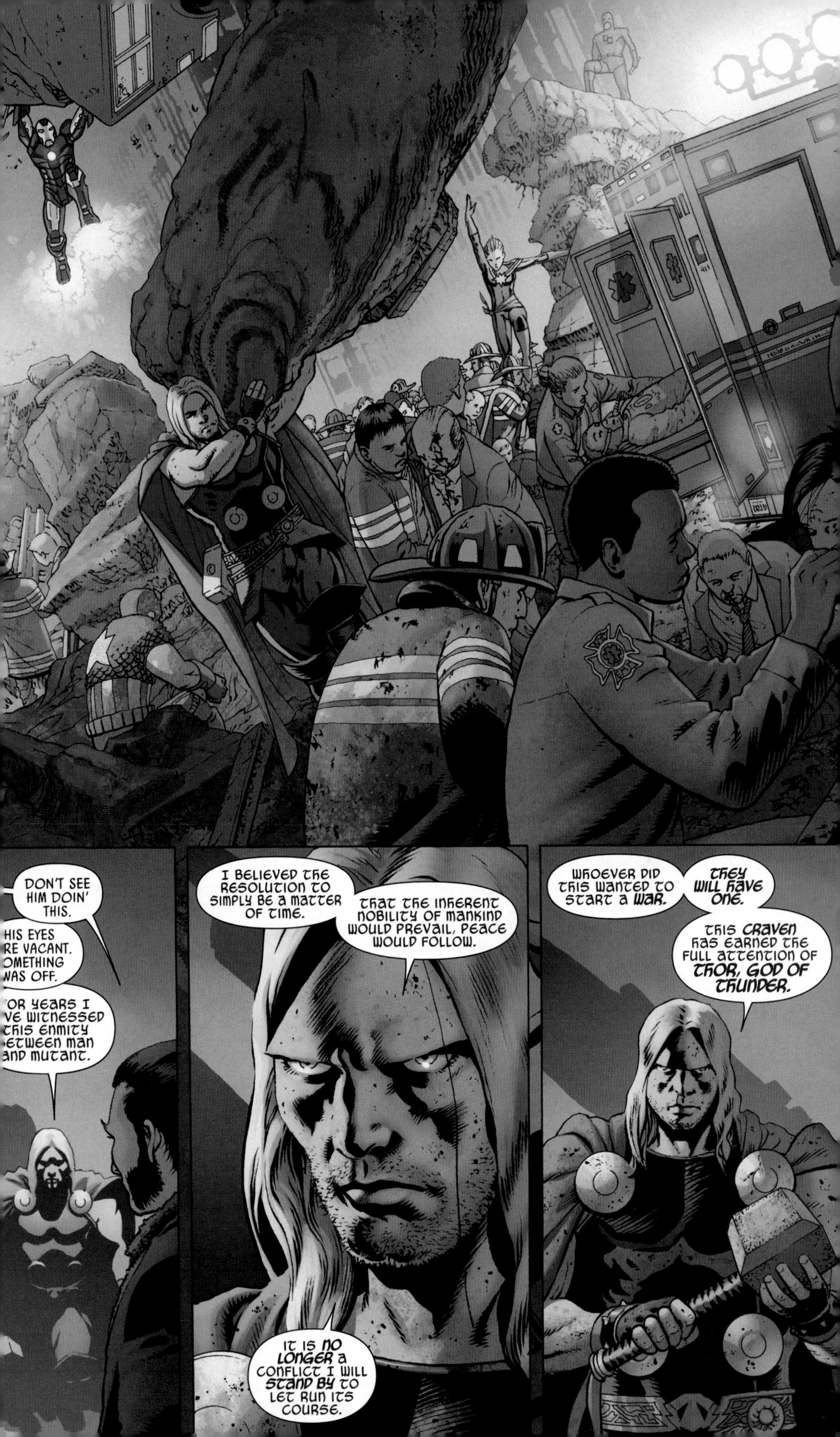
DON'T SEE HIM DOIN' THIS.
HIS EYES RE VACANT. OMETHING WAS OFF.
OR YEARS I VE WITNESSED THIS ENMITY ETWEEN MAN AND MUTANT.
I BELIEVED THE RESOLUTION TO SIMPLY BE A MATTER OF TIME.
THAT THE INHERENT NOBILITY OF MANKIND WOULD PREVAIL, PEACE WOULD FOLLOW.
IT IS NO LONGER A CONFLICT I WILL STAND BY TO LET RUN ITS COURSE.
WHOEVER DID THIS WANTED TO START A WAR.
THEY WILL HAVE ONE.
THIS CRAVEN HAS EARNED THE FULL ATTENTION OF THOR, GOD OF THUNDER.

WE **WILL** FIND WHO WAS BEHIND THIS, AND WE **WILL** AVENGE OUR FALLEN, THOR.

BUT, NOW-- **RIGHT NOW**--OUR FIRST PRIORITY IS TO **PREVENT** MORE BLOODSHED.

TO ENSURE **NO ONE** USES THIS CATASTROPHE TO FURTHER AN AGENDA OF HATRED.

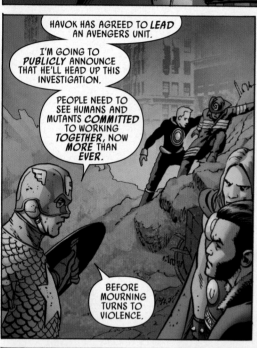

HAVOK HAS AGREED TO **LEAD** AN AVENGERS UNIT.

I'M GOING TO **PUBLICLY** ANNOUNCE THAT HE'LL HEAD UP THIS INVESTIGATION.

PEOPLE NEED TO SEE HUMANS AND MUTANTS **COMMITTED** TO WORKING **TOGETHER**, NOW **MORE** THAN **EVER**.

BEFORE MOURNING TURNS TO VIOLENCE.

LOT OF PEOPLE **DEAD** AT THE HANDS OF A **MUTANT** AND YOU WANT THE **BROTHER** OF A MUTANT NEARLY **TOOK OVER THE PLANET** TO HEAD UP **THE AVENGERS'** RESPONSE TO **THIS**?

GONNA **PISS** FOLKS OFF, STEVE.

GONNA GET MUTANTS **KILLED**.

I THOUGHT YOU'D BE **SUPPORTIVE** OF THIS, LOGAN.

COULDN'T'VE THOUGHT I'D BE **TOO** SUPPORTIVE GIVEN YOU **DIDN'T** BRING IT UP WITH ME FIRST.

LOGAN, **THIS** IS WHY CHARLES PUT HIS STUDENTS IN **UNIFORMS** AND SENT THEM OUT INTO THE WORLD. TO **PROTECT** AND **SERVE**--

--TO WIN **HEARTS AND MINDS**.

ALEX SUMMERS IS A **STRONG** AND **ETHICAL** MAN, A **PROVEN** LEADER.

A MAN WHO NORMAL PEOPLE CAN **IDENTIFY** WITH, AS WE NAVIGATE THIS.

PICKIN' THE PRETTY MUTANTS TO BE OUR PUBLIC FACE, STEVE?

HE WON'T FRIGHTEN PEOPLE, I WON'T LIE, THAT'S **IMPORTANT**.

WHAT MATTERS **MOST** IS THAT HE'S A GOOD MAN.

THE MUTANT COMMUNITY NEEDS--

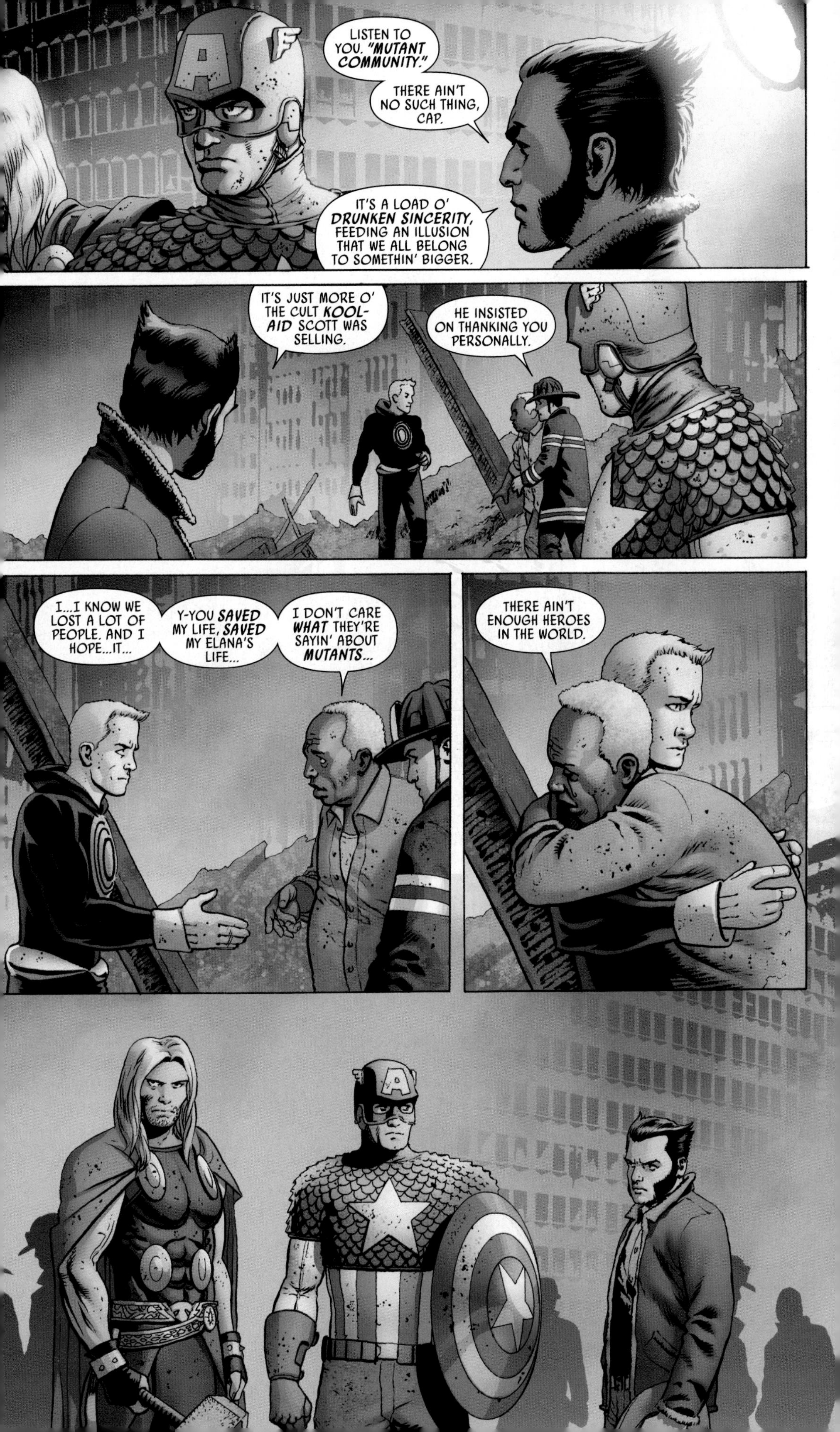
LISTEN TO YOU. "MUTANT COMMUNITY."
THERE AIN'T NO SUCH THING, CAP.
IT'S A LOAD O' DRUNKEN SINCERITY, FEEDING AN ILLUSION THAT WE ALL BELONG TO SOMETHIN' BIGGER.
IT'S JUST MORE O' THE CULT KOOL-AID SCOTT WAS SELLING.
HE INSISTED ON THANKING YOU PERSONALLY.
I...I KNOW WE LOST A LOT OF PEOPLE. AND I HOPE...IT...
Y-YOU SAVED MY LIFE, SAVED MY ELANA'S LIFE...
I DON'T CARE WHAT THEY'RE SAYIN' ABOUT MUTANTS...
THERE AIN'T ENOUGH HEROES IN THE WORLD.

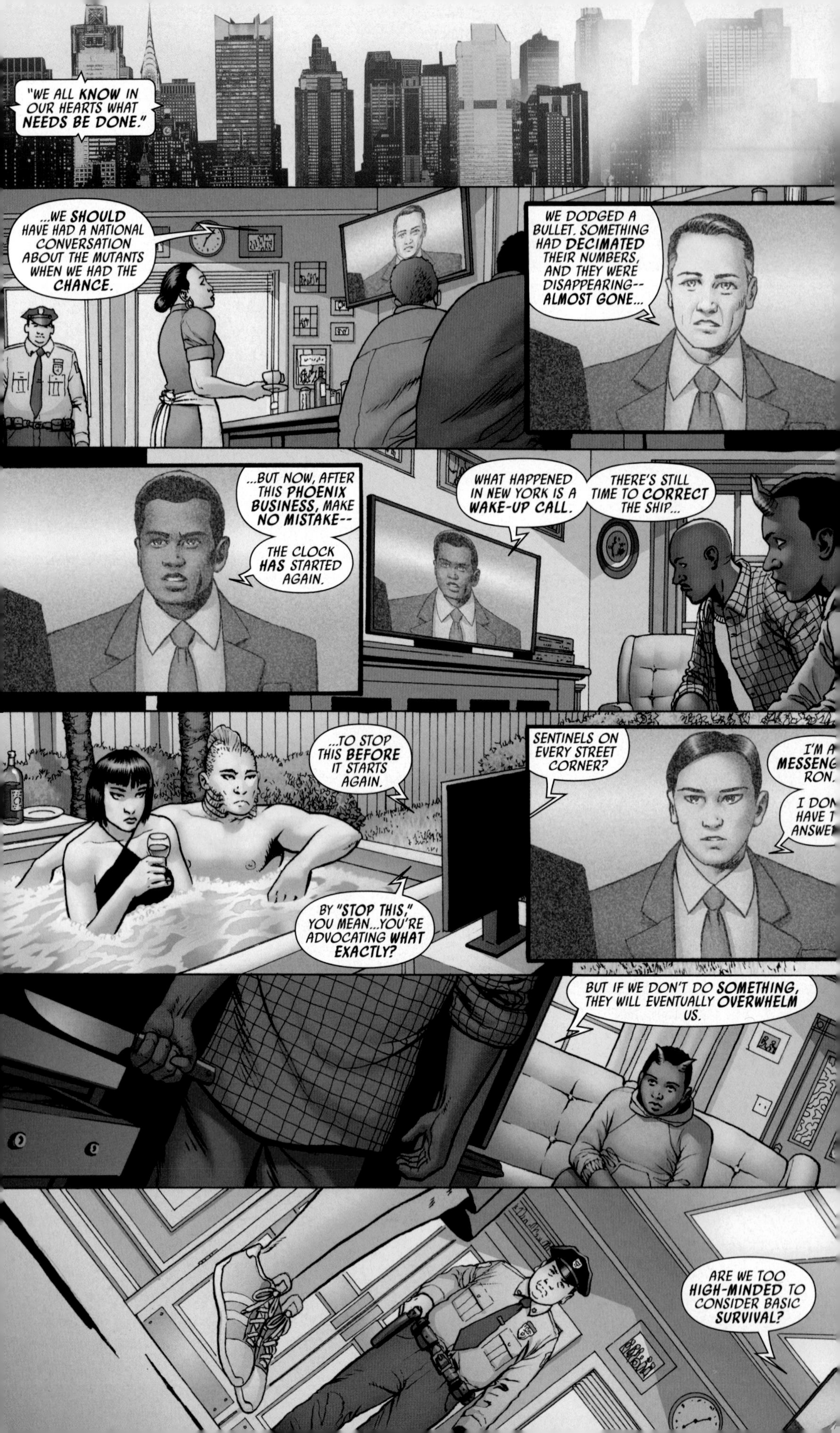
"WE ALL KNOW IN OUR HEARTS WHAT NEEDS BE DONE."
...WE SHOULD HAVE HAD A NATIONAL CONVERSATION ABOUT THE MUTANTS WHEN WE HAD THE CHANCE.
WE DODGED A BULLET. SOMETHING HAD DECIMATED THEIR NUMBERS, AND THEY WERE DISAPPEARING-- ALMOST GONE...
...BUT NOW, AFTER THIS PHOENIX BUSINESS, MAKE NO MISTAKE--
THE CLOCK HAS STARTED AGAIN.
WHAT HAPPENED IN NEW YORK IS A WAKE-UP CALL.
THERE'S STILL TIME TO CORRECT THE SHIP...
...TO STOP THIS BEFORE IT STARTS AGAIN.
BY "STOP THIS," YOU MEAN...YOU'RE ADVOCATING WHAT EXACTLY?
SENTINELS ON EVERY STREET CORNER?
I'M A MESSENG RON.
I DON HAVE T ANSWE
BUT IF WE DON'T DO SOMETHING, THEY WILL EVENTUALLY OVERWHELM US.
ARE WE TOO HIGH-MINDED TO CONSIDER BASIC SURVIVAL?

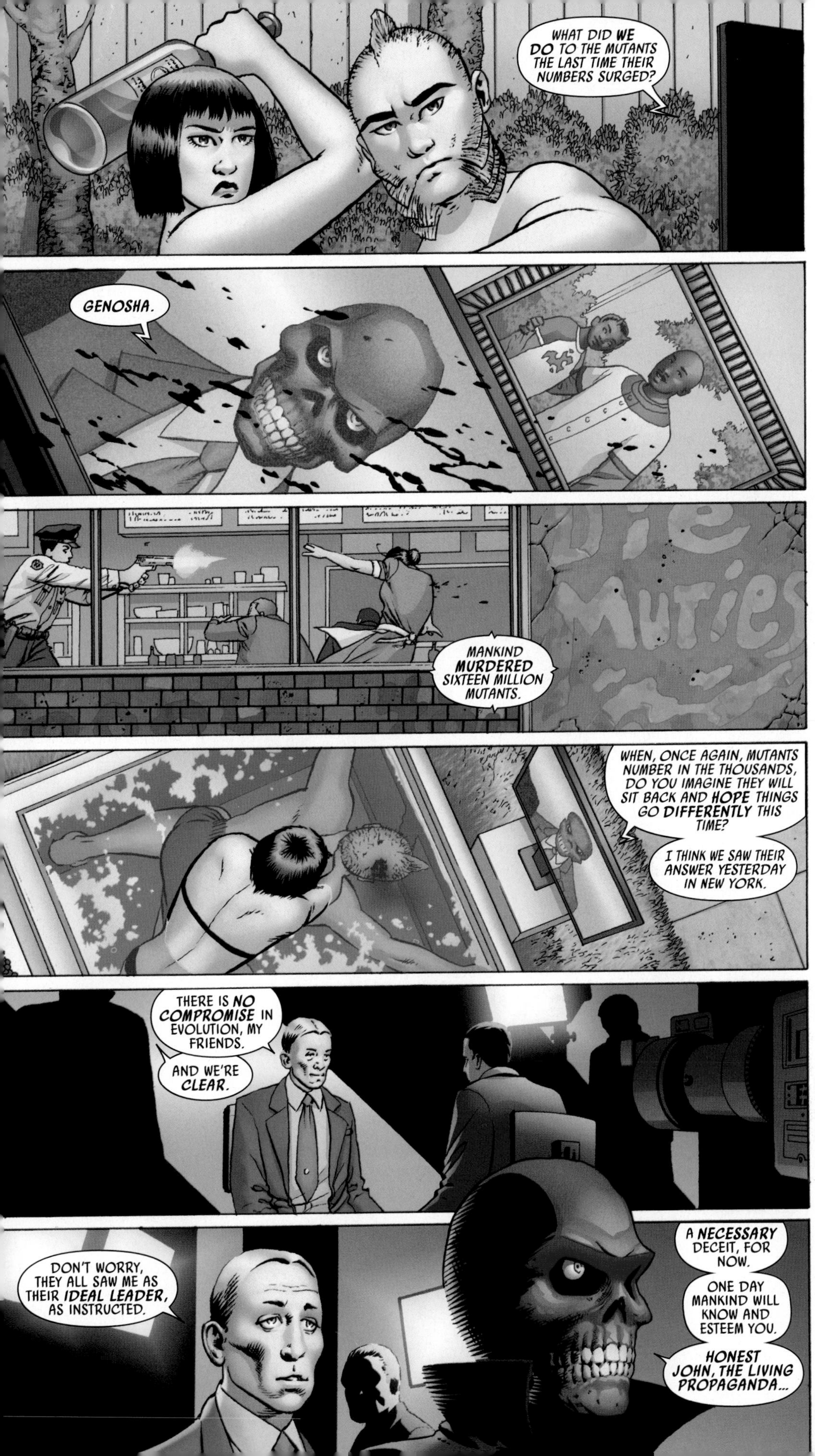
WHAT DID WE DO TO THE MUTANTS THE LAST TIME THEIR NUMBERS SURGED?
GENOSHA.
DIE MUTIES
MANKIND MURDERED SIXTEEN MILLION MUTANTS.
WHEN, ONCE AGAIN, MUTANTS NUMBER IN THE THOUSANDS, DO YOU IMAGINE THEY WILL SIT BACK AND HOPE THINGS GO DIFFERENTLY THIS TIME?
I THINK WE SAW THEIR ANSWER YESTERDAY IN NEW YORK.
THERE IS NO COMPROMISE IN EVOLUTION, MY FRIENDS.
AND WE'RE CLEAR.
DON'T WORRY, THEY ALL SAW ME AS THEIR IDEAL LEADER, AS INSTRUCTED.
A NECESSARY DECEIT, FOR NOW.
ONE DAY MANKIND WILL KNOW AND ESTEEM YOU.
HONEST JOHN, THE LIVING PROPAGANDA...

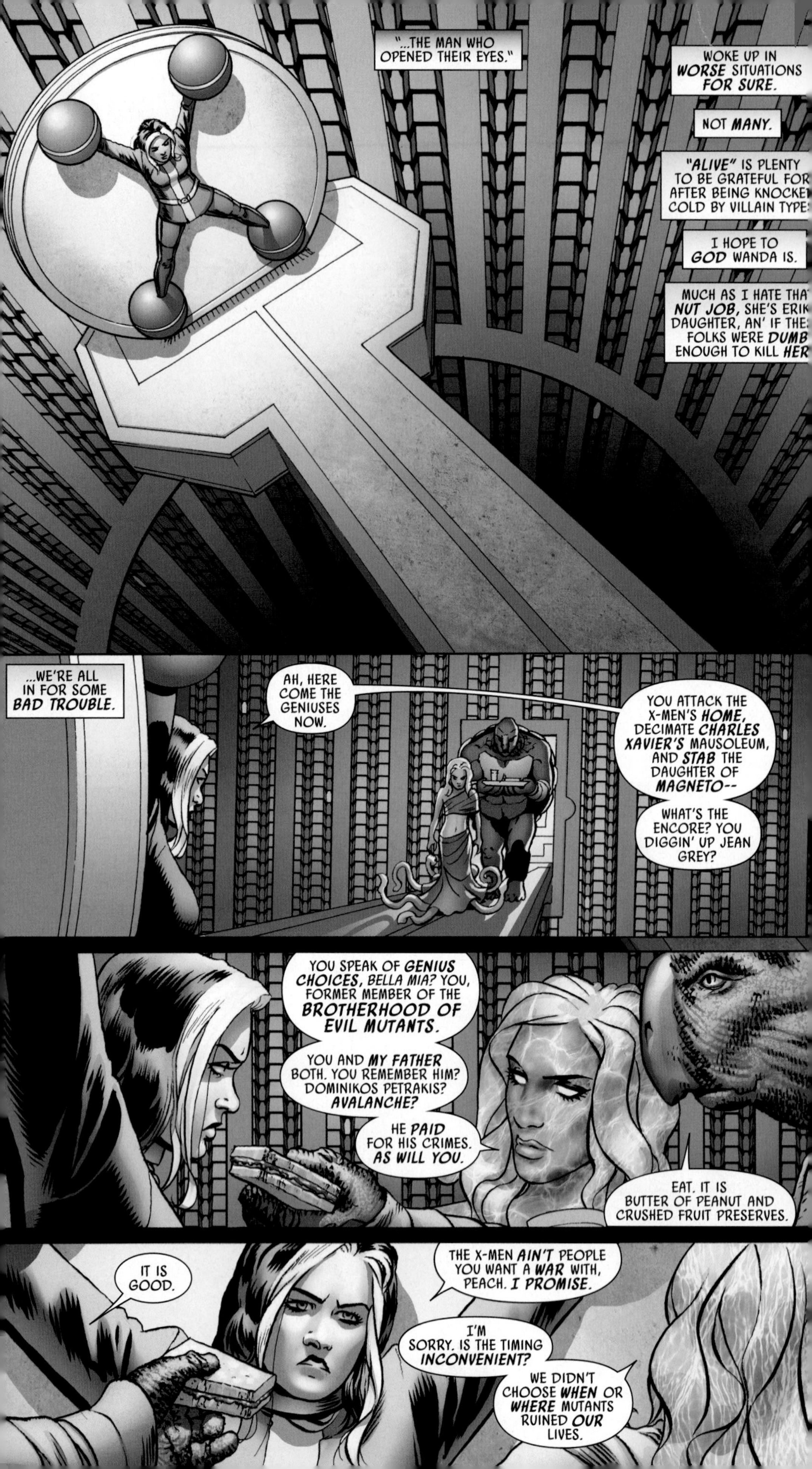
"...THE MAN WHO OPENED THEIR EYES."
WOKE UP IN WORSE SITUATIONS FOR SURE.
NOT MANY.
"ALIVE" IS PLENTY TO BE GRATEFUL FOR AFTER BEING KNOCKED COLD BY VILLAIN TYPES.
I HOPE TO GOD WANDA IS.
MUCH AS I HATE THAT NUT JOB, SHE'S ERIK'S DAUGHTER, AN' IF THESE FOLKS WERE DUMB ENOUGH TO KILL HER
...WE'RE ALL IN FOR SOME BAD TROUBLE.
AH, HERE COME THE GENIUSES NOW.
YOU ATTACK THE X-MEN'S HOME, DECIMATE CHARLES XAVIER'S MAUSOLEUM, AND STAB THE DAUGHTER OF MAGNETO--
WHAT'S THE ENCORE? YOU DIGGIN' UP JEAN GREY?
YOU SPEAK OF GENIUS CHOICES, BELLA MIA? YOU, FORMER MEMBER OF THE BROTHERHOOD OF EVIL MUTANTS.
YOU AND MY FATHER BOTH. YOU REMEMBER HIM? DOMINIKOS PETRAKIS? AVALANCHE?
HE PAID FOR HIS CRIMES. AS WILL YOU.
EAT. IT IS BUTTER OF PEANUT AND CRUSHED FRUIT PRESERVES.
IT IS GOOD.
THE X-MEN AIN'T PEOPLE YOU WANT A WAR WITH, PEACH. I PROMISE.
I'M SORRY. IS THE TIMING INCONVENIENT?
WE DIDN'T CHOOSE WHEN OR WHERE MUTANTS RUINED OUR LIVES.

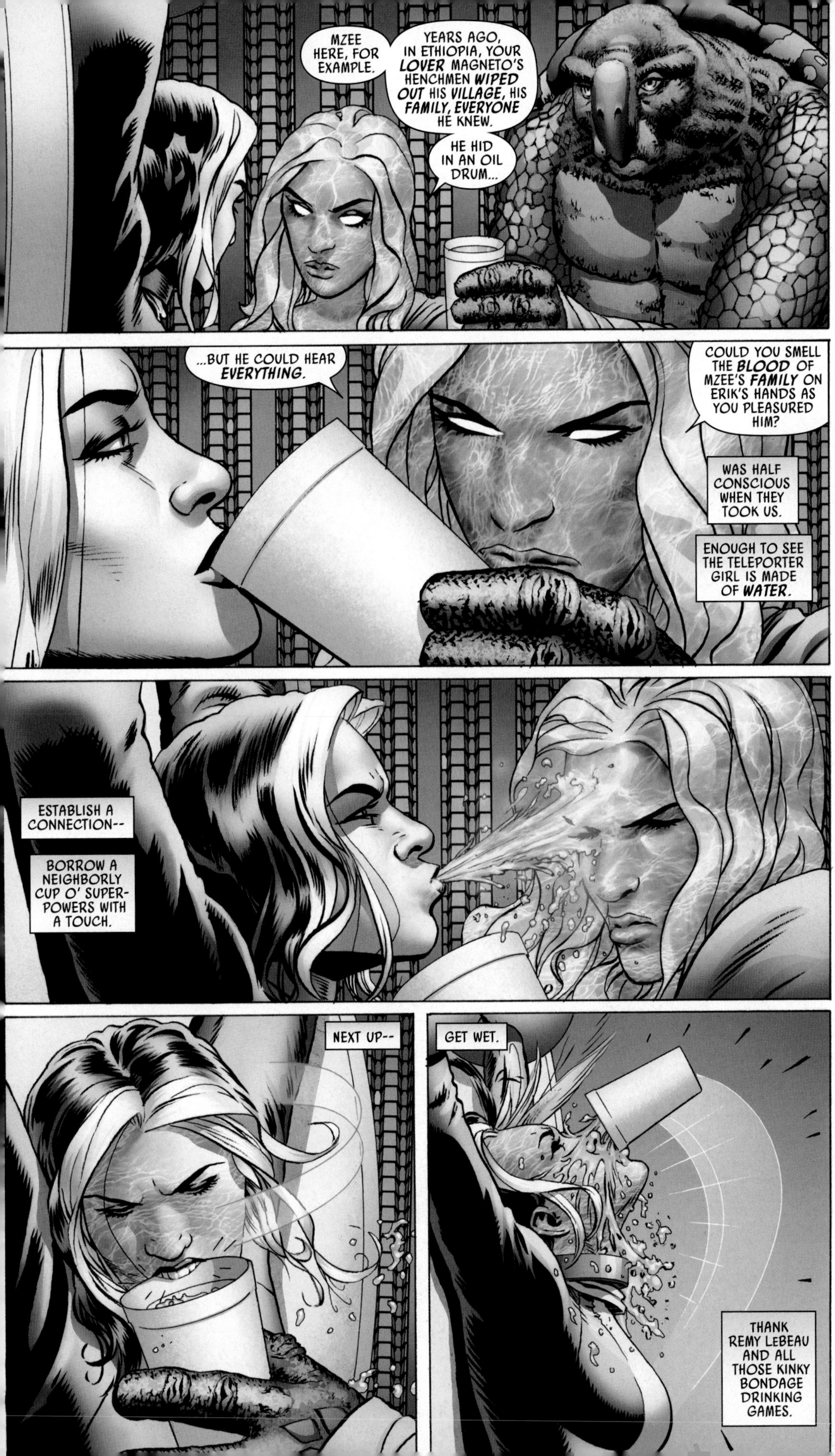
MZEE HERE, FOR EXAMPLE.
YEARS AGO, IN ETHIOPIA, YOUR LOVER MAGNETO'S HENCHMEN WIPED OUT HIS VILLAGE, HIS FAMILY, EVERYONE HE KNEW.
HE HID IN AN OIL DRUM...
...BUT HE COULD HEAR EVERYTHING.
COULD YOU SMELL THE BLOOD OF MZEE'S FAMILY ON ERIK'S HANDS AS YOU PLEASURED HIM?
WAS HALF CONSCIOUS WHEN THEY TOOK US.
ENOUGH TO SEE THE TELEPORTER GIRL IS MADE OF WATER.
ESTABLISH A CONNECTION--
BORROW A NEIGHBORLY CUP O' SUPER-POWERS WITH A TOUCH.
NEXT UP--
GET WET.
THANK REMY LEBEAU AND ALL THOSE KINKY BONDAGE DRINKING GAMES.

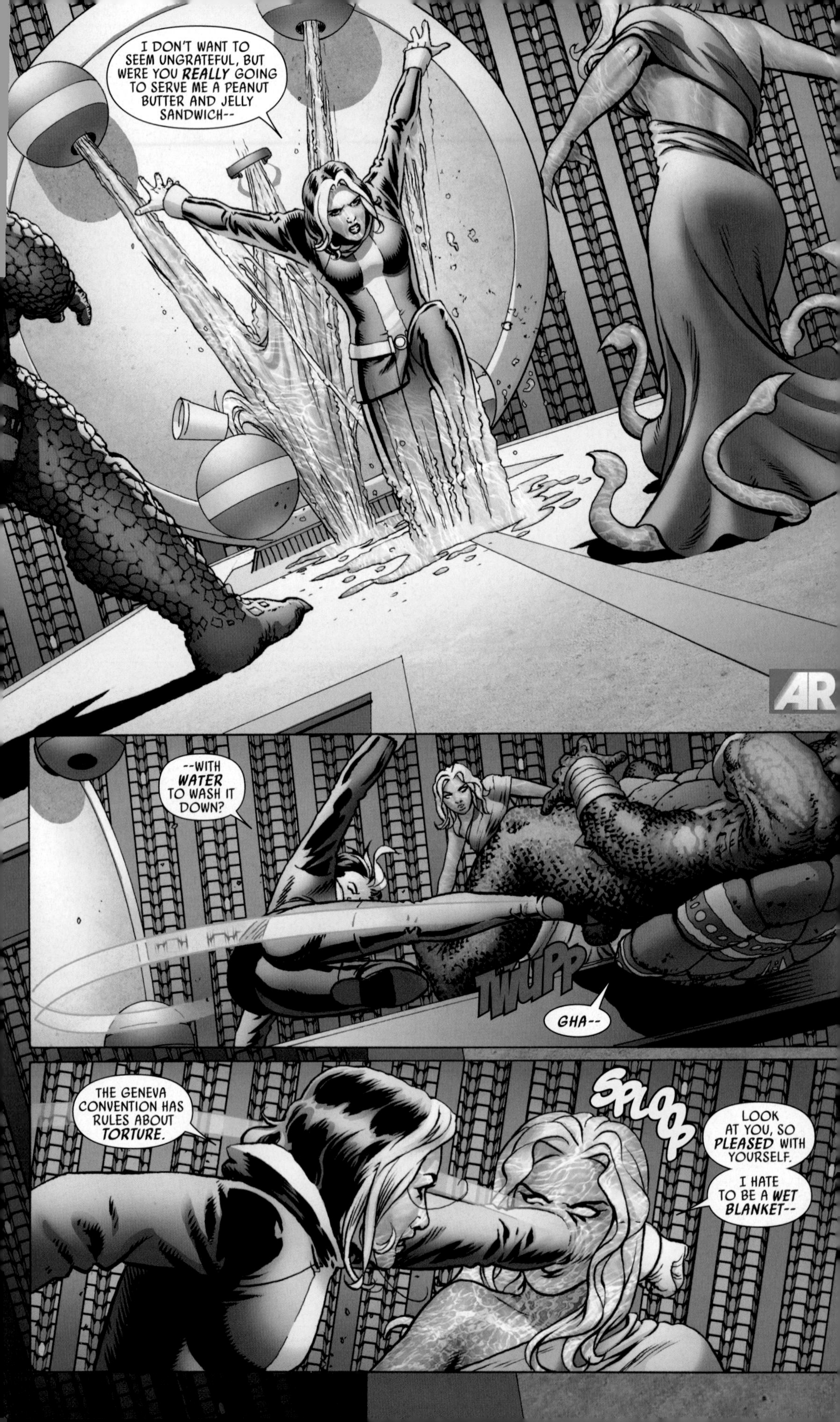
I DON'T WANT TO SEEM UNGRATEFUL, BUT WERE YOU REALLY GOING TO SERVE ME A PEANUT BUTTER AND JELLY SANDWICH--
--WITH WATER TO WASH IT DOWN?
TWUPP
GHA--
THE GENEVA CONVENTION HAS RULES ABOUT TORTURE.
SPLOOP
LOOK AT YOU, SO PLEASED WITH YOURSELF.
I HATE TO BE A WET BLANKET--

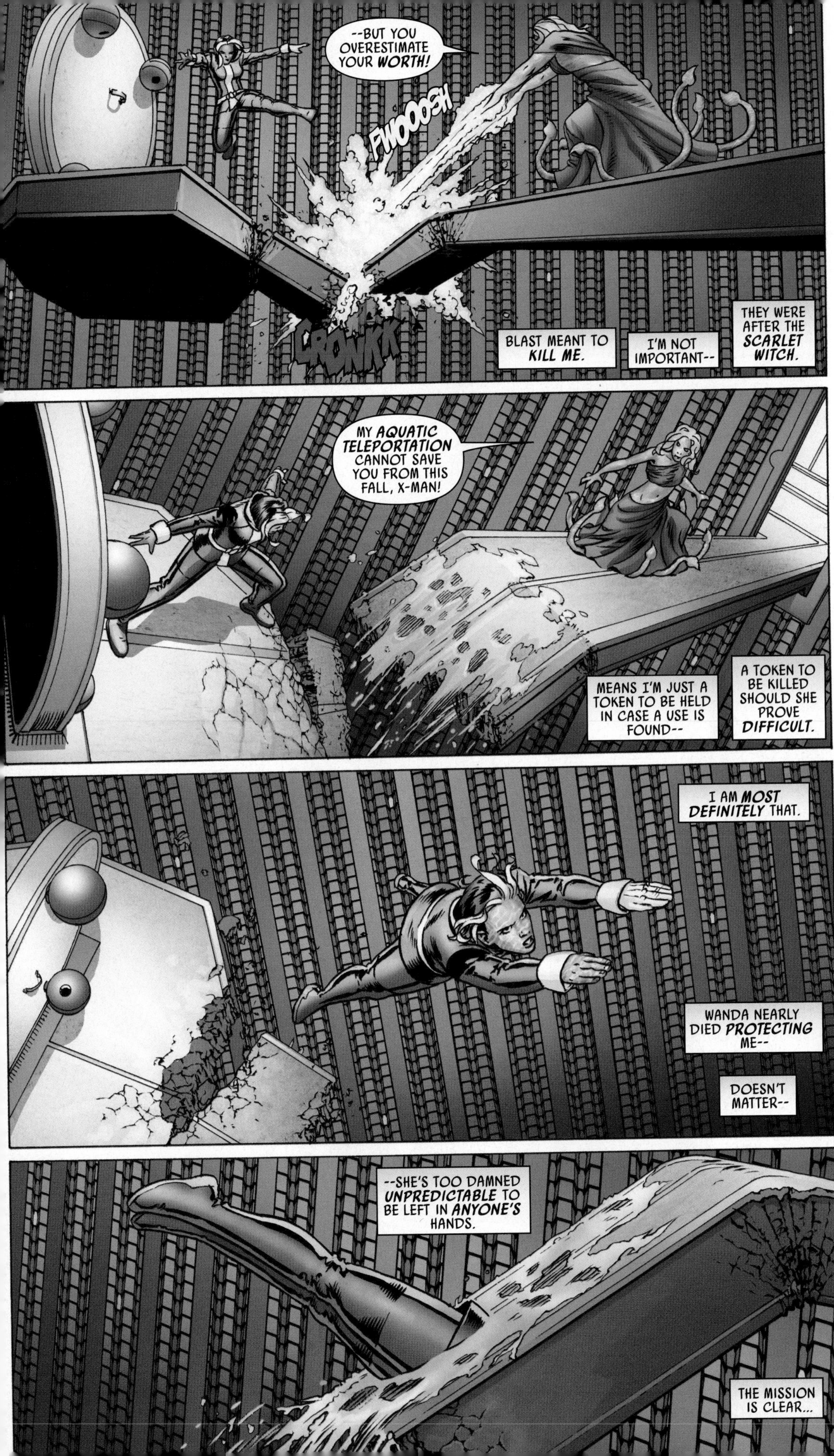
--BUT YOU OVERESTIMATE YOUR WORTH!
FWOOOOSH
CRONKK
BLAST MEANT TO KILL ME.
I'M NOT IMPORTANT--
THEY WERE AFTER THE SCARLET WITCH.
MY AQUATIC TELEPORTATION CANNOT SAVE YOU FROM THIS FALL, X-MAN!
MEANS I'M JUST A TOKEN TO BE HELD IN CASE A USE IS FOUND--
A TOKEN TO BE KILLED SHOULD SHE PROVE DIFFICULT.
I AM MOST DEFINITELY THAT.
WANDA NEARLY DIED PROTECTING ME--
DOESN'T MATTER--
--SHE'S TOO DAMNED UNPREDICTABLE TO BE LEFT IN ANYONE'S HANDS.
THE MISSION IS CLEAR...

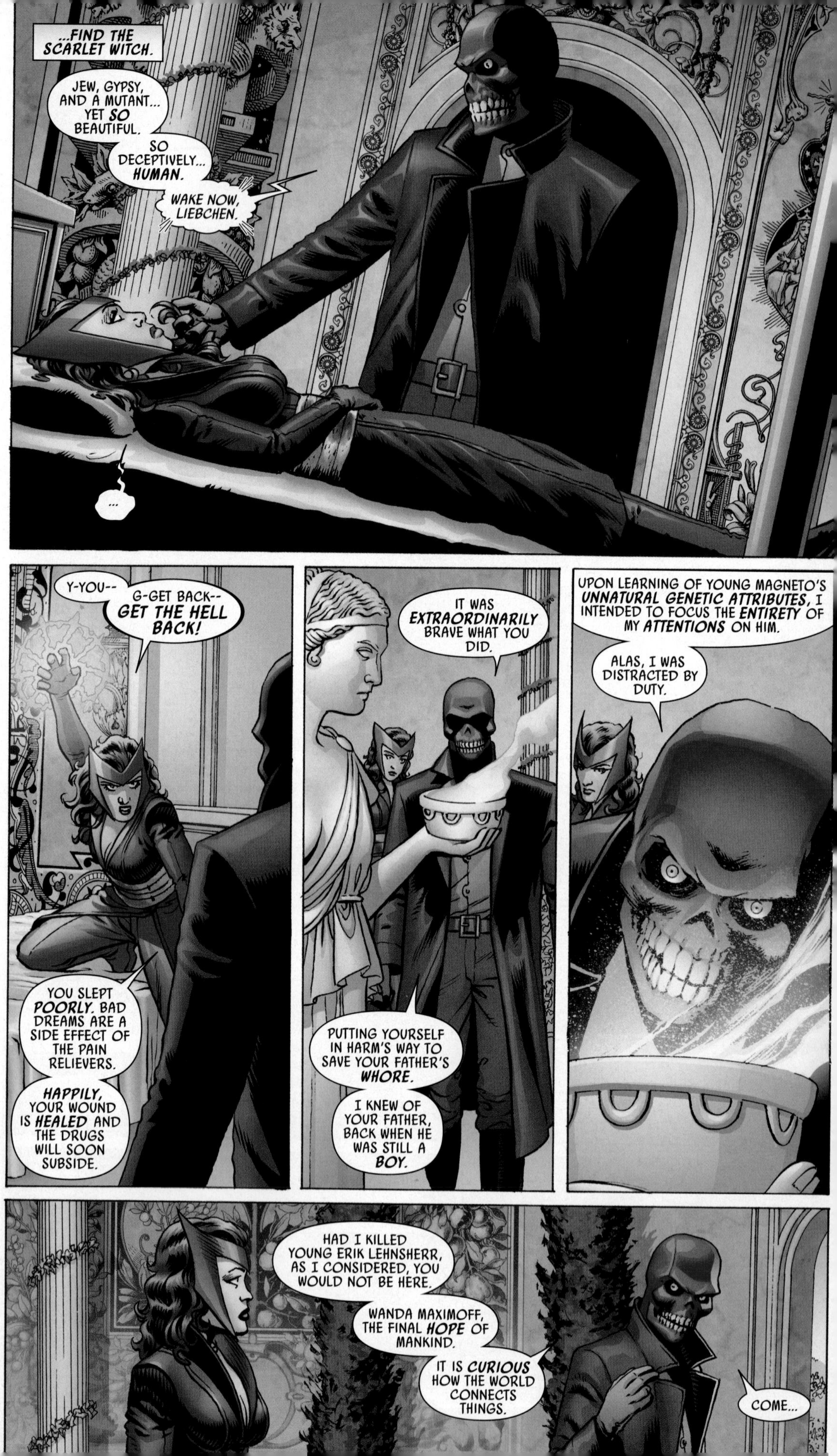
...FIND THE SCARLET WITCH.
JEW, GYPSY, AND A MUTANT... YET SO BEAUTIFUL.
SO DECEPTIVELY... HUMAN.
WAKE NOW, LIEBCHEN.
...
Y-YOU--
G-GET BACK-- GET THE HELL BACK!
YOU SLEPT POORLY. BAD DREAMS ARE A SIDE EFFECT OF THE PAIN RELIEVERS.
HAPPILY, YOUR WOUND IS HEALED AND THE DRUGS WILL SOON SUBSIDE.
IT WAS EXTRAORDINARILY BRAVE WHAT YOU DID.
PUTTING YOURSELF IN HARM'S WAY TO SAVE YOUR FATHER'S WHORE.
I KNEW OF YOUR FATHER, BACK WHEN HE WAS STILL A BOY.
UPON LEARNING OF YOUNG MAGNETO'S UNNATURAL GENETIC ATTRIBUTES, I INTENDED TO FOCUS THE ENTIRETY OF MY ATTENTIONS ON HIM.
ALAS, I WAS DISTRACTED BY DUTY.
HAD I KILLED YOUNG ERIK LEHNSHERR, AS I CONSIDERED, YOU WOULD NOT BE HERE.
WANDA MAXIMOFF, THE FINAL HOPE OF MANKIND.
IT IS CURIOUS HOW THE WORLD CONNECTS THINGS.
COME...

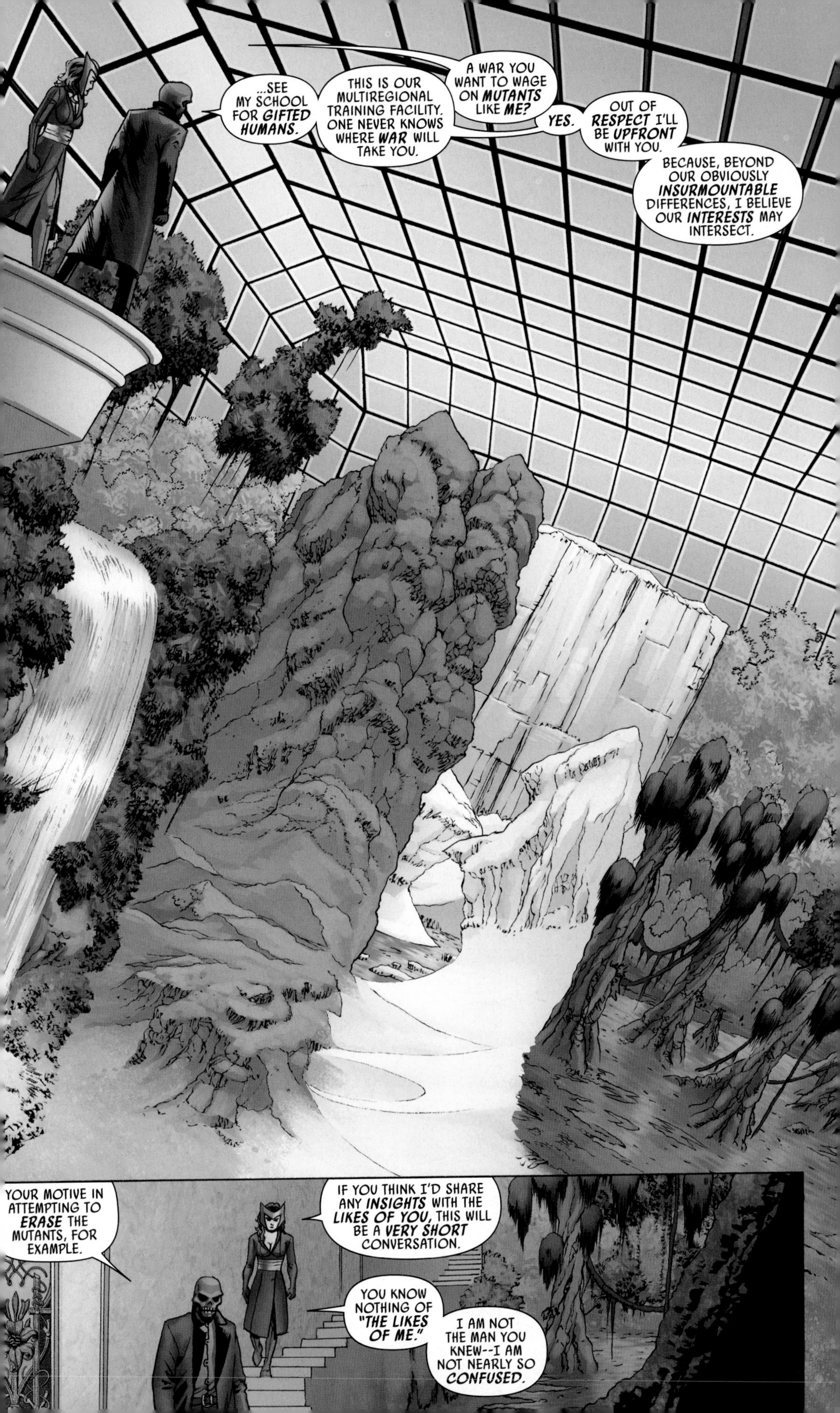
...SEE MY SCHOOL FOR GIFTED HUMANS.
THIS IS OUR MULTIREGIONAL TRAINING FACILITY. ONE NEVER KNOWS WHERE WAR WILL TAKE YOU.
A WAR YOU WANT TO WAGE ON MUTANTS LIKE ME?
YES.
OUT OF RESPECT I'LL BE UPFRONT WITH YOU.
BECAUSE, BEYOND OUR OBVIOUSLY INSURMOUNTABLE DIFFERENCES, I BELIEVE OUR INTERESTS MAY INTERSECT.
YOUR MOTIVE IN ATTEMPTING TO ERASE THE MUTANTS, FOR EXAMPLE.
IF YOU THINK I'D SHARE ANY INSIGHTS WITH THE LIKES OF YOU, THIS WILL BE A VERY SHORT CONVERSATION.
YOU KNOW NOTHING OF "THE LIKES OF ME."
I AM NOT THE MAN YOU KNEW--I AM NOT NEARLY SO CONFUSED.

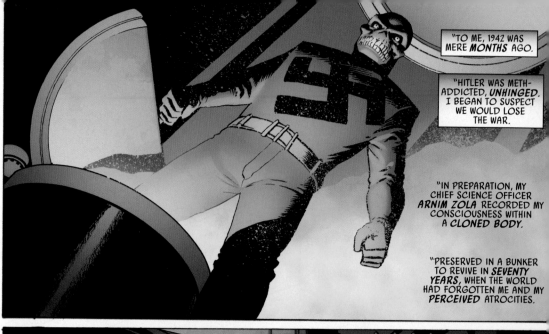

"TO ME, 1942 WAS MERE *MONTHS* AGO.

"HITLER WAS METH-ADDICTED, *UNHINGED*. I BEGAN TO SUSPECT WE WOULD LOSE THE WAR.

"IN PREPARATION, MY CHIEF SCIENCE OFFICER *ARNIM ZOLA* RECORDED MY CONSCIOUSNESS WITHIN A *CLONED BODY*.

"PRESERVED IN A BUNKER TO REVIVE IN *SEVENTY YEARS*, WHEN THE WORLD HAD FORGOTTEN ME AND MY *PERCEIVED* ATROCITIES.

"I AWOKE TO AN ALL-TOO-FAMILIAR WORLD STAGE.

"IN *AMERICA*, I SAW THE SAME *EMBERS* THAT *BURNED* IN GERMANY BEFORE THE *WAR*.

"A *FRIGHTENED* POPULATION OF TOTEM WORSHIPERS, LIVING IN *DECLINE*, *FLINCHING* AT SHADOWS--ALL *HUNGRILY* LOOKING FOR SOMEONE TO *BLAME*."

MUTANTS ARE THE ULTIMATE *INVADING FOREIGNERS*.

YOU ARE *THEIR GREATEST FEAR*-- AND *RIGHTFULLY* SO.

I SUSPECT YOU *MUST* AGREE--IN SOME PART OF YOUR SOUL--TO HAVE DONE WHAT YOU DID.

I WAS LOST...

MY CHILDREN *DEAD*, AND MY FATHER, HE NEEDED TO *SEE*...

NEEDED TO SEE THAT OUR WORLD WAS BETTER OFF WITHOUT MUTANTS.

NO...

YES.

YOU'VE *NEVER* BELONGED IN *THEIR* WORLD, WANDA. YOU SEE THEM FOR THE *DANGER* THEY ARE.

DEEP DOWN YOU WANT TO LIVE IN A WORLD *FREE* OF MUTANTS.

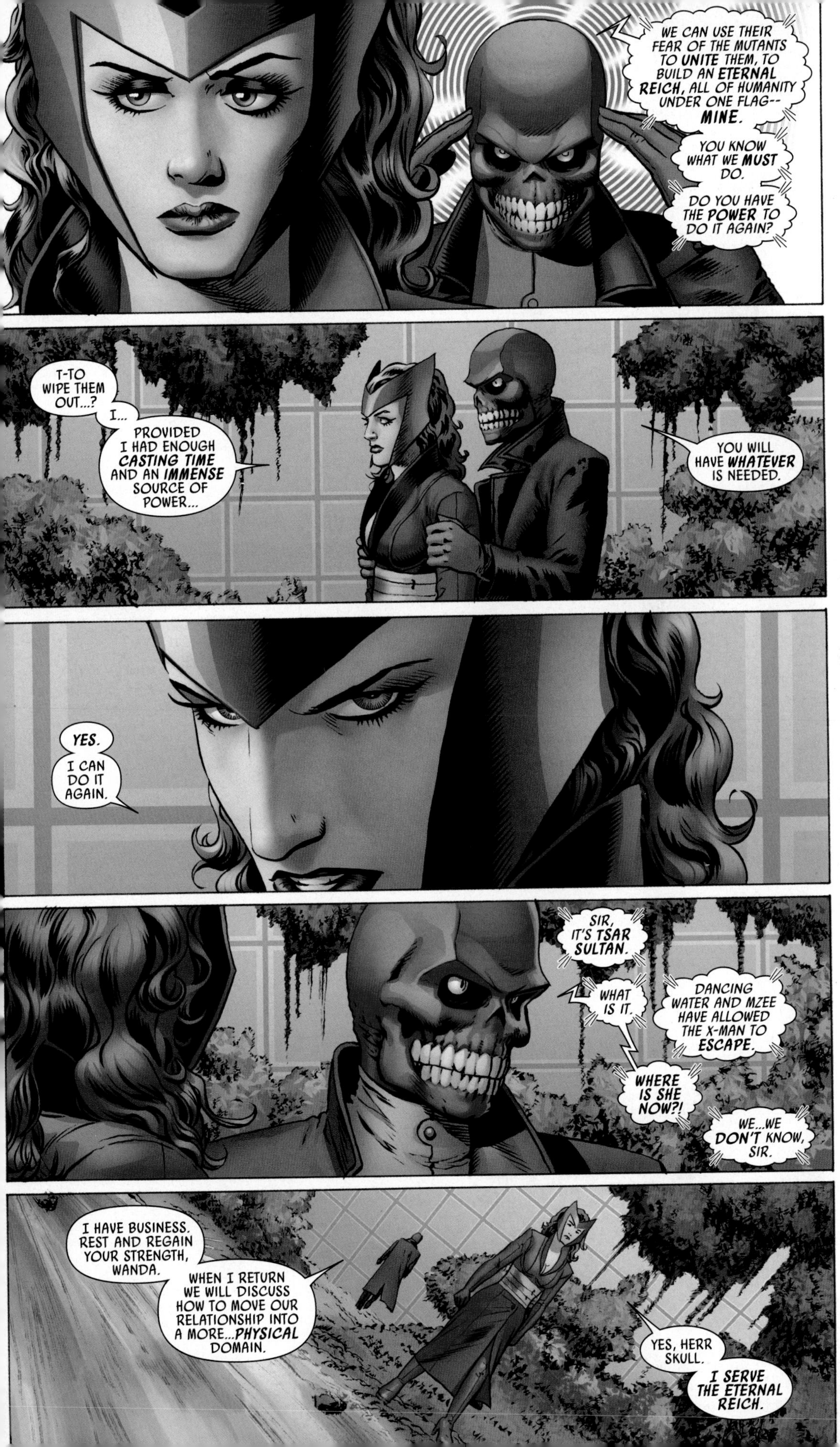
WE CAN USE THEIR FEAR OF THE MUTANTS TO UNITE THEM, TO BUILD AN ETERNAL REICH, ALL OF HUMANITY UNDER ONE FLAG-- MINE.
YOU KNOW WHAT WE MUST DO.
DO YOU HAVE THE POWER TO DO IT AGAIN?
T-TO WIPE THEM OUT...?
I...
PROVIDED I HAD ENOUGH CASTING TIME AND AN IMMENSE SOURCE OF POWER...
YOU WILL HAVE WHATEVER IS NEEDED.
YES.
I CAN DO IT AGAIN.
SIR, IT'S TSAR SULTAN.
WHAT IS IT.
DANCING WATER AND MZEE HAVE ALLOWED THE X-MAN TO ESCAPE.
WHERE IS SHE NOW?!
WE...WE DON'T KNOW, SIR.
I HAVE BUSINESS. REST AND REGAIN YOUR STRENGTH, WANDA.
WHEN I RETURN WE WILL DISCUSS HOW TO MOVE OUR RELATIONSHIP INTO A MORE...PHYSICAL DOMAIN.
YES, HERR SKULL.
I SERVE THE ETERNAL REICH.

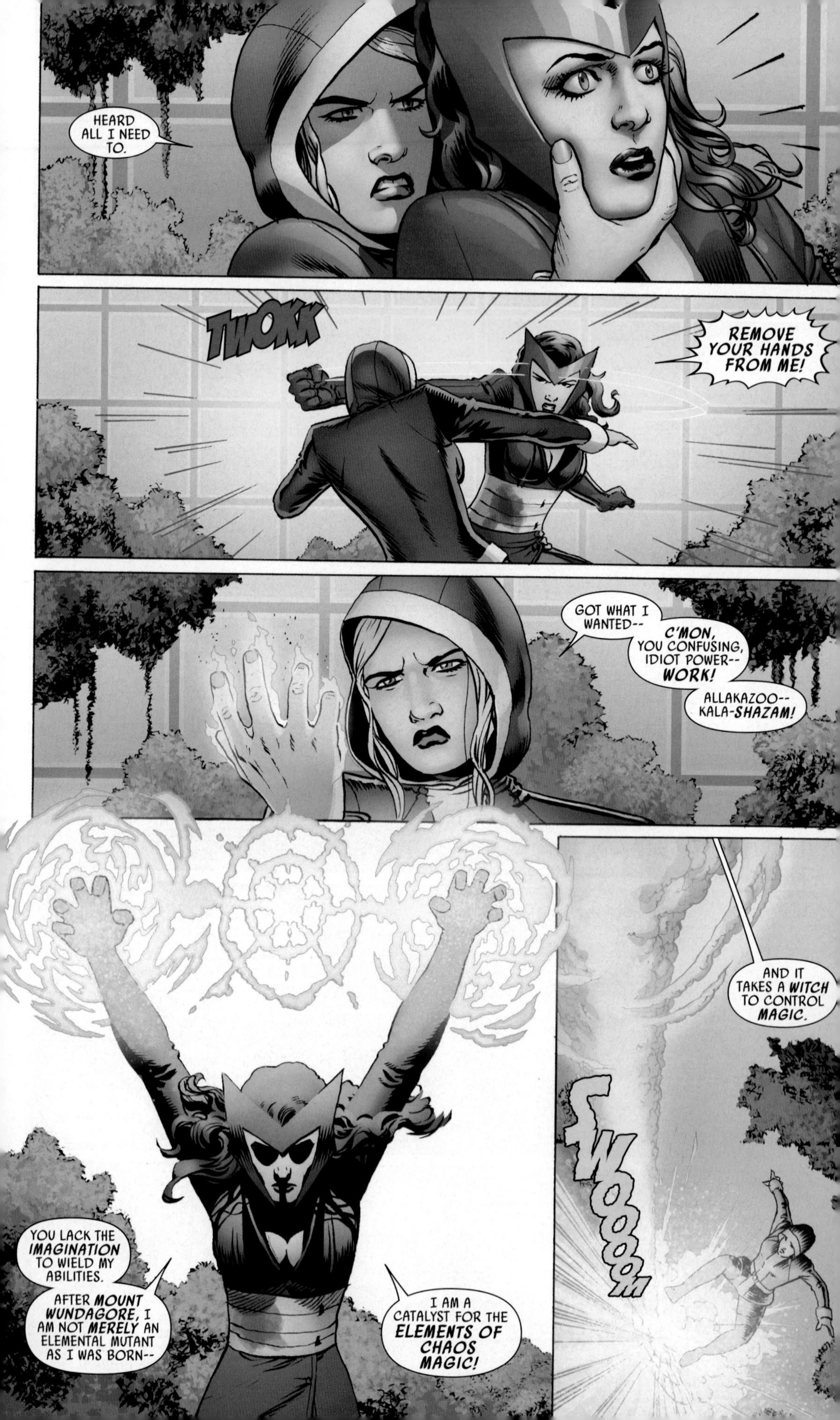
HEARD ALL I NEED TO.
TWOKK
REMOVE YOUR HANDS FROM ME!
GOT WHAT I WANTED-- C'MON, YOU CONFUSING, IDIOT POWER-- WORK!
ALLAKAZOO-- KALA-SHAZAM!
YOU LACK THE IMAGINATION TO WIELD MY ABILITIES.
AFTER MOUNT WUNDAGORE, I AM NOT MERELY AN ELEMENTAL MUTANT AS I WAS BORN--
I AM A CATALYST FOR THE ELEMENTS OF CHAOS MAGIC!
AND IT TAKES A WITCH TO CONTROL MAGIC.
FWOOOOM

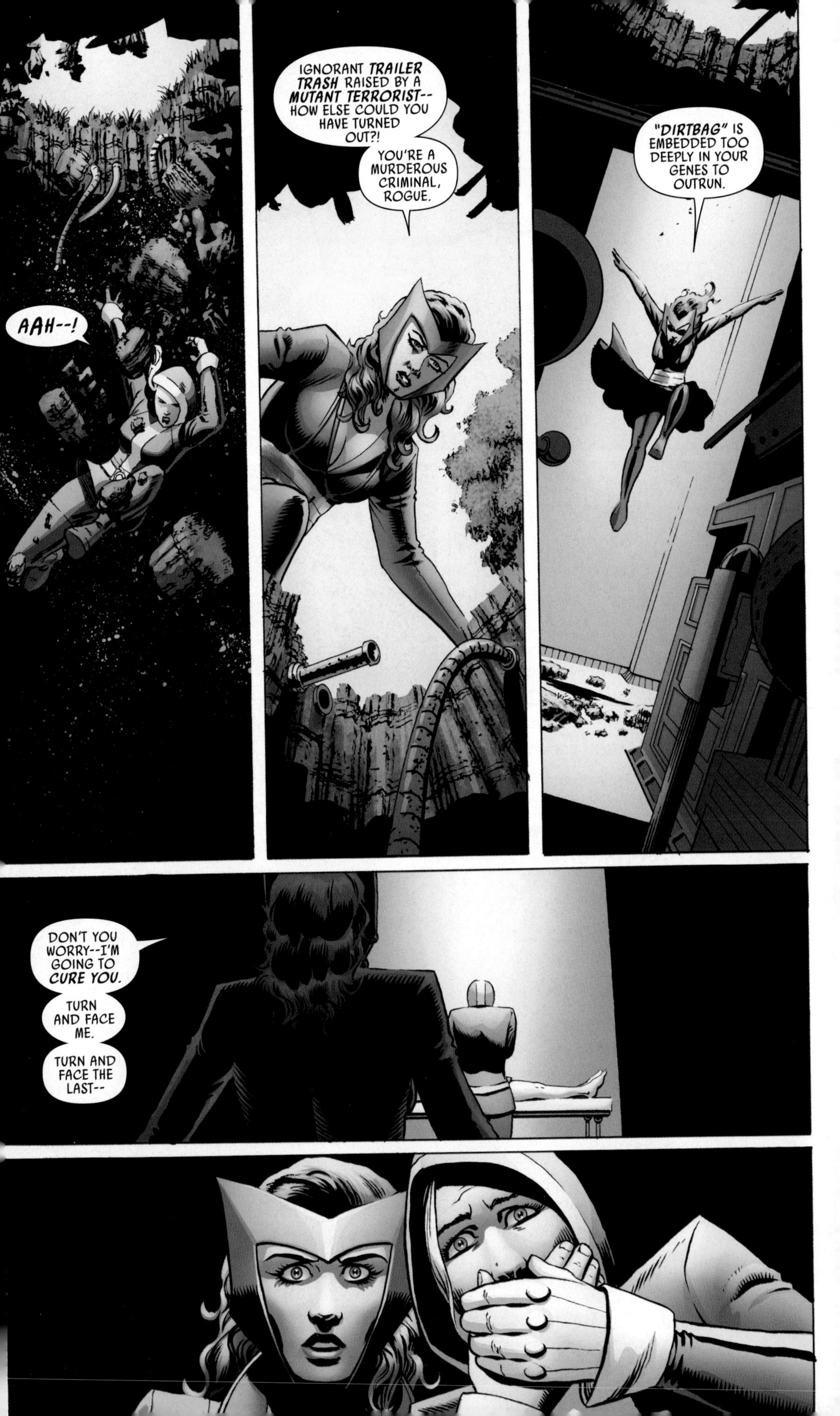
AAH--!
IGNORANT TRAILER TRASH RAISED BY A MUTANT TERRORIST-- HOW ELSE COULD YOU HAVE TURNED OUT?!
YOU'RE A MURDEROUS CRIMINAL, ROGUE.
"DIRTBAG" IS EMBEDDED TOO DEEPLY IN YOUR GENES TO OUTRUN.
DON'T YOU WORRY--I'M GOING TO CURE YOU.
TURN AND FACE ME.
TURN AND FACE THE LAST--

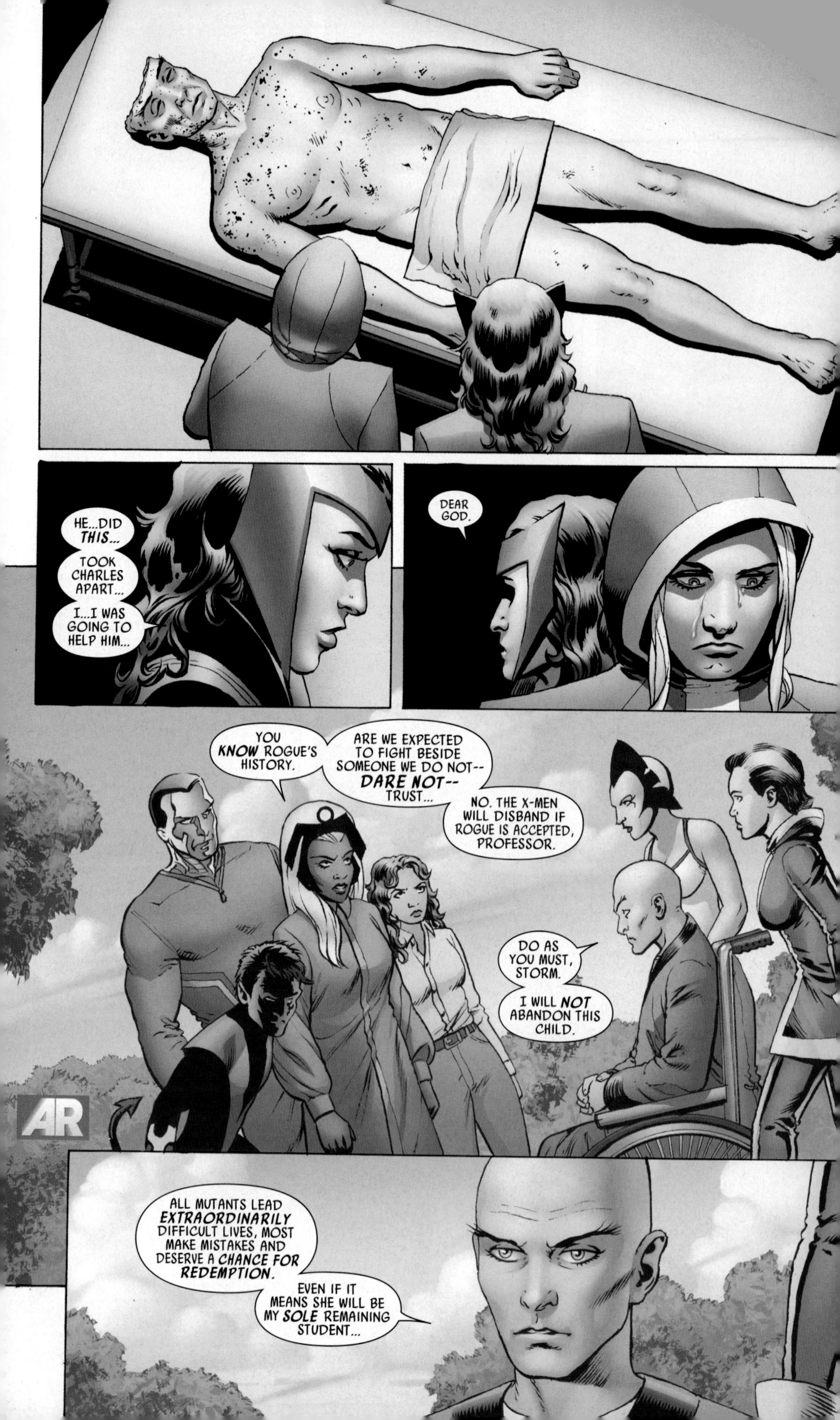
HE...DID THIS...
TOOK CHARLES APART...
I...I WAS GOING TO HELP HIM...
DEAR GOD.
YOU KNOW ROGUE'S HISTORY.
ARE WE EXPECTED TO FIGHT BESIDE SOMEONE WE DO NOT-- DARE NOT-- TRUST...
NO. THE X-MEN WILL DISBAND IF ROGUE IS ACCEPTED, PROFESSOR.
DO AS YOU MUST, STORM.
I WILL NOT ABANDON THIS CHILD.
ALL MUTANTS LEAD EXTRAORDINARILY DIFFICULT LIVES, MOST MAKE MISTAKES AND DESERVE A CHANCE FOR REDEMPTION.
EVEN IF IT MEANS SHE WILL BE MY SOLE REMAINING STUDENT...

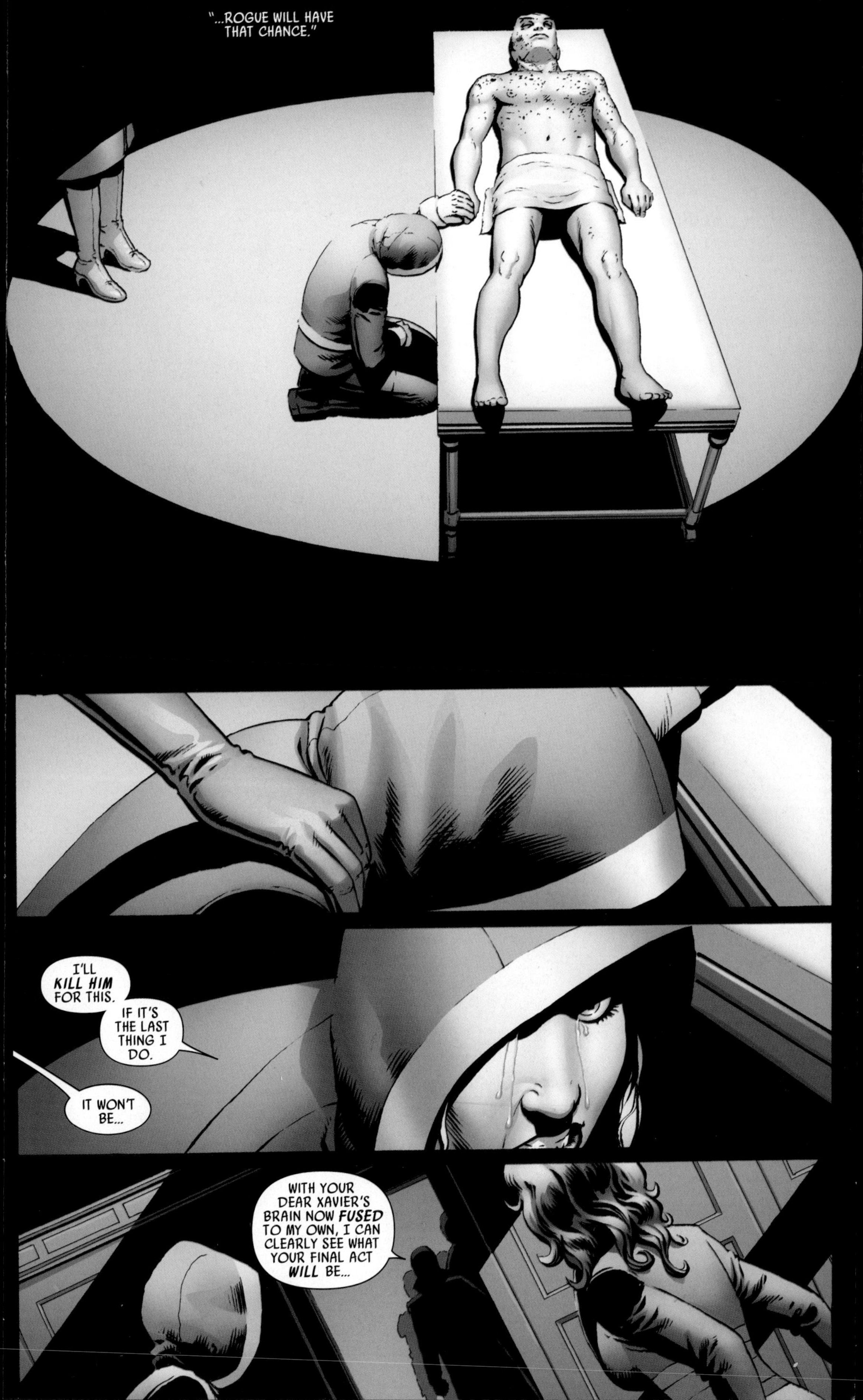
"...ROGUE WILL HAVE THAT CHANCE."
I'LL KILL HIM FOR THIS.
IF IT'S THE LAST THING I DO.
IT WON'T BE...
WITH YOUR DEAR XAVIER'S BRAIN NOW FUSED TO MY OWN, I CAN CLEARLY SEE WHAT YOUR FINAL ACT WILL BE...

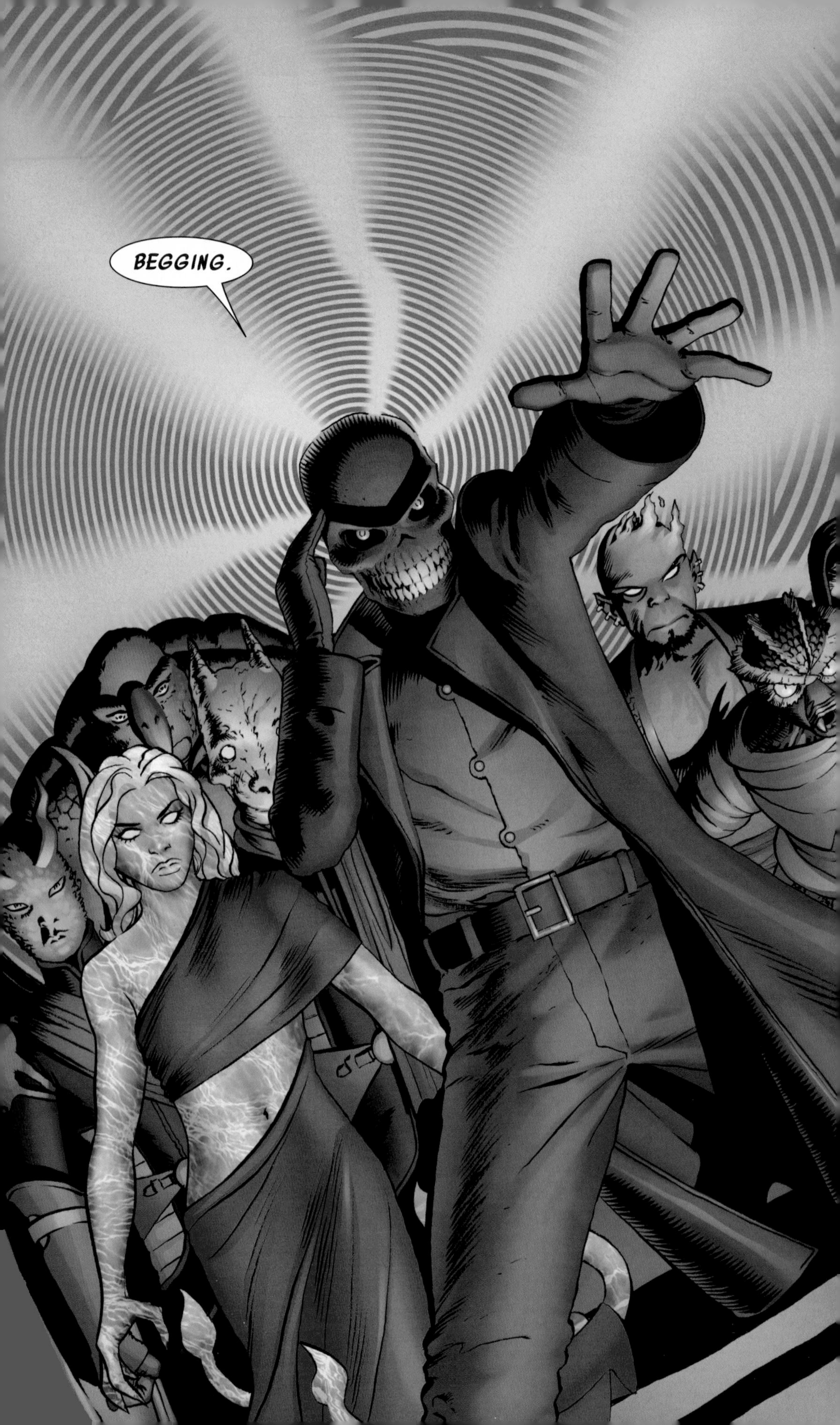
BEGGING.

UNCANNY AVENGERS #1 VARIANT BY SARA PICHELLI & MARTE GRACIA

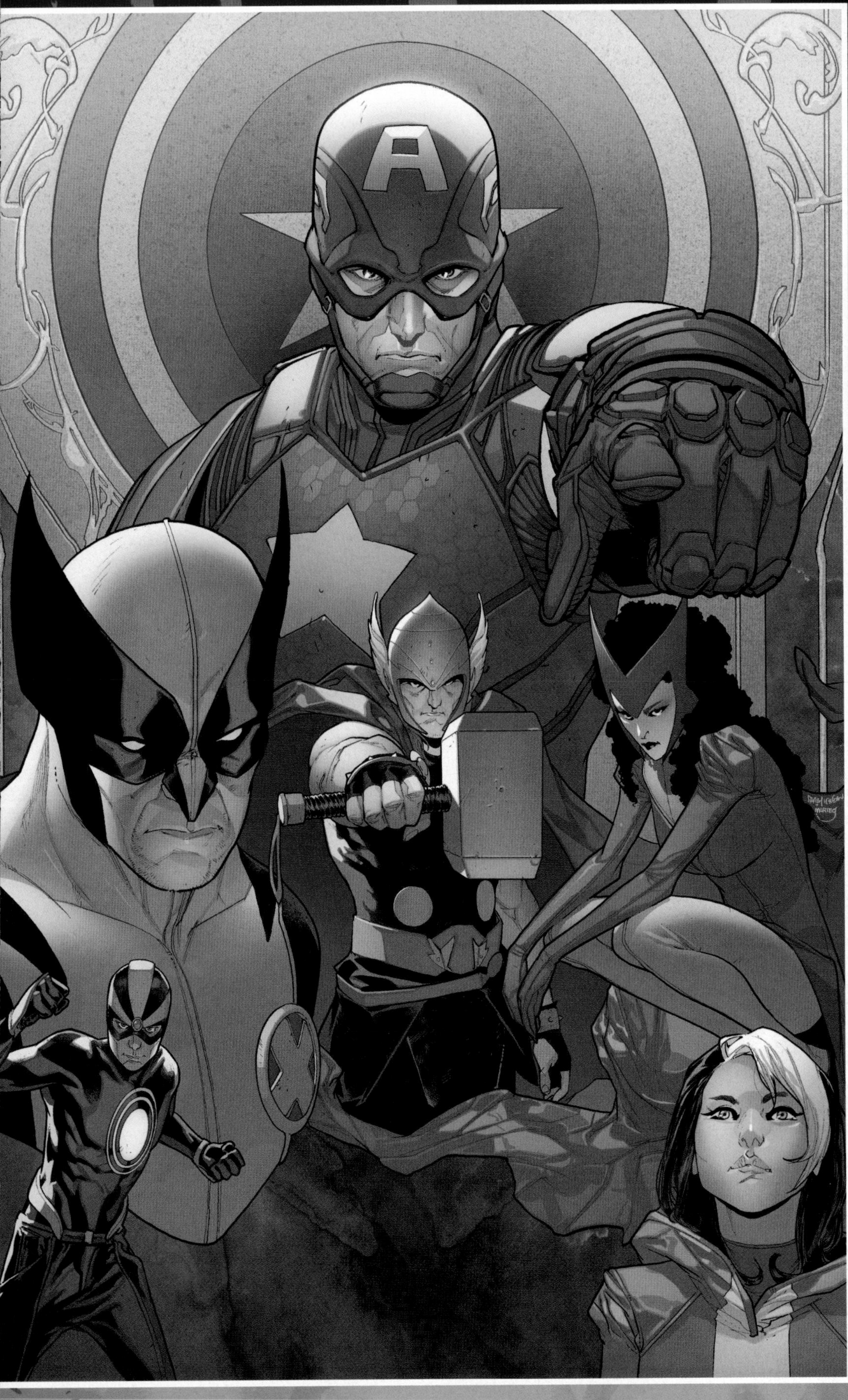

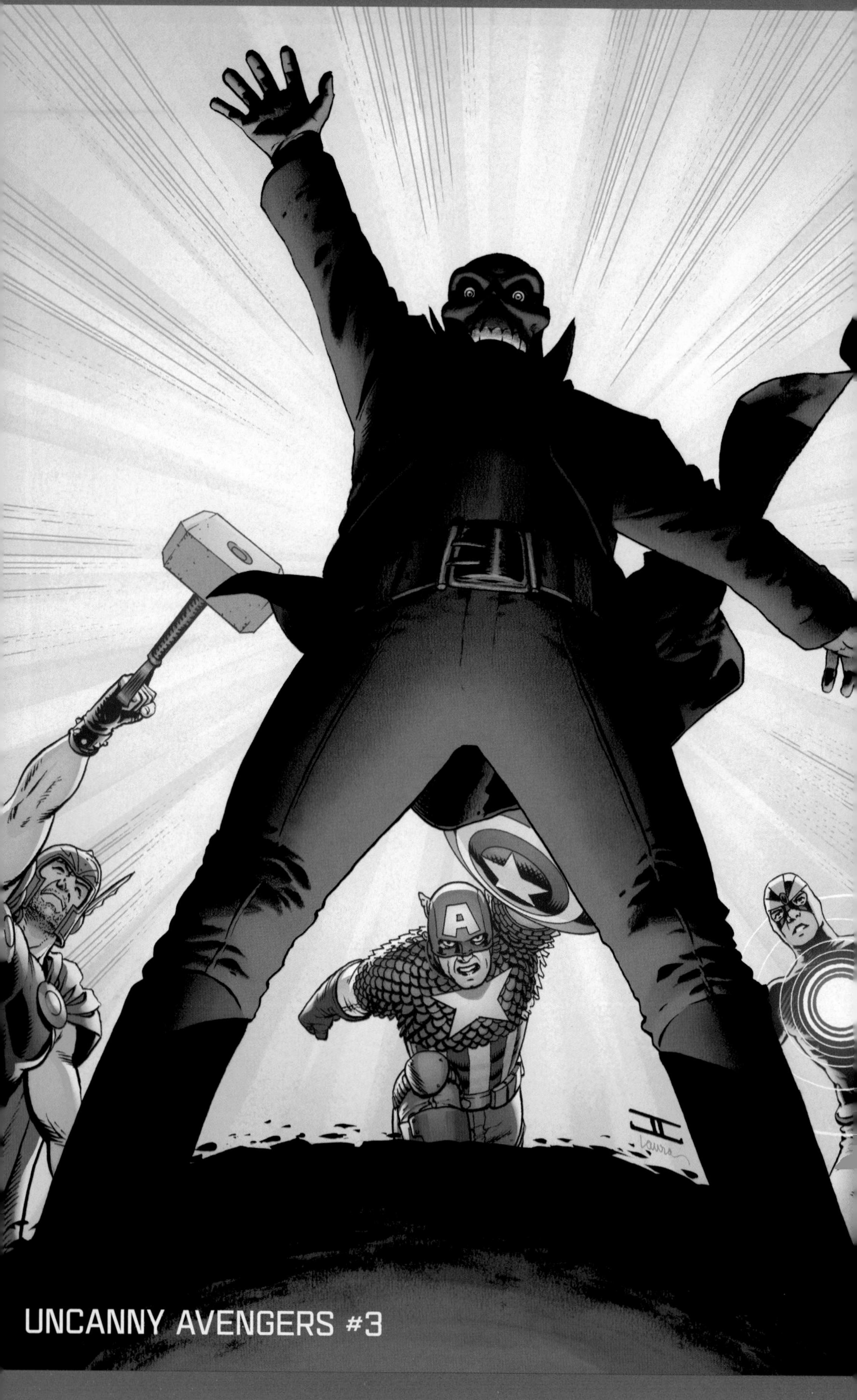

UNCANNY AVENGERS #3

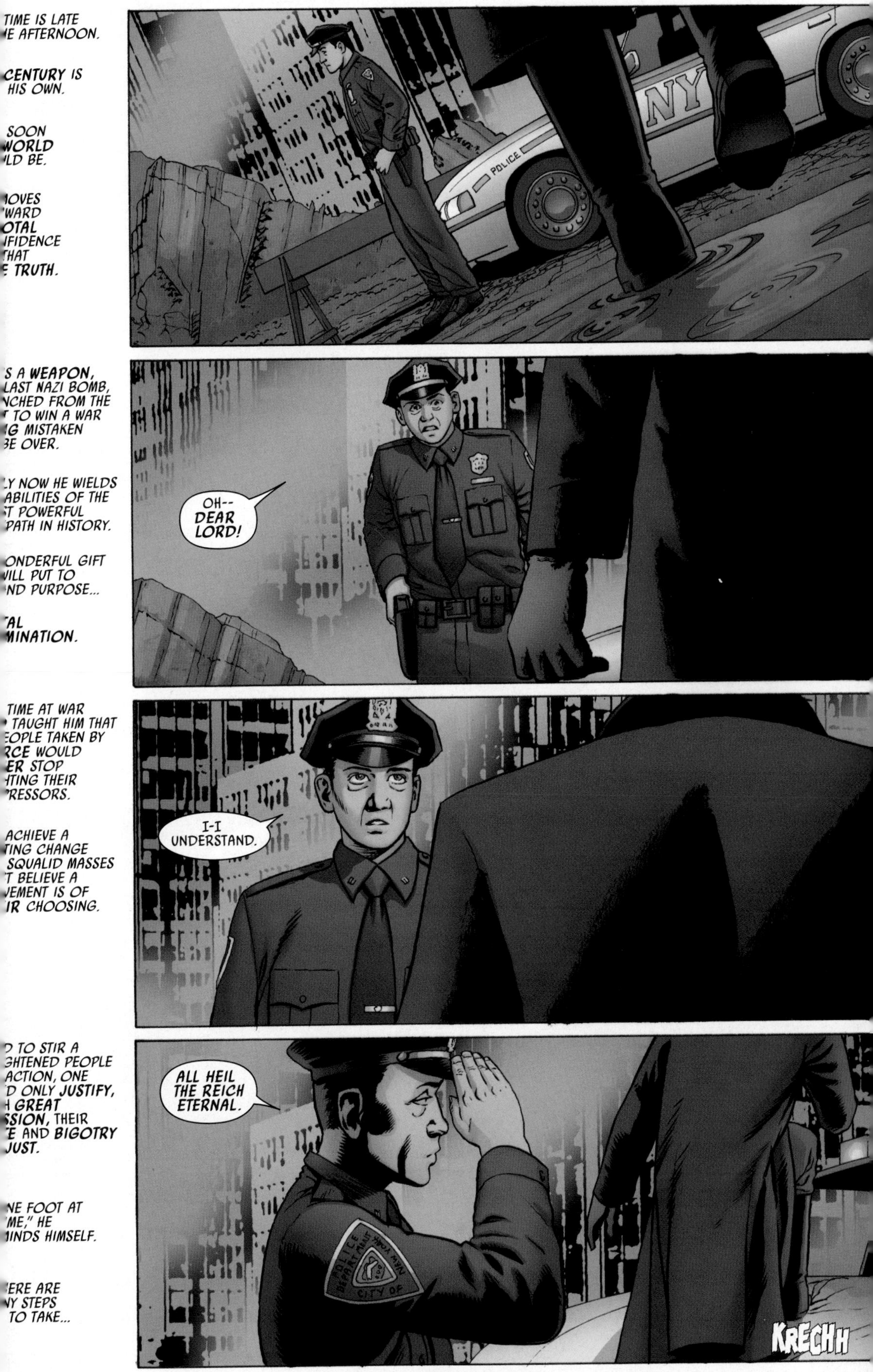
TIME IS LATE
IE AFTERNOON.
CENTURY IS
HIS OWN.
SOON
WORLD
ILD BE.
IOVES
WARD
OTAL
IFIDENCE
THAT
TRUTH.
POLICE
NY
S A WEAPON,
LAST NAZI BOMB,
NCHED FROM THE
TO WIN A WAR
G MISTAKEN
BE OVER.
Y NOW HE WIELDS
ABILITIES OF THE
T POWERFUL
PATH IN HISTORY.
ONDERFUL GIFT
VILL PUT TO
ND PURPOSE...
AL
MINATION.
OH-- DEAR LORD!
TIME AT WAR
TAUGHT HIM THAT
EOPLE TAKEN BY
RCE WOULD
ER STOP
ITING THEIR
RESSORS.
ACHIEVE A
TING CHANGE
SQUALID MASSES
T BELIEVE A
VEMENT IS OF
IR CHOOSING.
I-I UNDERSTAND.
D TO STIR A
GHTENED PEOPLE
ACTION, ONE
D ONLY JUSTIFY,
H GREAT
SSION, THEIR
E AND BIGOTRY
JUST.
NE FOOT AT
ME," HE
IINDS HIMSELF.
ERE ARE
NY STEPS
TO TAKE...
ALL HEIL THE REICH ETERNAL.
KRECHH

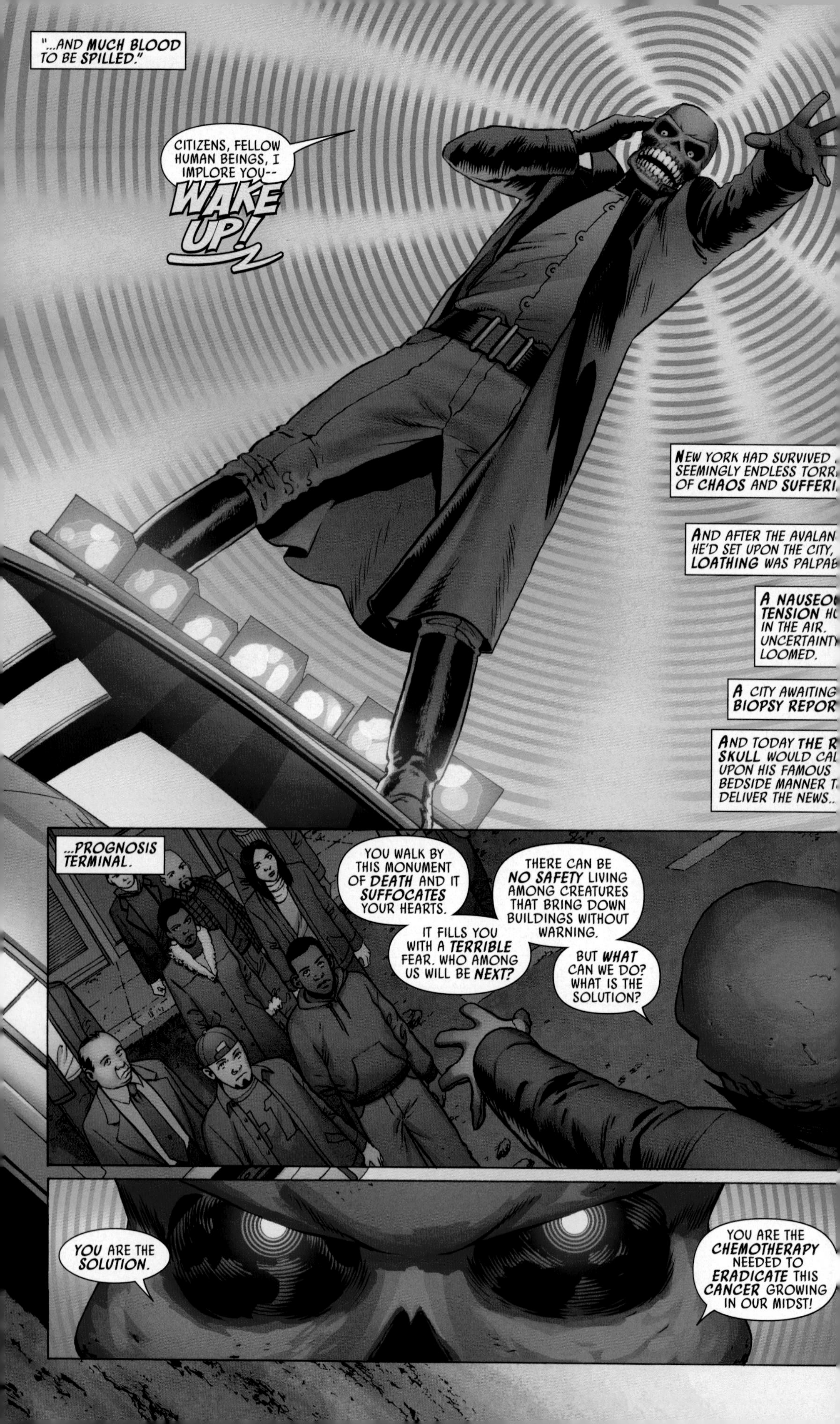
"...AND MUCH BLOOD TO BE SPILLED."
CITIZENS, FELLOW HUMAN BEINGS, I IMPLORE YOU-- WAKE UP!
NEW YORK HAD SURVIVED . SEEMINGLY ENDLESS TORR OF CHAOS AND SUFFERI
AND AFTER THE AVALAN HE'D SET UPON THE CITY, LOATHING WAS PALPAB
A NAUSEO TENSION H IN THE AIR. UNCERTAINTY LOOMED.
A CITY AWAITING BIOPSY REPOR
AND TODAY THE R SKULL WOULD CAL UPON HIS FAMOUS BEDSIDE MANNER T DELIVER THE NEWS...
...PROGNOSIS TERMINAL.
YOU WALK BY THIS MONUMENT OF DEATH AND IT SUFFOCATES YOUR HEARTS.
IT FILLS YOU WITH A TERRIBLE FEAR. WHO AMONG US WILL BE NEXT?
THERE CAN BE NO SAFETY LIVING AMONG CREATURES THAT BRING DOWN BUILDINGS WITHOUT WARNING.
BUT WHAT CAN WE DO? WHAT IS THE SOLUTION?
YOU ARE THE SOLUTION.
YOU ARE THE CHEMOTHERAPY NEEDED TO ERADICATE THIS CANCER GROWING IN OUR MIDST!

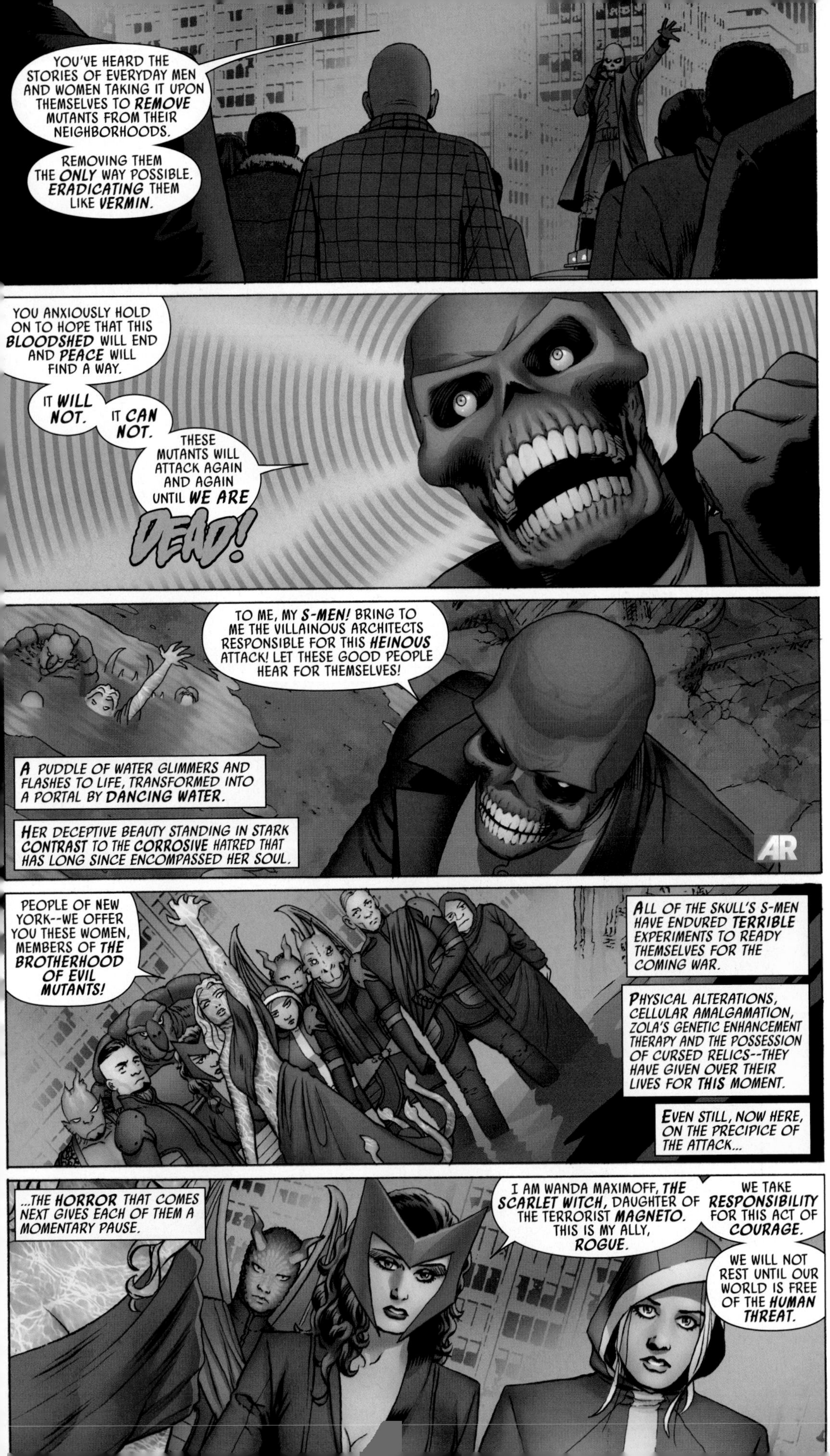

YOU'VE HEARD THE STORIES OF EVERYDAY MEN AND WOMEN TAKING IT UPON THEMSELVES TO REMOVE MUTANTS FROM THEIR NEIGHBORHOODS.
REMOVING THEM THE ONLY WAY POSSIBLE. ERADICATING THEM LIKE VERMIN.
YOU ANXIOUSLY HOLD ON TO HOPE THAT THIS BLOODSHED WILL END AND PEACE WILL FIND A WAY.
IT WILL NOT.
IT CAN NOT.
THESE MUTANTS WILL ATTACK AGAIN AND AGAIN UNTIL WE ARE DEAD!
TO ME, MY S-MEN! BRING TO ME THE VILLAINOUS ARCHITECTS RESPONSIBLE FOR THIS HEINOUS ATTACK! LET THESE GOOD PEOPLE HEAR FOR THEMSELVES!
A PUDDLE OF WATER GLIMMERS AND FLASHES TO LIFE, TRANSFORMED INTO A PORTAL BY DANCING WATER.
HER DECEPTIVE BEAUTY STANDING IN STARK CONTRAST TO THE CORROSIVE HATRED THAT HAS LONG SINCE ENCOMPASSED HER SOUL.
PEOPLE OF NEW YORK--WE OFFER YOU THESE WOMEN, MEMBERS OF THE BROTHERHOOD OF EVIL MUTANTS!
ALL OF THE SKULL'S S-MEN HAVE ENDURED TERRIBLE EXPERIMENTS TO READY THEMSELVES FOR THE COMING WAR.
PHYSICAL ALTERATIONS, CELLULAR AMALGAMATION, ZOLA'S GENETIC ENHANCEMENT THERAPY AND THE POSSESSION OF CURSED RELICS--THEY HAVE GIVEN OVER THEIR LIVES FOR THIS MOMENT.
EVEN STILL, NOW HERE, ON THE PRECIPICE OF THE ATTACK...
...THE HORROR THAT COMES NEXT GIVES EACH OF THEM A MOMENTARY PAUSE.
I AM WANDA MAXIMOFF, THE SCARLET WITCH, DAUGHTER OF THE TERRORIST MAGNETO. THIS IS MY ALLY, ROGUE.
WE TAKE RESPONSIBILITY FOR THIS ACT OF COURAGE.
WE WILL NOT REST UNTIL OUR WORLD IS FREE OF THE HUMAN THREAT.

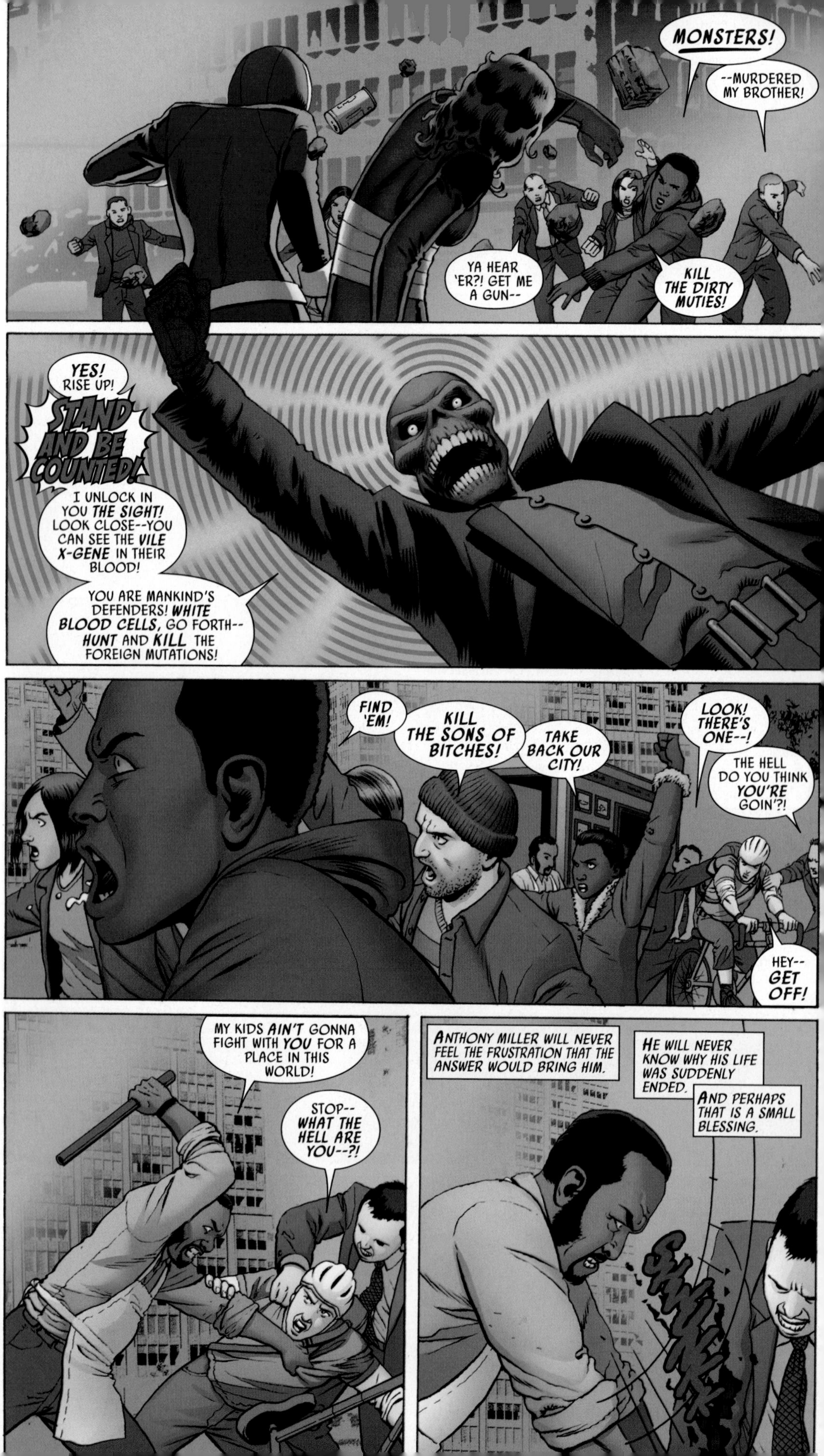
MONSTERS!
--MURDERED MY BROTHER!
YA HEAR 'ER?! GET ME A GUN--
KILL THE DIRTY MUTIES!
YES! RISE UP!
STAND AND BE COUNTED!
I UNLOCK IN YOU THE SIGHT! LOOK CLOSE--YOU CAN SEE THE VILE X-GENE IN THEIR BLOOD!
YOU ARE MANKIND'S DEFENDERS! WHITE BLOOD CELLS, GO FORTH-- HUNT AND KILL THE FOREIGN MUTATIONS!
FIND 'EM!
KILL THE SONS OF BITCHES!
TAKE BACK OUR CITY!
LOOK! THERE'S ONE--!
THE HELL DO YOU THINK YOU'RE GOIN'?!
HEY-- GET OFF!
MY KIDS AIN'T GONNA FIGHT WITH YOU FOR A PLACE IN THIS WORLD!
STOP-- WHAT THE HELL ARE YOU--?!
ANTHONY MILLER WILL NEVER FEEL THE FRUSTRATION THAT THE ANSWER WOULD BRING HIM.
HE WILL NEVER KNOW WHY HIS LIFE WAS SUDDENLY ENDED.
AND PERHAPS THAT IS A SMALL BLESSING.

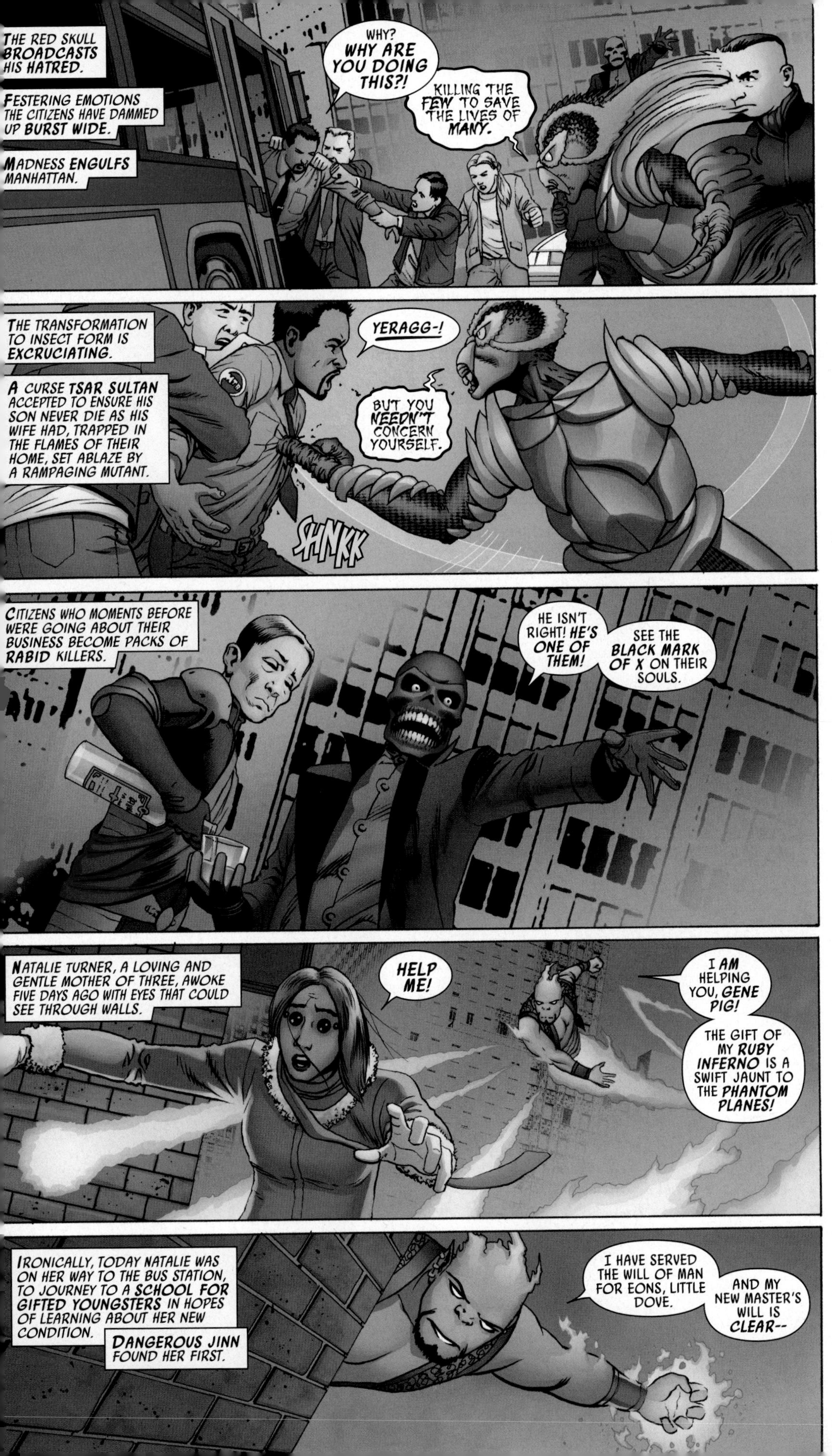
THE RED SKULL BROADCASTS HIS HATRED.
FESTERING EMOTIONS THE CITIZENS HAVE DAMMED UP BURST WIDE.
MADNESS ENGULFS MANHATTAN.
WHY? WHY ARE YOU DOING THIS?!
KILLING THE FEW TO SAVE THE LIVES OF MANY.
THE TRANSFORMATION TO INSECT FORM IS EXCRUCIATING.
A CURSE TSAR SULTAN ACCEPTED TO ENSURE HIS SON NEVER DIE AS HIS WIFE HAD, TRAPPED IN THE FLAMES OF THEIR HOME, SET ABLAZE BY A RAMPAGING MUTANT.
YERAGG-!
BUT YOU NEEDN'T CONCERN YOURSELF.
SHNKK
CITIZENS WHO MOMENTS BEFORE WERE GOING ABOUT THEIR BUSINESS BECOME PACKS OF RABID KILLERS.
HE ISN'T RIGHT! HE'S ONE OF THEM!
SEE THE BLACK MARK OF X ON THEIR SOULS.
NATALIE TURNER, A LOVING AND GENTLE MOTHER OF THREE, AWOKE FIVE DAYS AGO WITH EYES THAT COULD SEE THROUGH WALLS.
HELP ME!
I AM HELPING YOU, GENE PIG!
THE GIFT OF MY RUBY INFERNO IS A SWIFT JAUNT TO THE PHANTOM PLANES!
IRONICALLY, TODAY NATALIE WAS ON HER WAY TO THE BUS STATION, TO JOURNEY TO A SCHOOL FOR GIFTED YOUNGSTERS IN HOPES OF LEARNING ABOUT HER NEW CONDITION.
DANGEROUS JINN FOUND HER FIRST.
I HAVE SERVED THE WILL OF MAN FOR EONS, LITTLE DOVE.
AND MY NEW MASTER'S WILL IS CLEAR--

SKWOKK

THE SHIELD'S OWNER TOWERS BEFORE THE PANICKED MUTANT GIRL. THE VERY SIGHT OF THE MAN CALMS HER FRIGHT.

COMMANDER SUMMERS, HOW TO PROCEED?

ALEX SUMMERS BRIEFLY CONSIDERS TO WHOM HE IS GIVING ORDERS...

...BUT THERE IS NO TIME FOR NERVES HERE.

GET THE GIRL TO SAFETY.

LOGAN, PUT US ON THE TRAIL OF THE ATTACKERS.

AIN'T GONNA BE TOO HARD, HAVOK...

"...ENTIRE CITY IS OUT FOR MUTANT BLOOD."

THIS ONE'S GOT THE MARK!

I CAN SEE IT-- CRUSH HIS SKULL!

PLEASE-- PLEASE DON'T!

PETER BROWN TOLD HIS MOTHER H[...] PICK UP HIS YOUNGER BROTHER FR[...] PHYSICAL THERAPY IN TIME FOR DINNER[...]

WHEN THE BOY'S TREATMENT WENT LONG, PETER TOOK A WALK.

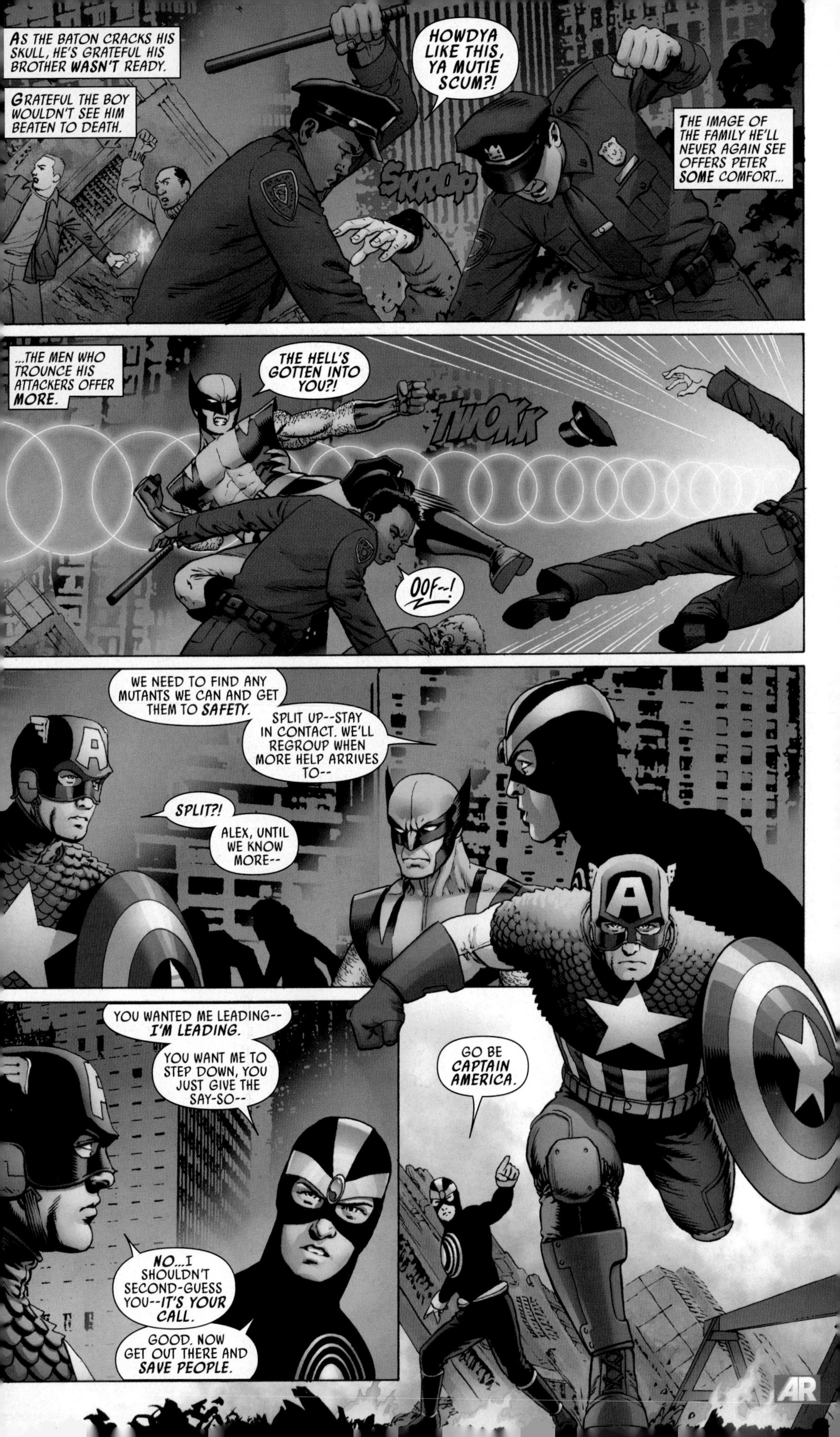
AS THE BATON CRACKS HIS SKULL, HE'S GRATEFUL HIS BROTHER WASN'T READY.
GRATEFUL THE BOY WOULDN'T SEE HIM BEATEN TO DEATH.
HOWDYA LIKE THIS, YA MUTIE SCUM?!
SKROP
THE IMAGE OF THE FAMILY HE'LL NEVER AGAIN SEE OFFERS PETER SOME COMFORT...
...THE MEN WHO TROUNCE HIS ATTACKERS OFFER MORE.
THE HELL'S GOTTEN INTO YOU?!
TWOKK
OOF--!
WE NEED TO FIND ANY MUTANTS WE CAN AND GET THEM TO SAFETY.
SPLIT UP--STAY IN CONTACT. WE'LL REGROUP WHEN MORE HELP ARRIVES TO--
SPLIT?!
ALEX, UNTIL WE KNOW MORE--
YOU WANTED ME LEADING-- I'M LEADING.
YOU WANT ME TO STEP DOWN, YOU JUST GIVE THE SAY-SO--
NO...I SHOULDN'T SECOND-GUESS YOU--IT'S YOUR CALL.
GOOD. NOW GET OUT THERE AND SAVE PEOPLE.
GO BE CAPTAIN AMERICA.

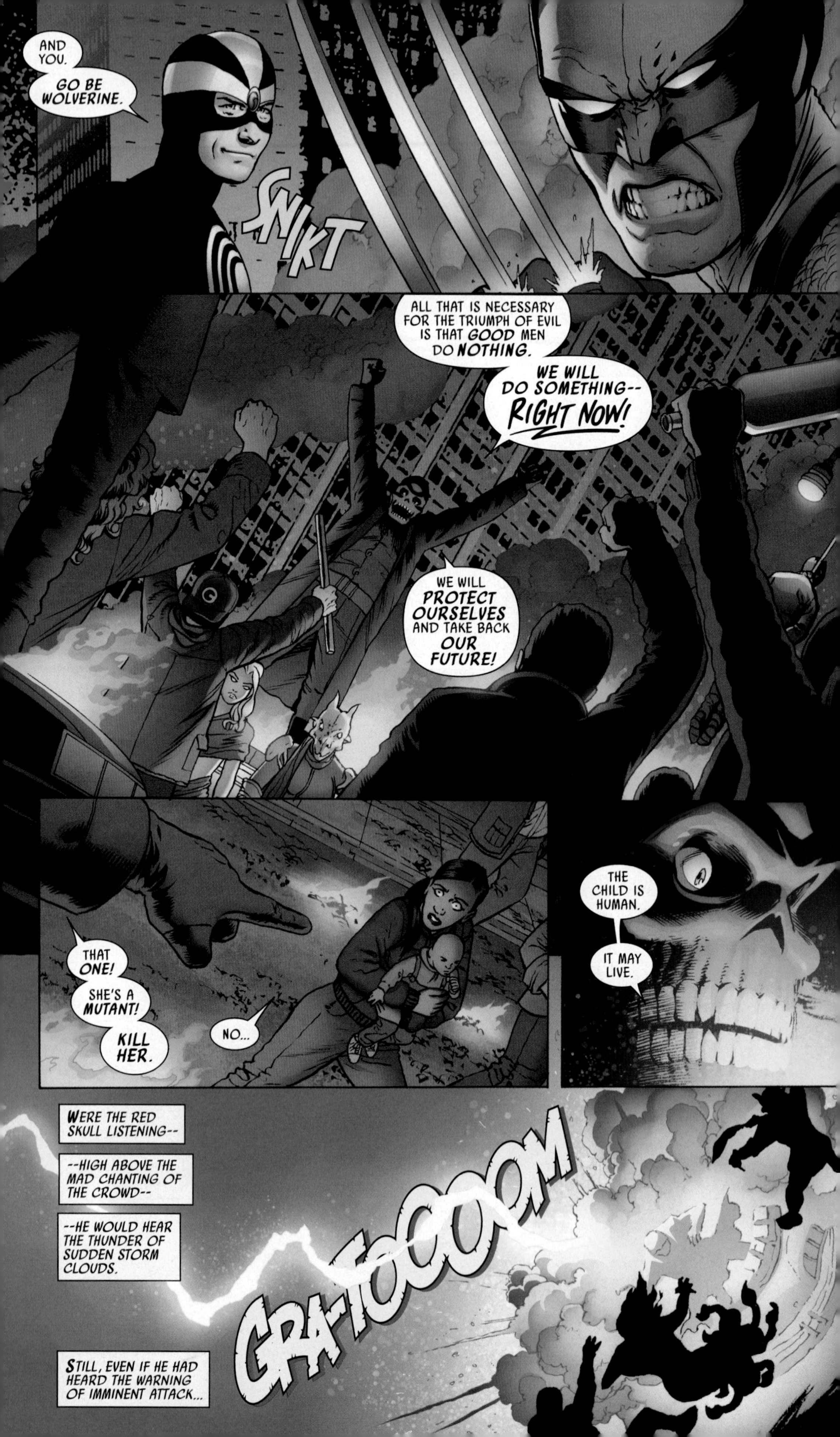
AND YOU.
GO BE WOLVERINE.
SNIKT
ALL THAT IS NECESSARY FOR THE TRIUMPH OF EVIL IS THAT GOOD MEN DO NOTHING.
WE WILL DO SOMETHING-- RIGHT NOW!
WE WILL PROTECT OURSELVES AND TAKE BACK OUR FUTURE!
THAT ONE!
SHE'S A MUTANT!
KILL HER.
NO...
THE CHILD IS HUMAN.
IT MAY LIVE.
WERE THE RED SKULL LISTENING--
--HIGH ABOVE THE MAD CHANTING OF THE CROWD--
--HE WOULD HEAR THE THUNDER OF SUDDEN STORM CLOUDS.
GRA-TOOOOOM
STILL, EVEN IF HE HAD HEARD THE WARNING OF IMMINENT ATTACK...

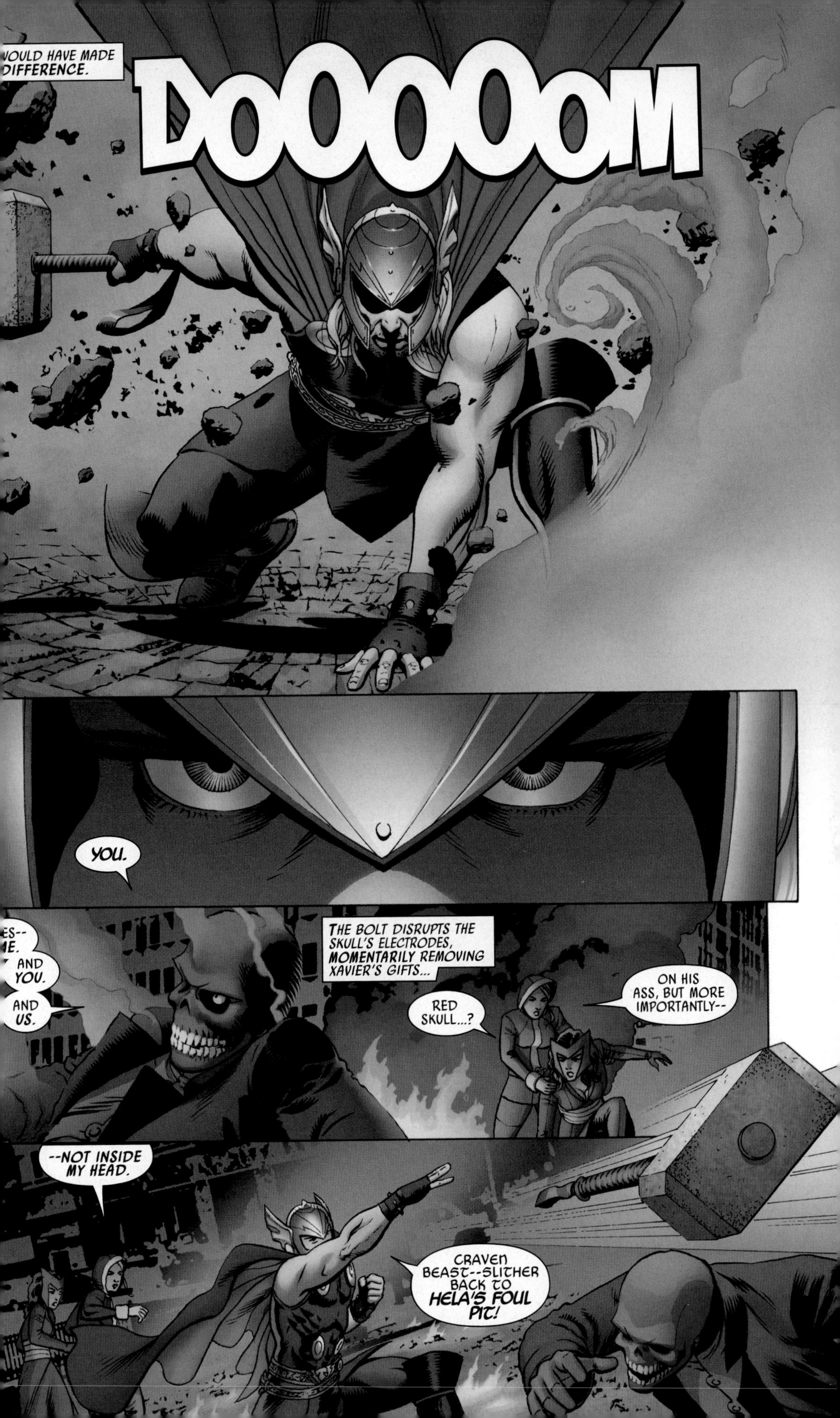

WOULD HAVE MADE
DIFFERENCE.
DOOOOOM
YOU.
ES--
ME.
AND
YOU.
AND
US.
THE BOLT DISRUPTS THE SKULL'S ELECTRODES, MOMENTARILY REMOVING XAVIER'S GIFTS...
RED SKULL...?
ON HIS ASS, BUT MORE IMPORTANTLY--
--NOT INSIDE MY HEAD.
CRAVEN BEAST--SLITHER BACK TO HELA'S FOUL PIT!

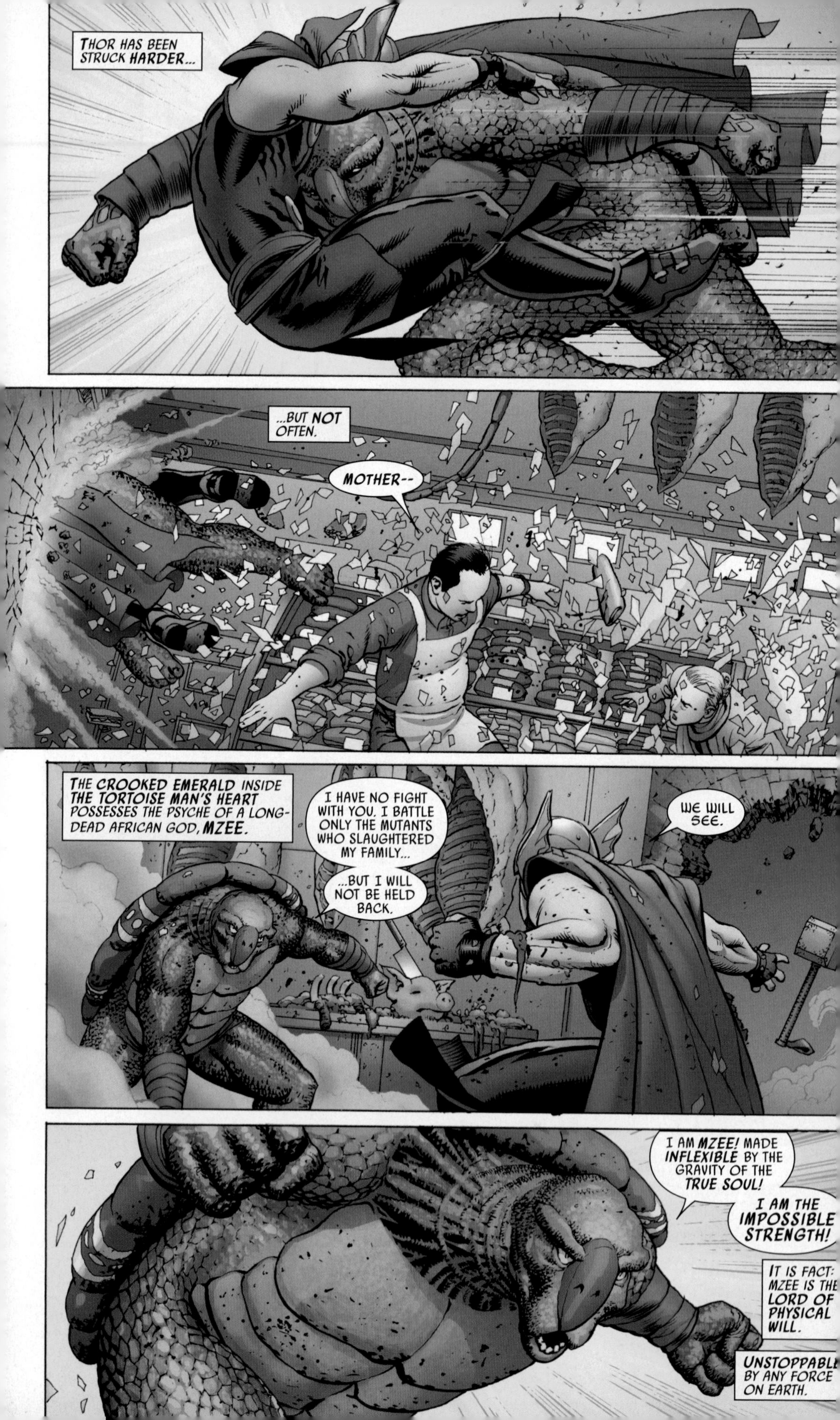
THOR HAS BEEN STRUCK HARDER...
...BUT NOT OFTEN.
MOTHER--
THE CROOKED EMERALD INSIDE THE TORTOISE MAN'S HEART POSSESSES THE PSYCHE OF A LONG-DEAD AFRICAN GOD, MZEE.
I HAVE NO FIGHT WITH YOU. I BATTLE ONLY THE MUTANTS WHO SLAUGHTERED MY FAMILY...
...BUT I WILL NOT BE HELD BACK.
WE WILL SEE.
I AM MZEE! MADE INFLEXIBLE BY THE GRAVITY OF THE TRUE SOUL!
I AM THE IMPOSSIBLE STRENGTH!
IT IS FACT: MZEE IS THE LORD OF PHYSICAL WILL.
UNSTOPPABLE BY ANY FORCE ON EARTH.

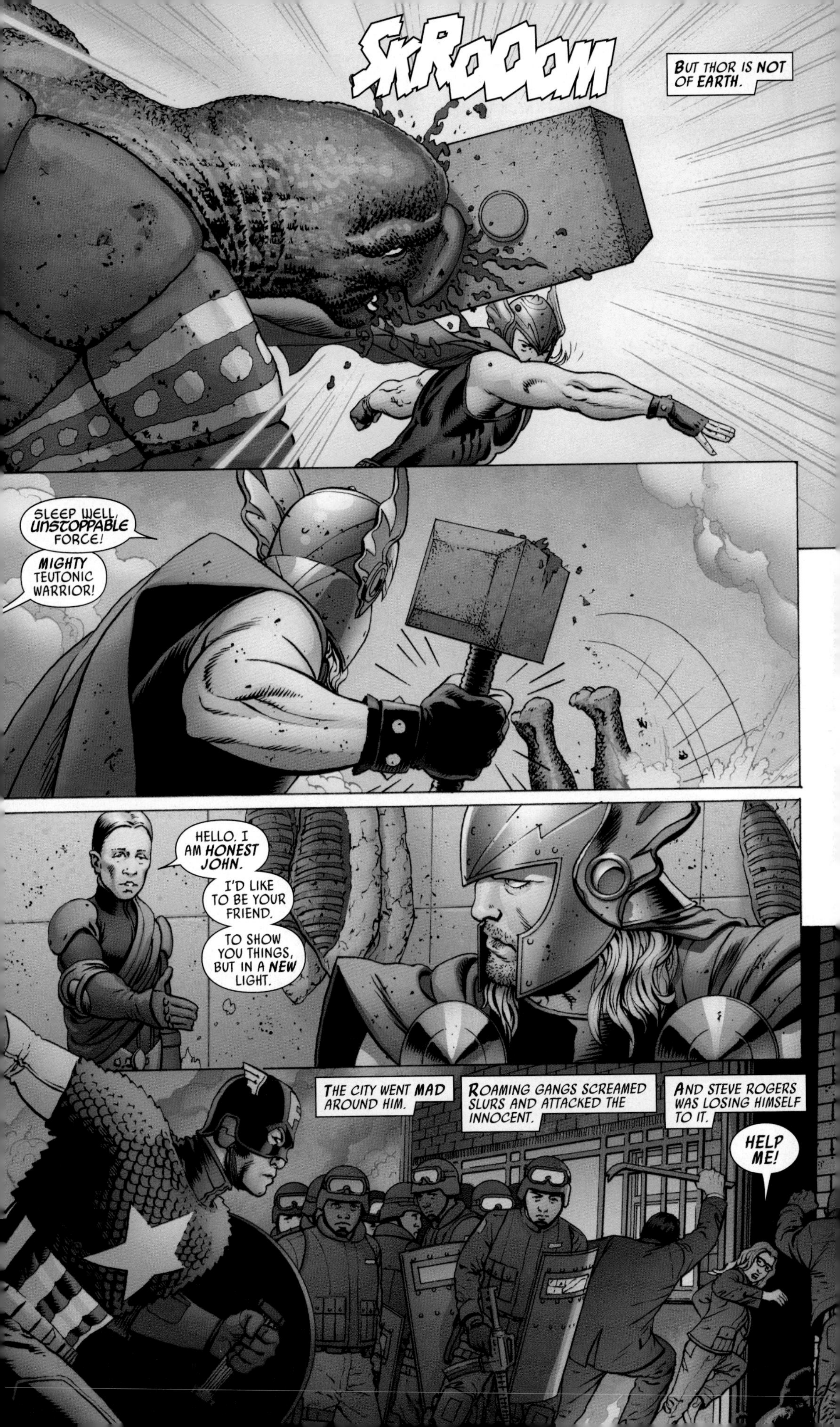
SKROOOM
BUT THOR IS NOT OF EARTH.
SLEEP WELL, UNSTOPPABLE FORCE!
MIGHTY TEUTONIC WARRIOR!
HELLO, I AM HONEST JOHN.
I'D LIKE TO BE YOUR FRIEND.
TO SHOW YOU THINGS, BUT IN A NEW LIGHT.
THE CITY WENT MAD AROUND HIM.
ROAMING GANGS SCREAMED SLURS AND ATTACKED THE INNOCENT.
AND STEVE ROGERS WAS LOSING HIMSELF TO IT.
HELP ME!

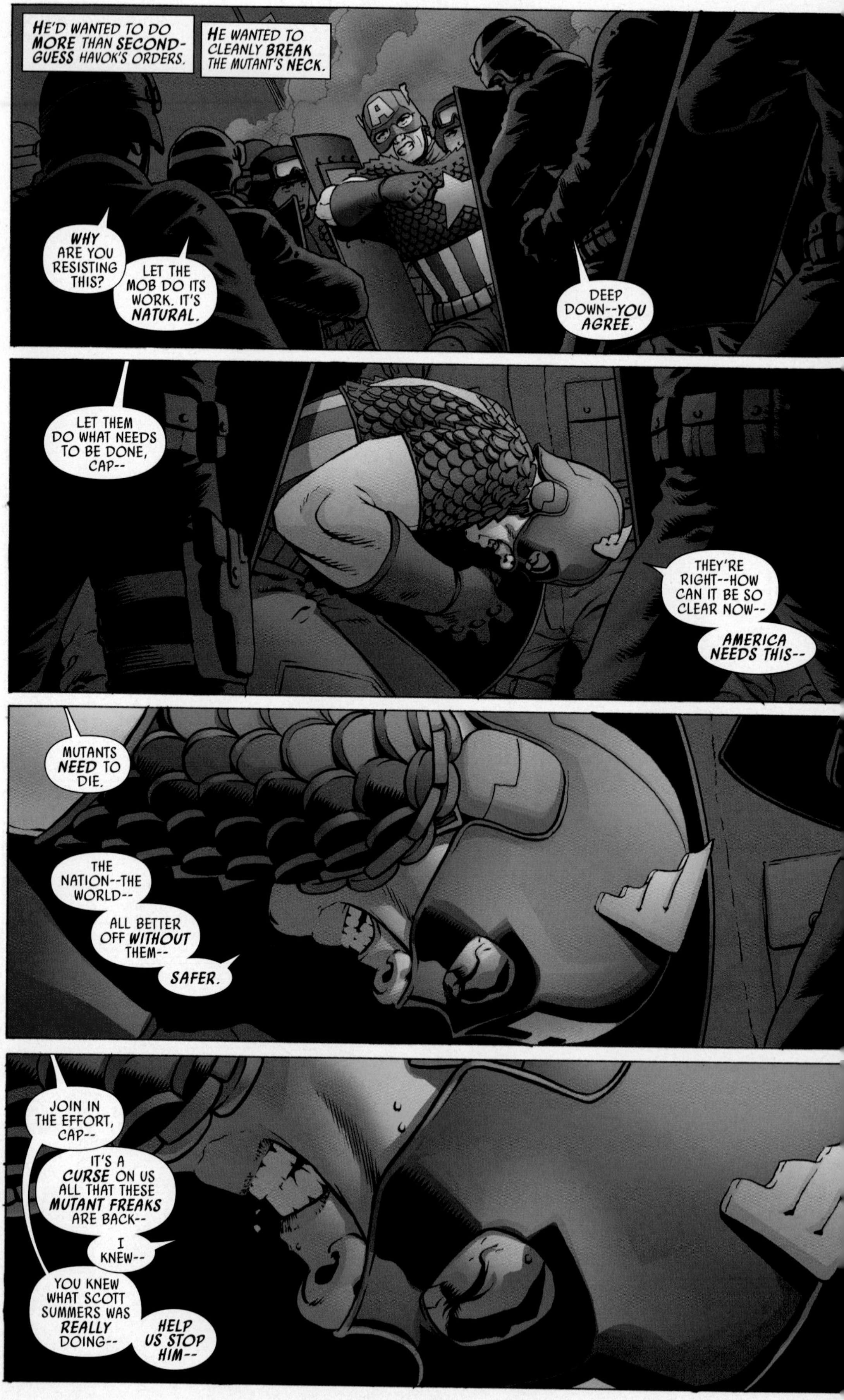
HE'D WANTED TO DO MORE THAN SECOND-GUESS HAVOK'S ORDERS.
HE WANTED TO CLEANLY BREAK THE MUTANT'S NECK.
WHY ARE YOU RESISTING THIS?
LET THE MOB DO ITS WORK. IT'S NATURAL.
DEEP DOWN--YOU AGREE.
LET THEM DO WHAT NEEDS TO BE DONE, CAP--
THEY'RE RIGHT--HOW CAN IT BE SO CLEAR NOW--
AMERICA NEEDS THIS--
MUTANTS NEED TO DIE.
THE NATION--THE WORLD--
ALL BETTER OFF WITHOUT THEM--
SAFER.
JOIN IN THE EFFORT, CAP--
IT'S A CURSE ON US ALL THAT THESE MUTANT FREAKS ARE BACK--
I KNEW--
YOU KNEW WHAT SCOTT SUMMERS WAS REALLY DOING--
HELP US STOP HIM--

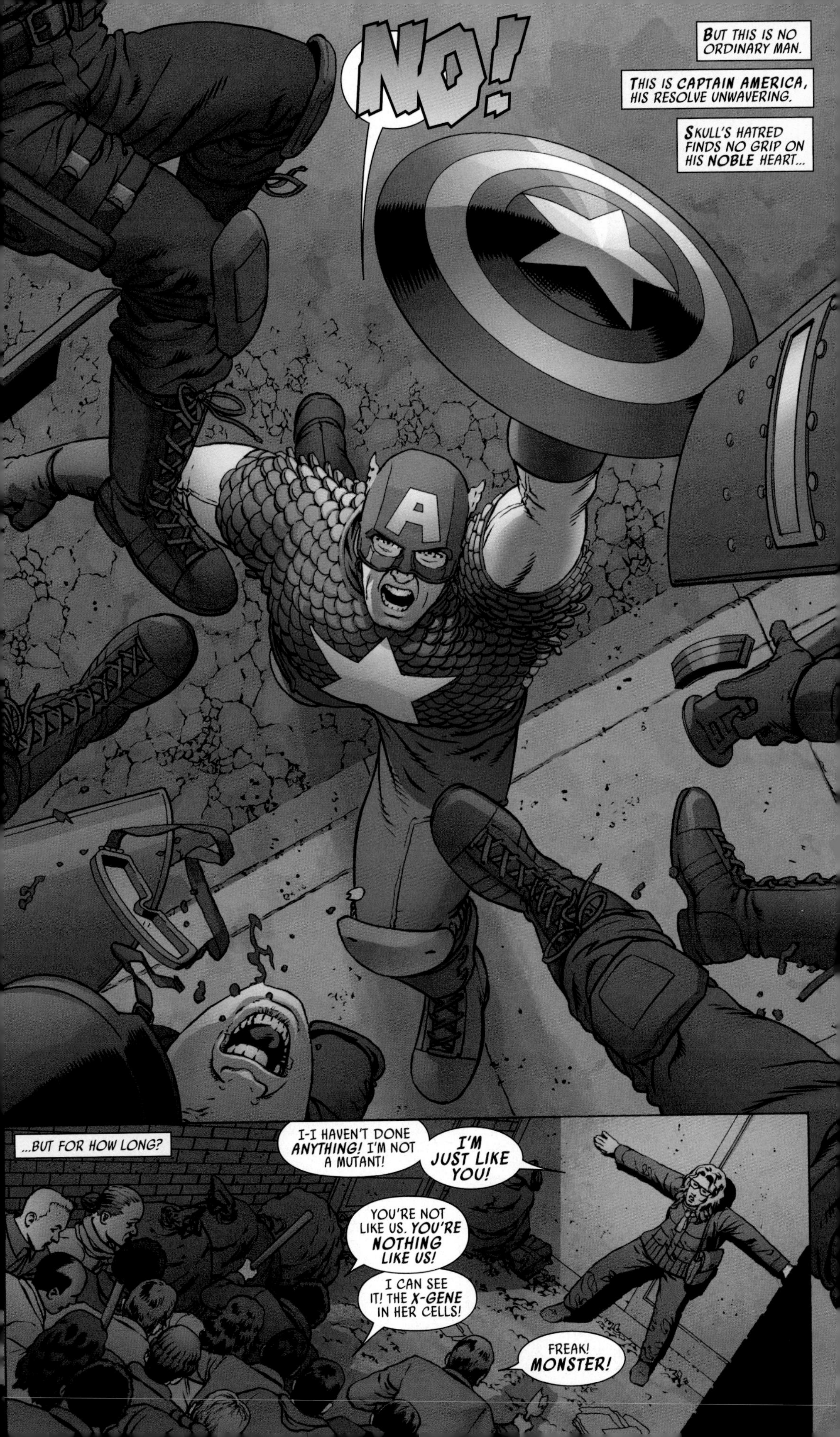
NO!
BUT THIS IS NO ORDINARY MAN.
THIS IS CAPTAIN AMERICA, HIS RESOLVE UNWAVERING.
SKULL'S HATRED FINDS NO GRIP ON HIS NOBLE HEART...
...BUT FOR HOW LONG?
I-I HAVEN'T DONE ANYTHING! I'M NOT A MUTANT!
I'M JUST LIKE YOU!
YOU'RE NOT LIKE US. YOU'RE NOTHING LIKE US!
I CAN SEE IT! THE X-GENE IN HER CELLS!
FREAK! MONSTER!

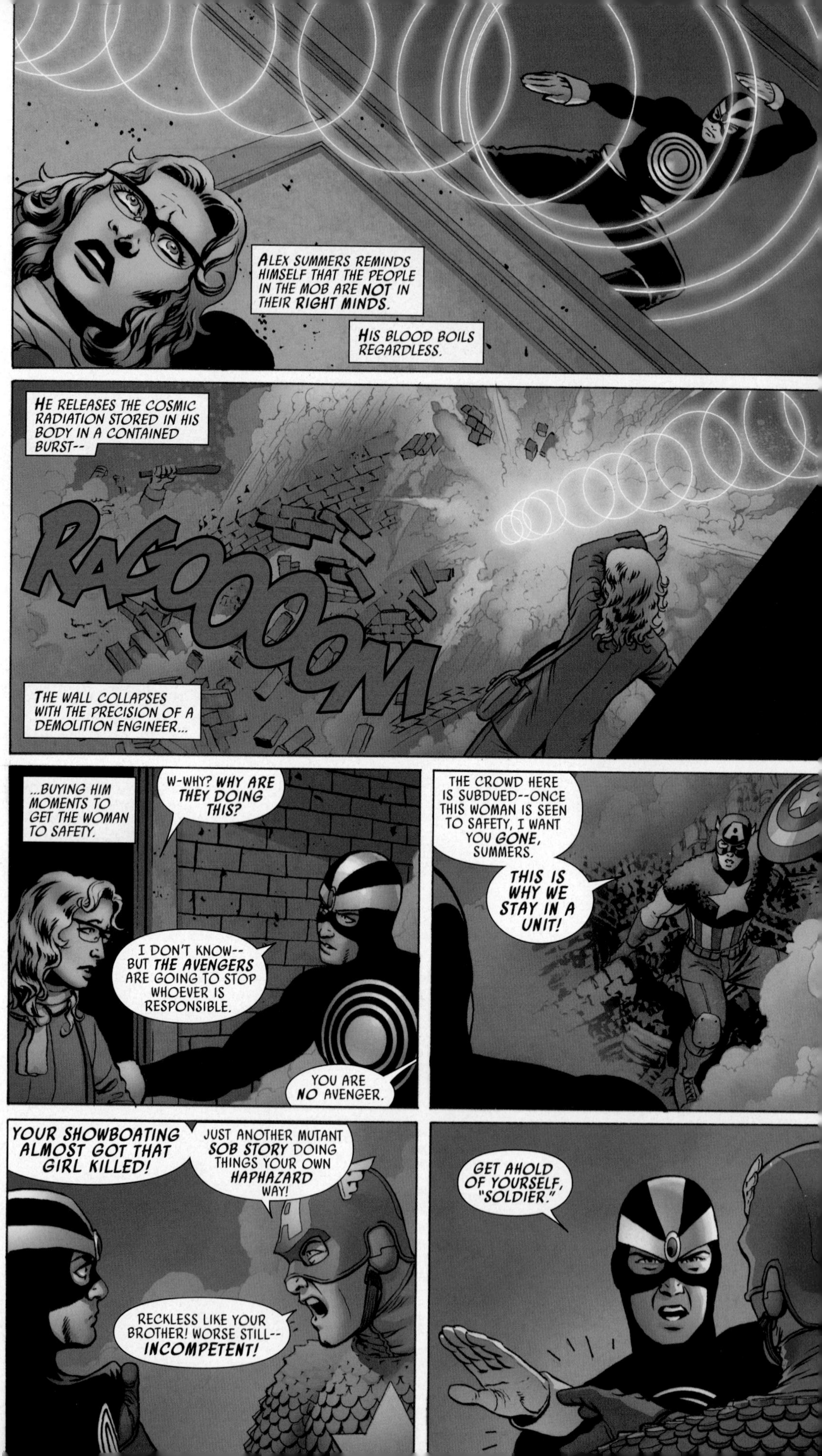
ALEX SUMMERS REMINDS HIMSELF THAT THE PEOPLE IN THE MOB ARE NOT IN THEIR RIGHT MINDS.
HIS BLOOD BOILS REGARDLESS.
HE RELEASES THE COSMIC RADIATION STORED IN HIS BODY IN A CONTAINED BURST--
RAGOOOOM
THE WALL COLLAPSES WITH THE PRECISION OF A DEMOLITION ENGINEER...
...BUYING HIM MOMENTS TO GET THE WOMAN TO SAFETY.
W-WHY? WHY ARE THEY DOING THIS?
I DON'T KNOW--BUT THE AVENGERS ARE GOING TO STOP WHOEVER IS RESPONSIBLE.
YOU ARE NO AVENGER.
THE CROWD HERE IS SUBDUED--ONCE THIS WOMAN IS SEEN TO SAFETY, I WANT YOU GONE, SUMMERS.
THIS IS WHY WE STAY IN A UNIT!
YOUR SHOWBOATING ALMOST GOT THAT GIRL KILLED!
JUST ANOTHER MUTANT SOB STORY DOING THINGS YOUR OWN HAPHAZARD WAY!
RECKLESS LIKE YOUR BROTHER! WORSE STILL--INCOMPETENT!
GET AHOLD OF YOURSELF, "SOLDIER."

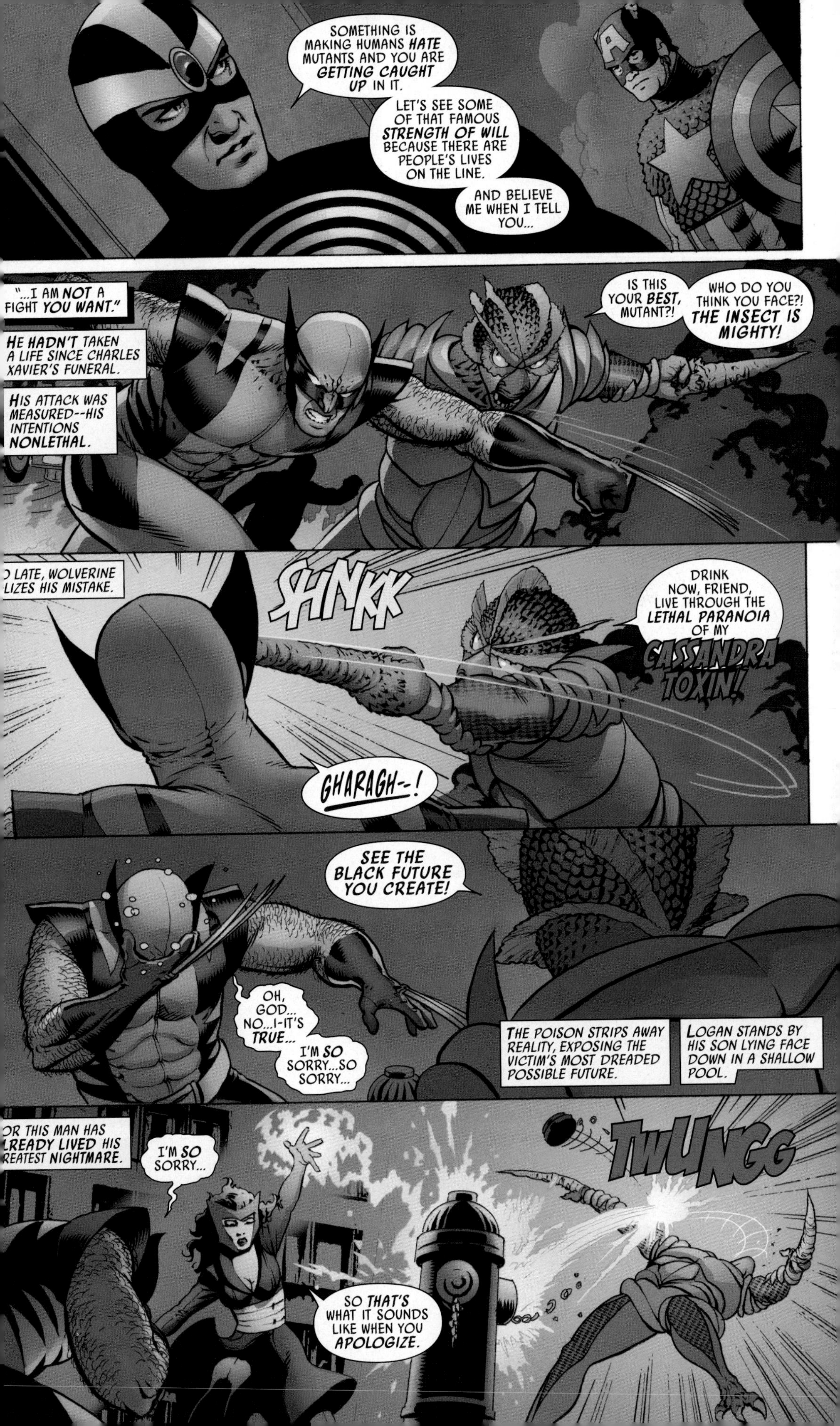

SOMETHING IS MAKING HUMANS HATE MUTANTS AND YOU ARE GETTING CAUGHT UP IN IT.
LET'S SEE SOME OF THAT FAMOUS STRENGTH OF WILL BECAUSE THERE ARE PEOPLE'S LIVES ON THE LINE.
AND BELIEVE ME WHEN I TELL YOU...
"...I AM NOT A FIGHT YOU WANT."
HE HADN'T TAKEN A LIFE SINCE CHARLES XAVIER'S FUNERAL.
HIS ATTACK WAS MEASURED--HIS INTENTIONS NONLETHAL.
IS THIS YOUR BEST, MUTANT?!
WHO DO YOU THINK YOU FACE?! THE INSECT IS MIGHTY!
LIZES HIS MISTAKE.
SHNKK
DRINK NOW, FRIEND, LIVE THROUGH THE LETHAL PARANOIA OF MY CASSANDRA TOXIN!
GHARAGH--!
SEE THE BLACK FUTURE YOU CREATE!
OH, GOD... NO...I-IT'S TRUE...
I'M SO SORRY...SO SORRY...
THE POISON STRIPS AWAY REALITY, EXPOSING THE VICTIM'S MOST DREADED POSSIBLE FUTURE.
LOGAN STANDS BY HIS SON LYING FACE DOWN IN A SHALLOW POOL.
OR THIS MAN HAS LREADY LIVED HIS REATEST NIGHTMARE.
I'M SO SORRY...
TWUNGG
SO THAT'S WHAT IT SOUNDS LIKE WHEN YOU APOLOGIZE.

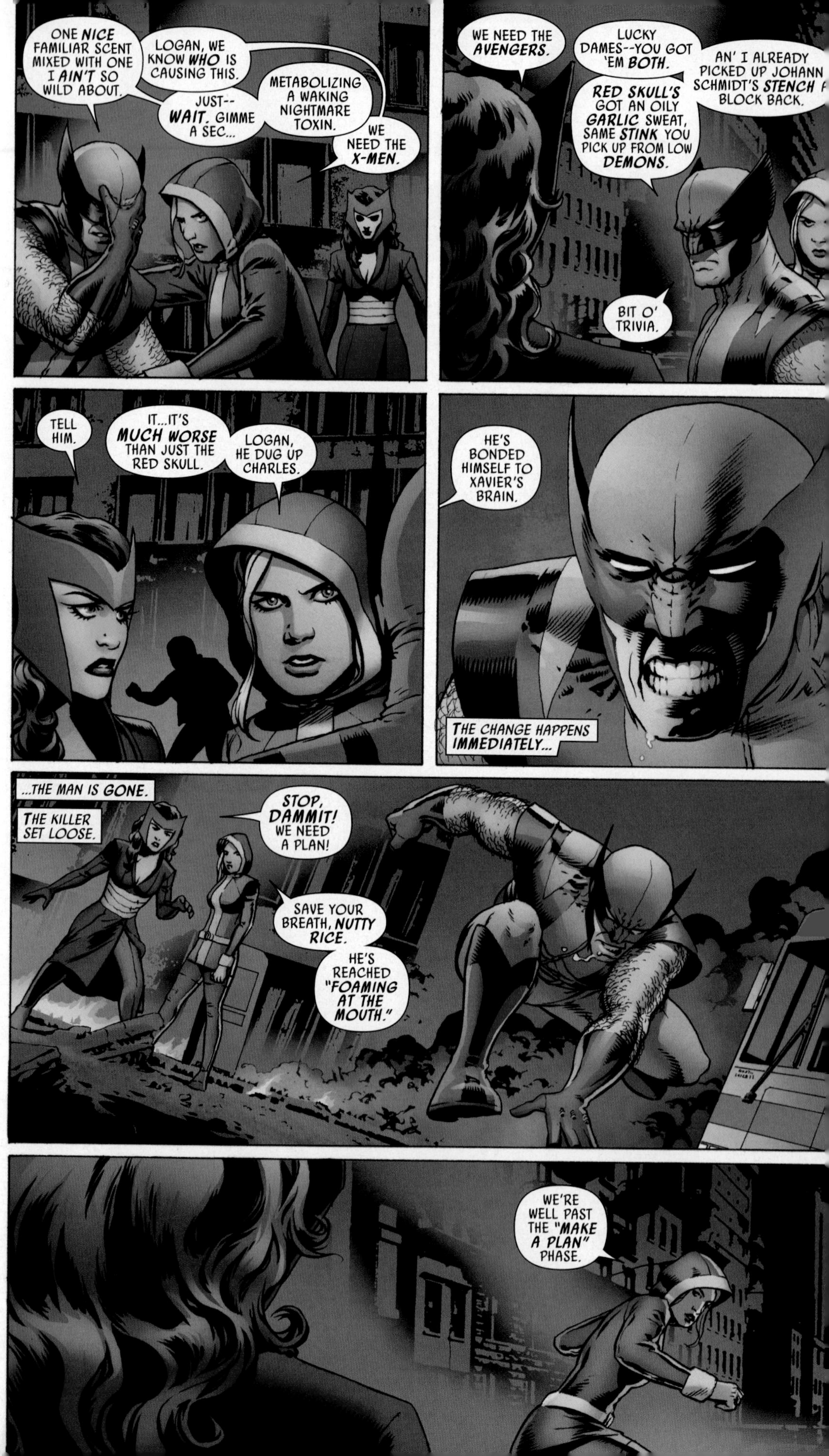

ONE NICE FAMILIAR SCENT MIXED WITH ONE I AIN'T SO WILD ABOUT.
LOGAN, WE KNOW WHO IS CAUSING THIS.
JUST-- WAIT. GIMME A SEC...
METABOLIZING A WAKING NIGHTMARE TOXIN.
WE NEED THE X-MEN.
WE NEED THE AVENGERS.
LUCKY DAMES--YOU GOT 'EM BOTH.
AN' I ALREADY PICKED UP JOHANN SCHMIDT'S STENCH A BLOCK BACK.
RED SKULL'S GOT AN OILY GARLIC SWEAT, SAME STINK YOU PICK UP FROM LOW DEMONS.
BIT O' TRIVIA.
TELL HIM.
IT...IT'S MUCH WORSE THAN JUST THE RED SKULL.
LOGAN, HE DUG UP CHARLES.
HE'S BONDED HIMSELF TO XAVIER'S BRAIN.
THE CHANGE HAPPENS IMMEDIATELY...
...THE MAN IS GONE.
THE KILLER SET LOOSE.
STOP, DAMMIT! WE NEED A PLAN!
SAVE YOUR BREATH, NUTTY RICE.
HE'S REACHED "FOAMING AT THE MOUTH."
WE'RE WELL PAST THE "MAKE A PLAN" PHASE.

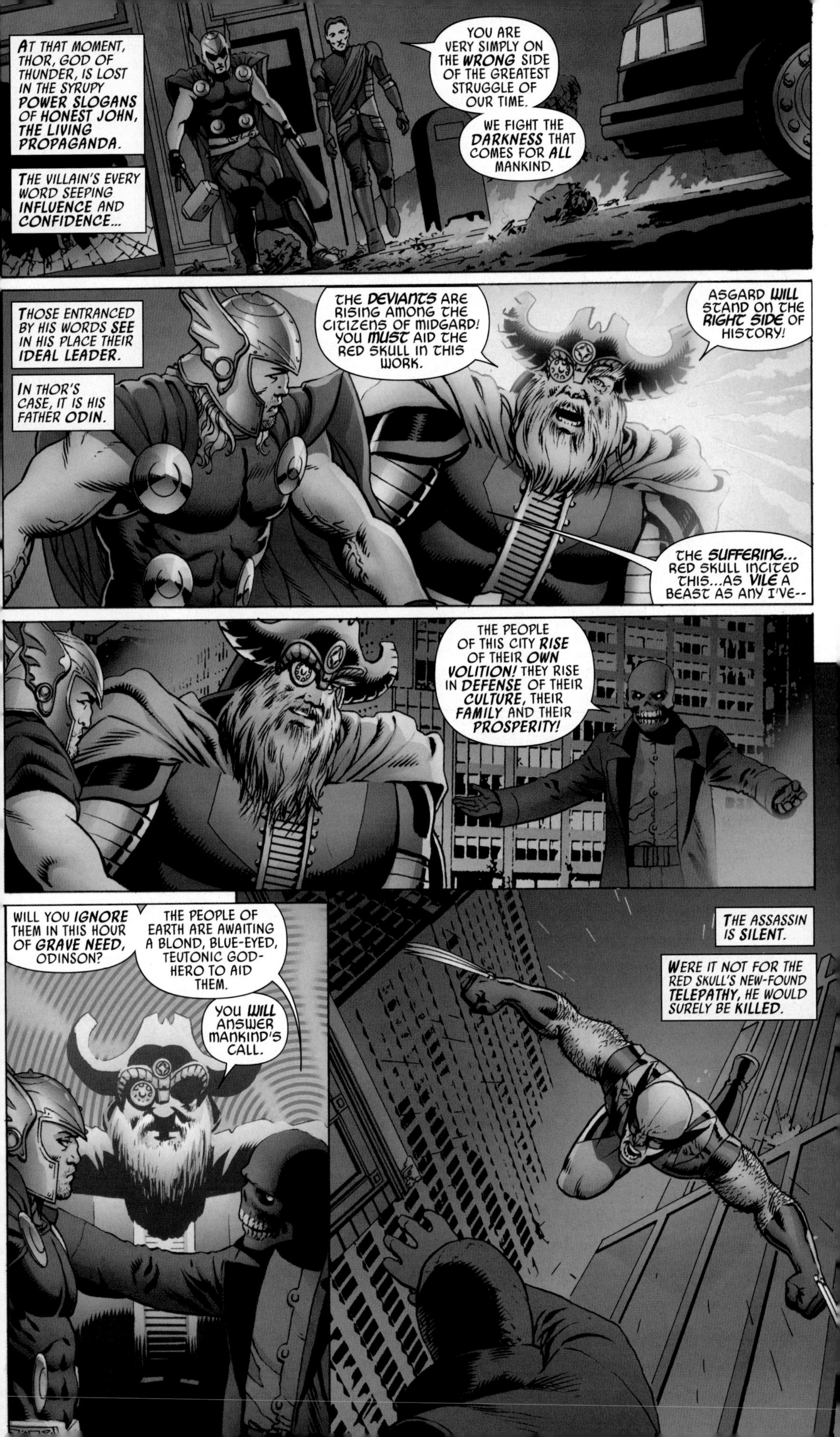
AT THAT MOMENT, THOR, GOD OF THUNDER, IS LOST IN THE SYRUPY POWER SLOGANS OF HONEST JOHN, THE LIVING PROPAGANDA.
THE VILLAIN'S EVERY WORD SEEPING INFLUENCE AND CONFIDENCE...
YOU ARE VERY SIMPLY ON THE WRONG SIDE OF THE GREATEST STRUGGLE OF OUR TIME.
WE FIGHT THE DARKNESS THAT COMES FOR ALL MANKIND.
THOSE ENTRANCED BY HIS WORDS SEE IN HIS PLACE THEIR IDEAL LEADER.
IN THOR'S CASE, IT IS HIS FATHER ODIN.
THE DEVIANTS ARE RISING AMONG THE CITIZENS OF MIDGARD! YOU MUST AID THE RED SKULL IN THIS WORK.
ASGARD WILL STAND ON THE RIGHT SIDE OF HISTORY!
THE SUFFERING... RED SKULL INCITED THIS...AS VILE A BEAST AS ANY I'VE--
THE PEOPLE OF THIS CITY RISE OF THEIR OWN VOLITION! THEY RISE IN DEFENSE OF THEIR CULTURE, THEIR FAMILY AND THEIR PROSPERITY!
WILL YOU IGNORE THEM IN THIS HOUR OF GRAVE NEED, ODINSON?
THE PEOPLE OF EARTH ARE AWAITING A BLOND, BLUE-EYED, TEUTONIC GOD-HERO TO AID THEM.
YOU WILL ANSWER MANKIND'S CALL.
THE ASSASSIN IS SILENT.
WERE IT NOT FOR THE RED SKULL'S NEW-FOUND TELEPATHY, HE WOULD SURELY BE KILLED.

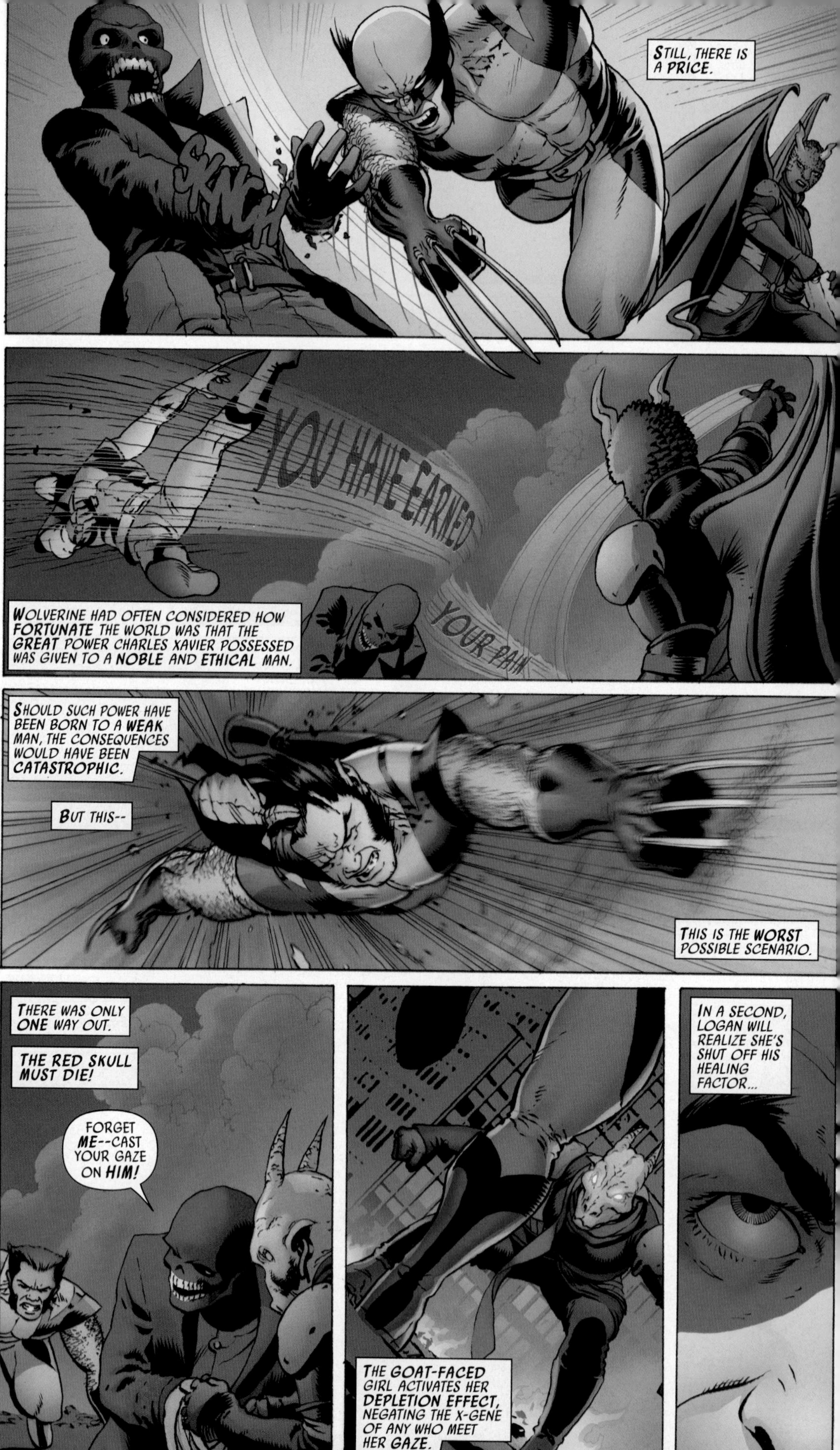
STILL, THERE IS A PRICE.
SKNCH
YOU HAVE EARNED
YOUR PAIN
WOLVERINE HAD OFTEN CONSIDERED HOW FORTUNATE THE WORLD WAS THAT THE GREAT POWER CHARLES XAVIER POSSESSED WAS GIVEN TO A NOBLE AND ETHICAL MAN.
SHOULD SUCH POWER HAVE BEEN BORN TO A WEAK MAN, THE CONSEQUENCES WOULD HAVE BEEN CATASTROPHIC.
BUT THIS--
THIS IS THE WORST POSSIBLE SCENARIO.
THERE WAS ONLY ONE WAY OUT.
THE RED SKULL MUST DIE!
FORGET ME--CAST YOUR GAZE ON HIM!
THE GOAT-FACED GIRL ACTIVATES HER DEPLETION EFFECT, NEGATING THE X-GENE OF ANY WHO MEET HER GAZE.
IN A SECOND, LOGAN WILL REALIZE SHE'S SHUT OFF HIS HEALING FACTOR...

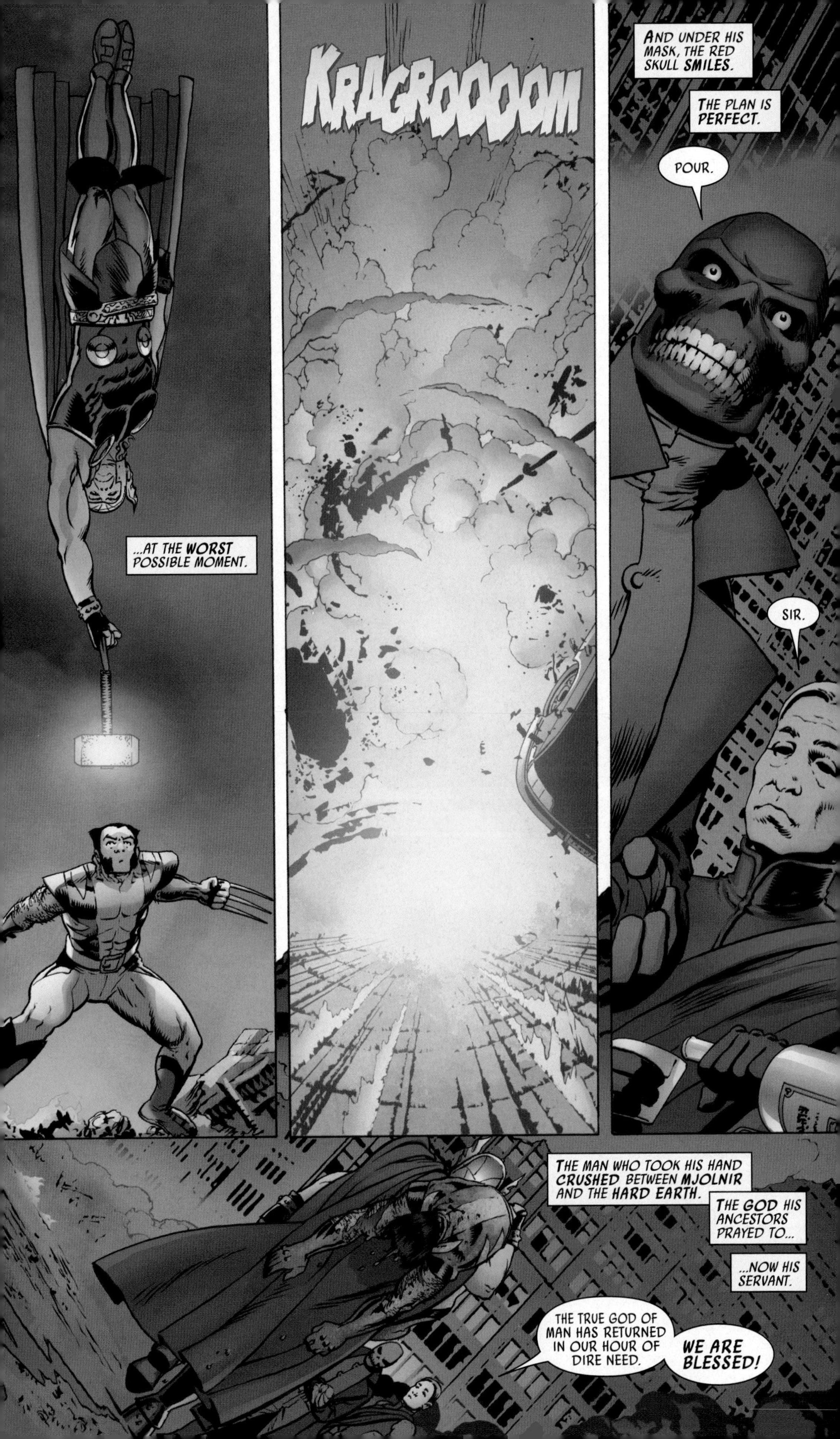
...AT THE WORST POSSIBLE MOMENT.
KRAGROOOOM
AND UNDER HIS MASK, THE RED SKULL SMILES.
THE PLAN IS PERFECT.
POUR.
SIR.
THE MAN WHO TOOK HIS HAND CRUSHED BETWEEN MJOLNIR AND THE HARD EARTH.
THE GOD HIS ANCESTORS PRAYED TO...
...NOW HIS SERVANT.
THE TRUE GOD OF MAN HAS RETURNED IN OUR HOUR OF DIRE NEED.
WE ARE BLESSED!

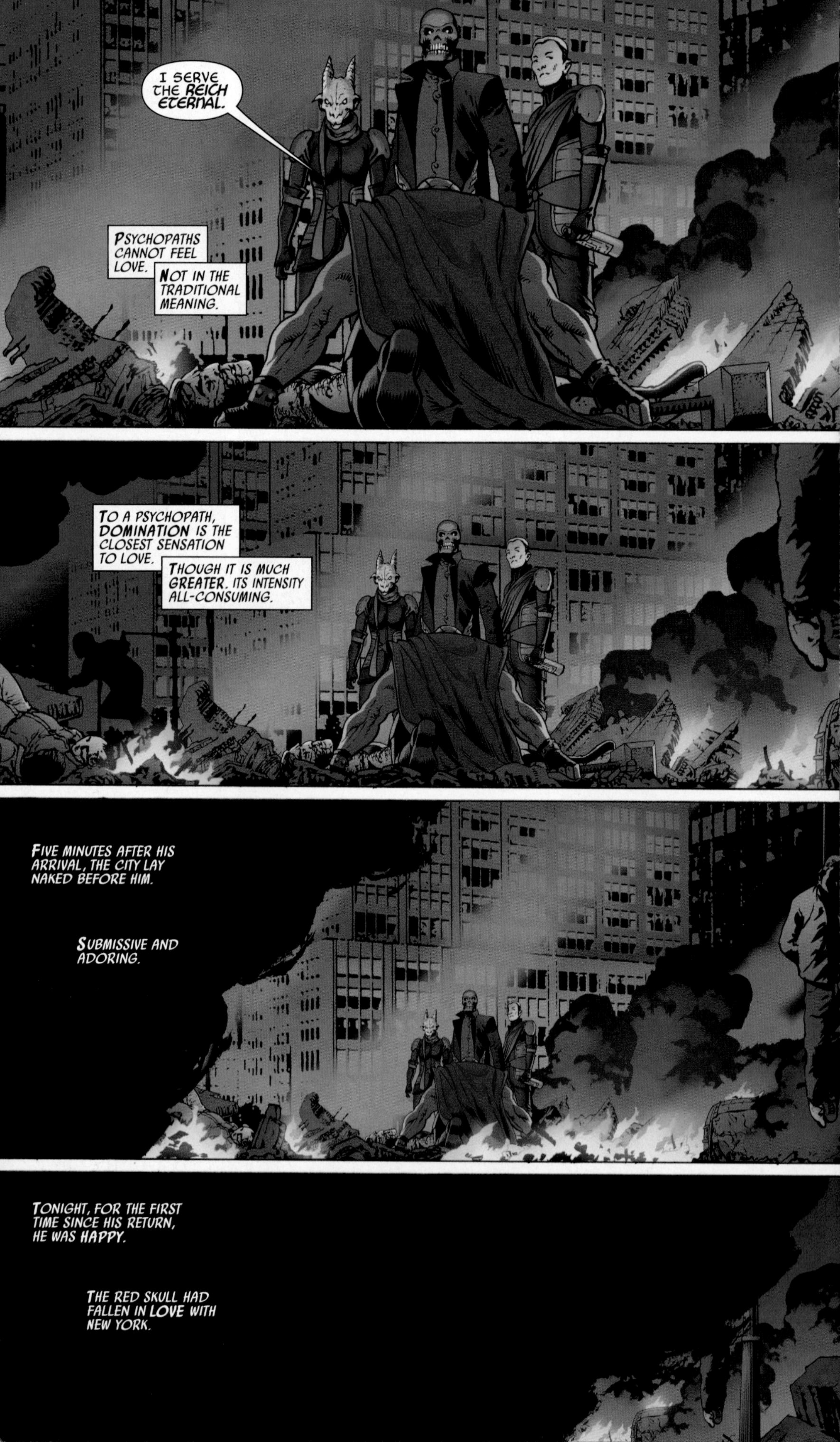
I SERVE THE REICH ETERNAL.
PSYCHOPATHS CANNOT FEEL LOVE.
NOT IN THE TRADITIONAL MEANING.
TO A PSYCHOPATH, DOMINATION IS THE CLOSEST SENSATION TO LOVE.
THOUGH IT IS MUCH GREATER. ITS INTENSITY ALL-CONSUMING.
FIVE MINUTES AFTER HIS ARRIVAL, THE CITY LAY NAKED BEFORE HIM.
SUBMISSIVE AND ADORING.
TONIGHT, FOR THE FIRST TIME SINCE HIS RETURN, HE WAS HAPPY.
THE RED SKULL HAD FALLEN IN LOVE WITH NEW YORK.

UNCANNY AVENGERS #1 HASTINGS VARIANT BY MARK TEXEIRA

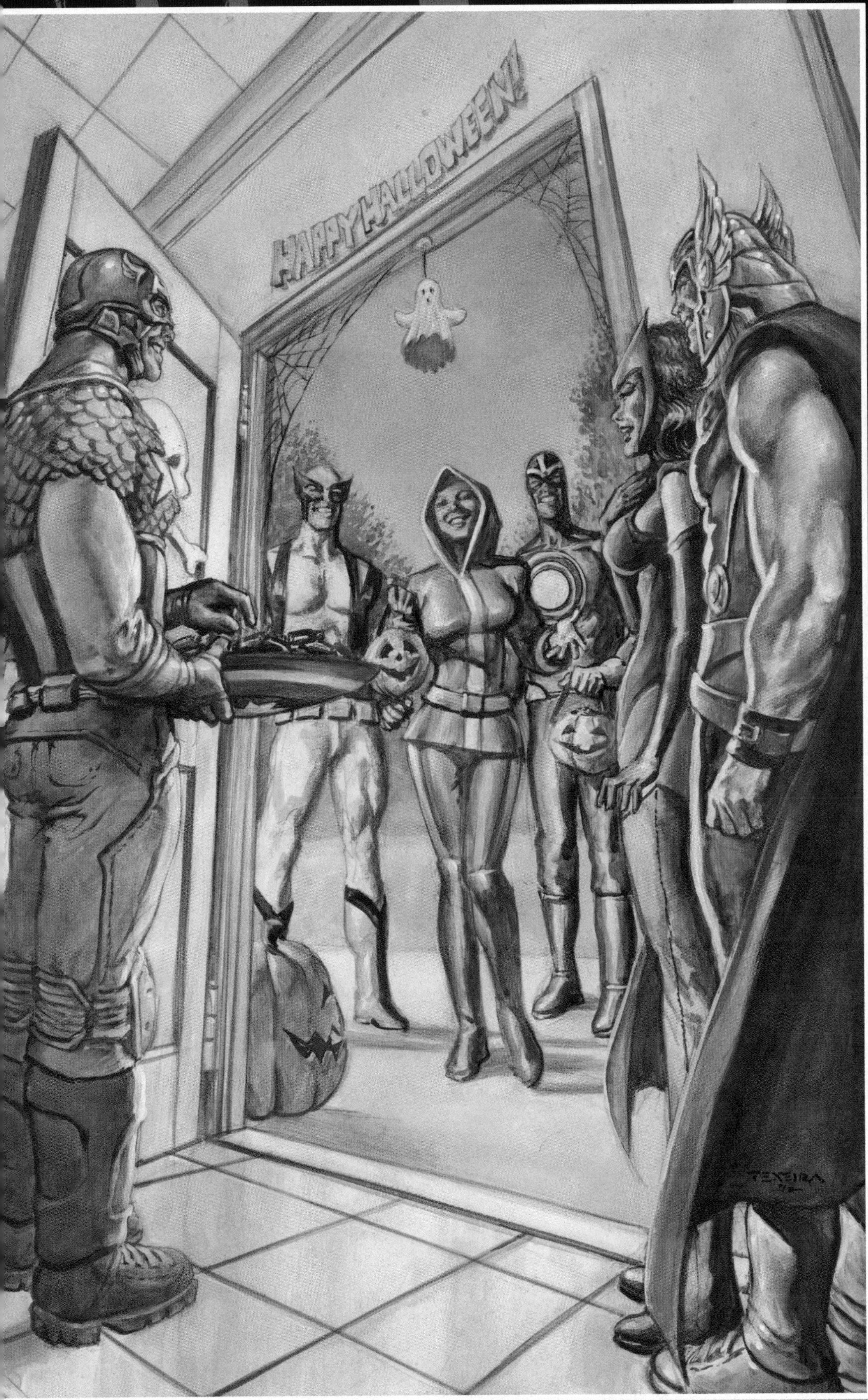
HAPPY HALLOWEEN!
TEXEIRA

UNCANNY AVENGERS #4

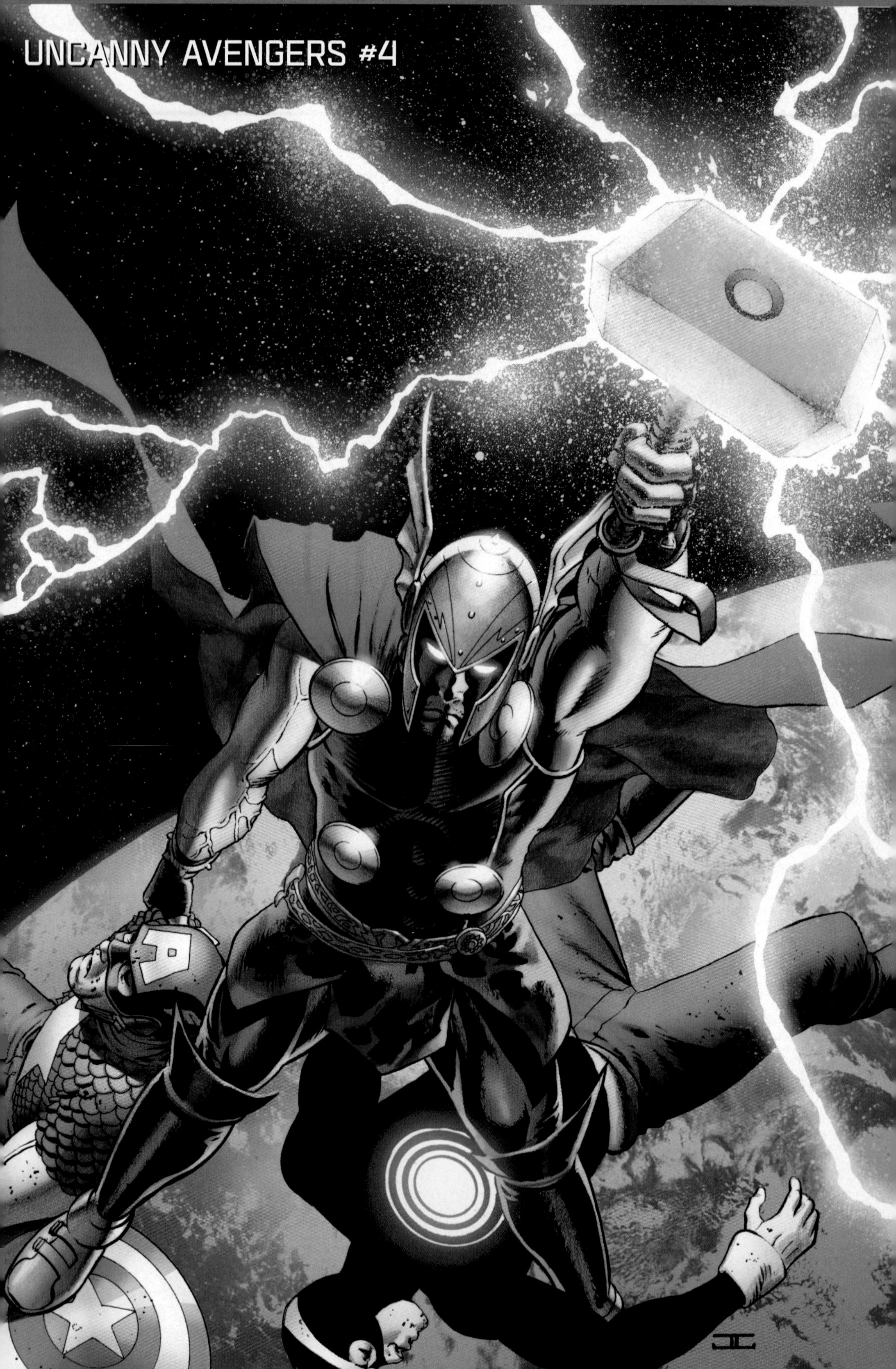

MINUTES AGO, THE SUMMERS FAMILY WAS RETURNING HOME FROM A VACATION IN ANCHORAGE, ALASKA.

NOW CHRISTOPHER SUMMERS FIGHTS BACK TEARS AS HE STRAPS HIS ELDEST SON SCOTT INTO THE ONLY INTACT PARACHUTE.

IT DOESN'T GO UNNOTICED BY YOUNGER BROTHER ALEX.

O-OKAY, DAD...I WILL.

YOU HOLD ON TO ALEX AS TIGHT AS YOU CAN, SCOTT, *YOU HEAR ME?*

BE *BOLD* AND *FEARLESS.* LOOK TO YOUR HEARTS FOR STRENGTH TO FACE THE FUTURE.

WHEN YOU CAN'T FIND IT THERE, LOOK TO *EACH OTHER.*

PROMISE ME YOU'LL TAKE CARE OF EACH OTHER. *PROMISE.*

WE WILL, MOM. I PROMISE.

ALEX CAN MANAGE ONLY A *WHIMPER,* HIS THROAT *SWOLLEN* IN GRIEF.

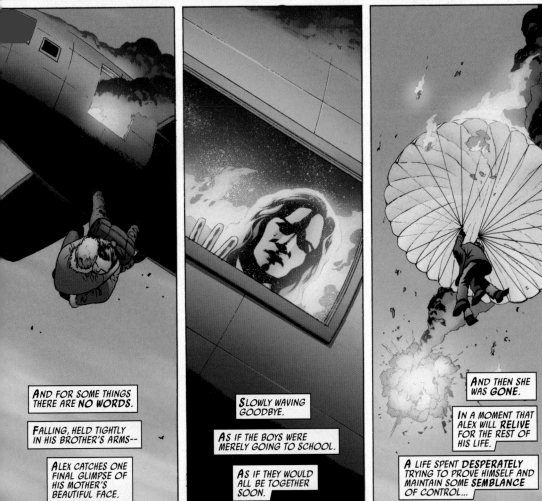

AND FOR SOME THINGS THERE ARE *NO WORDS.*

FALLING, HELD TIGHTLY IN HIS BROTHER'S ARMS--

ALEX CATCHES ONE FINAL GLIMPSE OF HIS MOTHER'S BEAUTIFUL FACE.

SLOWLY WAVING GOODBYE.

AS IF THE BOYS WERE MERELY GOING TO SCHOOL.

AS IF THEY WOULD ALL BE TOGETHER SOON.

AND THEN SHE WAS *GONE.*

IN A MOMENT THAT ALEX WILL *RELIVE* FOR THE REST OF HIS LIFE.

A LIFE SPENT *DESPERATELY* TRYING TO PROVE HIMSELF AND MAINTAIN SOME *SEMBLANCE* OF CONTROL...

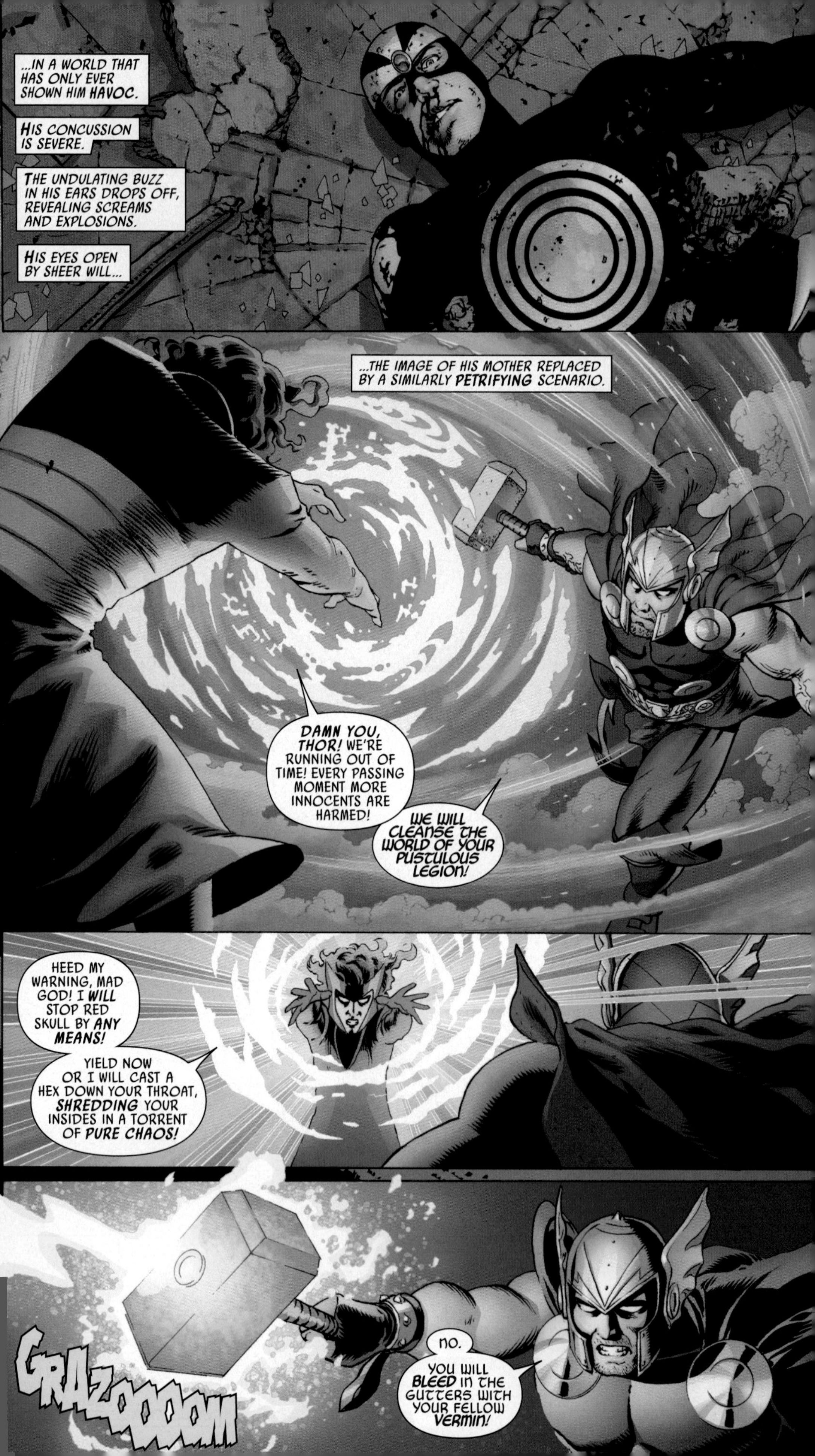
...IN A WORLD THAT HAS ONLY EVER SHOWN HIM HAVOC.
HIS CONCUSSION IS SEVERE.
THE UNDULATING BUZZ IN HIS EARS DROPS OFF, REVEALING SCREAMS AND EXPLOSIONS.
HIS EYES OPEN BY SHEER WILL...
...THE IMAGE OF HIS MOTHER REPLACED BY A SIMILARLY PETRIFYING SCENARIO.
DAMN YOU, THOR! WE'RE RUNNING OUT OF TIME! EVERY PASSING MOMENT MORE INNOCENTS ARE HARMED!
WE WILL CLEANSE THE WORLD OF YOUR PUSTULOUS LEGION!
HEED MY WARNING, MAD GOD! I WILL STOP RED SKULL BY ANY MEANS!
YIELD NOW OR I WILL CAST A HEX DOWN YOUR THROAT, SHREDDING YOUR INSIDES IN A TORRENT OF PURE CHAOS!
GRAZOOOOOM
no.
YOU WILL BLEED IN THE GUTTERS WITH YOUR FELLOW VERMIN!

ALL ENERGY CAN BE *EASILY* TRANSMOGRIFIED.

LIGHTNING SIMPLEST OF ALL.

WITHSTAND OUR WORST!

CAN YOUR *HEAD* WITHSTAND *MJOLNIR'S* SPITE?!

YOU RUSH HEADLONG? YOU ARE TRULY *OUT OF YOUR MIND*--

KRADOOM

--AND *CLEARLY DO NOT REMEMBER WHOM* YOU FACE!

I REMEMBER WELL THE FOE I FACE!

THE *MONSTER* WHO BENDS REALITY TO HER SUITING!

THKOM

AND I REMEMBER YOUR BLACK GIFTS REQUIRE *TIME* AND *REST*--

--OF WHICH YOU WILL HAVE *NEITHER!*

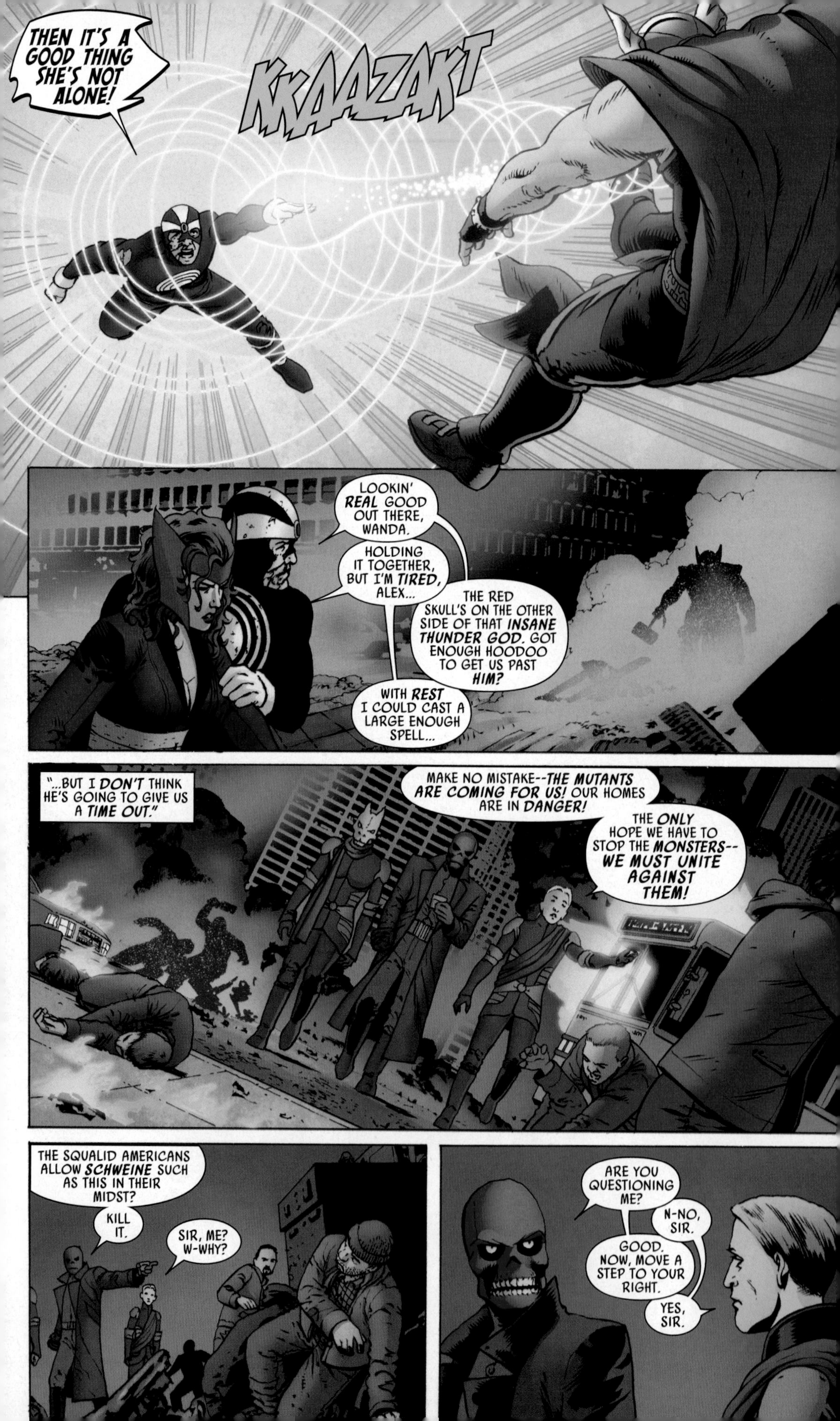
THEN IT'S A GOOD THING SHE'S NOT ALONE!
KKAAZAKT
LOOKIN' REAL GOOD OUT THERE, WANDA.
HOLDING IT TOGETHER, BUT I'M TIRED, ALEX...
THE RED SKULL'S ON THE OTHER SIDE OF THAT INSANE THUNDER GOD. GOT ENOUGH HOODOO TO GET US PAST HIM?
WITH REST I COULD CAST A LARGE ENOUGH SPELL...
"...BUT I DON'T THINK HE'S GOING TO GIVE US A TIME OUT."
MAKE NO MISTAKE--THE MUTANTS ARE COMING FOR US! OUR HOMES ARE IN DANGER!
THE ONLY HOPE WE HAVE TO STOP THE MONSTERS--WE MUST UNITE AGAINST THEM!
THE SQUALID AMERICANS ALLOW SCHWEINE SUCH AS THIS IN THEIR MIDST?
KILL IT.
SIR, ME? W-WHY?
ARE YOU QUESTIONING ME?
N-NO, SIR.
GOOD. NOW, MOVE A STEP TO YOUR RIGHT.
YES, SIR.

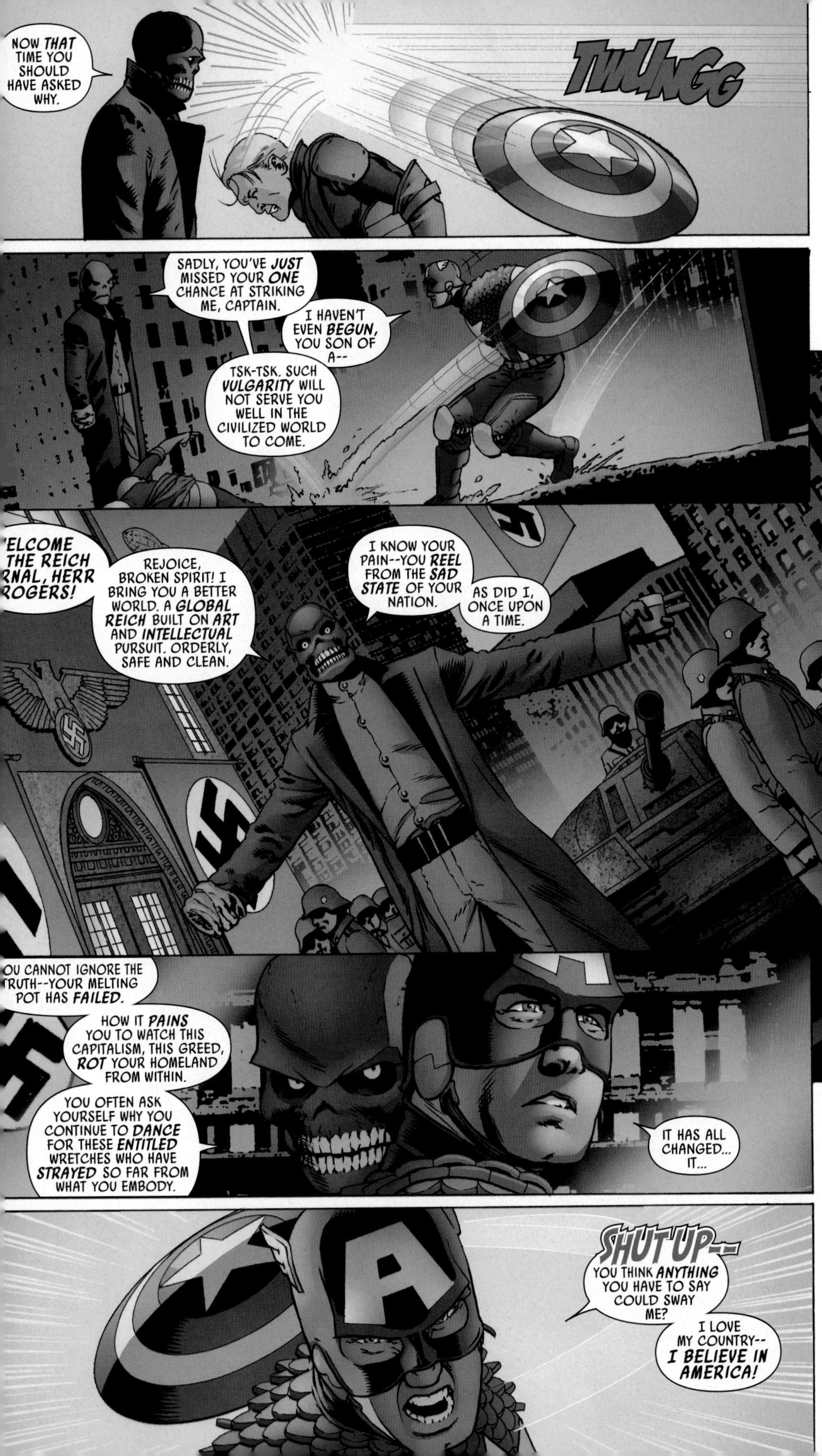

NOW THAT TIME YOU SHOULD HAVE ASKED WHY.
TWUNGG
SADLY, YOU'VE JUST MISSED YOUR ONE CHANCE AT STRIKING ME, CAPTAIN.
I HAVEN'T EVEN BEGUN, YOU SON OF A--
TSK-TSK. SUCH VULGARITY WILL NOT SERVE YOU WELL IN THE CIVILIZED WORLD TO COME.
REJOICE, BROKEN SPIRIT! I BRING YOU A BETTER WORLD. A GLOBAL REICH BUILT ON ART AND INTELLECTUAL PURSUIT. ORDERLY, SAFE AND CLEAN.
I KNOW YOUR PAIN--YOU REEL FROM THE SAD STATE OF YOUR NATION.
AS DID I, ONCE UPON A TIME.
HOW IT PAINS YOU TO WATCH THIS CAPITALISM, THIS GREED, ROT YOUR HOMELAND FROM WITHIN.
YOU OFTEN ASK YOURSELF WHY YOU CONTINUE TO DANCE FOR THESE ENTITLED WRETCHES WHO HAVE STRAYED SO FAR FROM WHAT YOU EMBODY.
IT HAS ALL CHANGED... IT...
SHUT UP--
YOU THINK ANYTHING YOU HAVE TO SAY COULD SWAY ME?
I LOVE MY COUNTRY-- I BELIEVE IN AMERICA!

CAPTAIN AMERICA'S BODY GOES LIMP.

HIS CEREBELLUM SHUT DOWN BY HIS HATED ENEMY.

IT'S LIKE THEY SAY-- THE BEST WAY TO SELL A LIE IS TO *BELIEVE* IT YOURSELF.

PLOKK

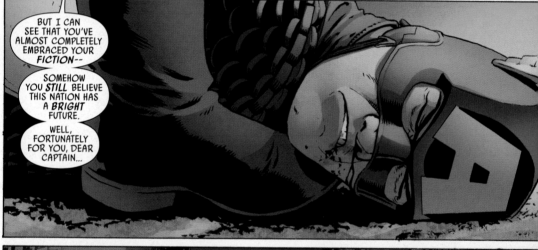

BUT I CAN SEE THAT YOU'VE ALMOST COMPLETELY EMBRACED YOUR *FICTION*--

SOMEHOW YOU *STILL* BELIEVE THIS NATION HAS A *BRIGHT* FUTURE.

WELL, FORTUNATELY FOR YOU, DEAR CAPTAIN...

...I AM HERE TO *ENSURE* IT.

YOU WILL BECOME THE FIGUREHEAD OF MY MOVEMENT.

WHEN THE PEOPLE SEE *YOU* HUNTING MUTANTS IN THE STREETS, THEY WILL RALLY BEHIND THEIR *NOBLE* HERO.

WE WILL DIRECT THEIR *RAGE* AND *FRUSTRATION* AT THIS *MINORITY*, GIVING A FACE TO THEIR PAIN.

A FACE THEY CAN *CRUSH*.

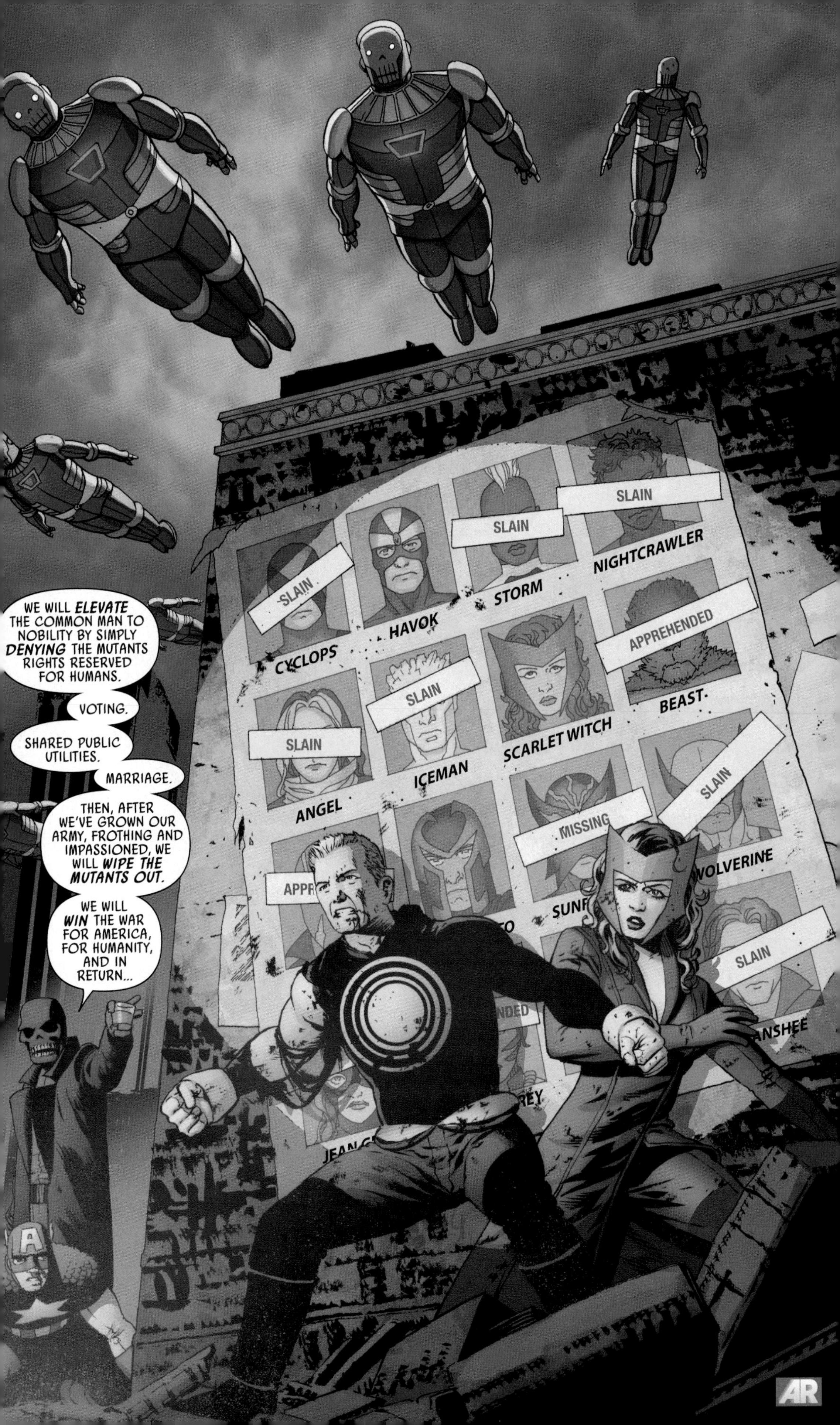

SLAIN
SLAIN
NIGHTCRAWLER
SLAIN
STORM
HAVOK
CYCLOPS
APPREHENDED
BEAST.
SLAIN
SCARLET WITCH
SLAIN
ICEMAN
ANGEL
SLAIN
MISSING
WOLVERINE
SLAIN
WE WILL *ELEVATE* THE COMMON MAN TO NOBILITY BY SIMPLY *DENYING* THE MUTANTS RIGHTS RESERVED FOR HUMANS.
VOTING.
SHARED PUBLIC UTILITIES.
MARRIAGE.
THEN, AFTER WE'VE GROWN OUR ARMY, FROTHING AND IMPASSIONED, WE WILL *WIPE THE MUTANTS OUT.*
WE WILL *WIN* THE WAR FOR AMERICA, FOR HUMANITY, AND IN RETURN...

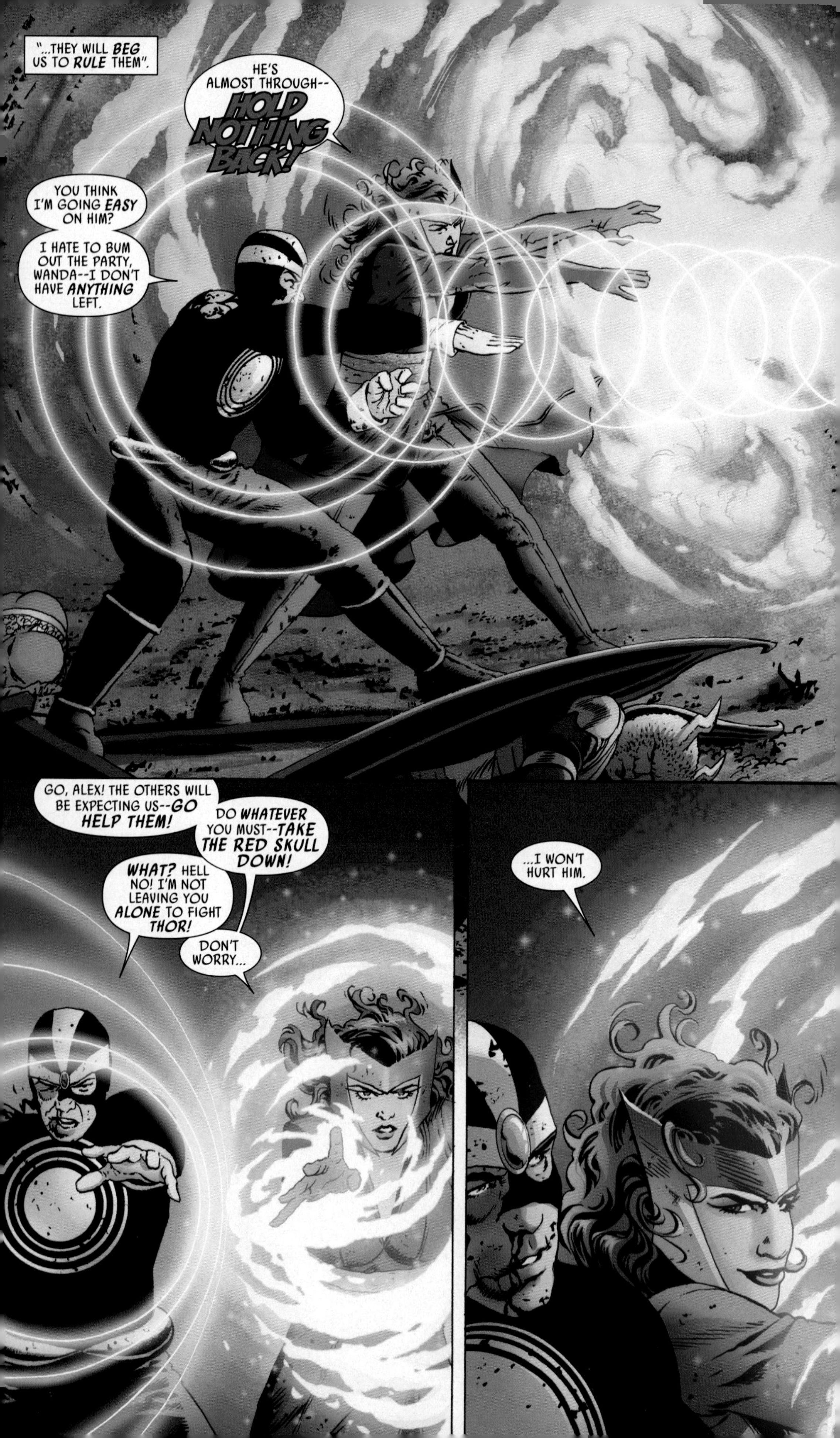
"...THEY WILL BEG US TO RULE THEM".
HE'S ALMOST THROUGH-- HOLD NOTHING BACK!
YOU THINK I'M GOING EASY ON HIM?
I HATE TO BUM OUT THE PARTY, WANDA--I DON'T HAVE ANYTHING LEFT.
GO, ALEX! THE OTHERS WILL BE EXPECTING US--GO HELP THEM!
DO WHATEVER YOU MUST--TAKE THE RED SKULL DOWN!
WHAT? HELL NO! I'M NOT LEAVING YOU ALONE TO FIGHT THOR!
DON'T WORRY...
...I WON'T HURT HIM.

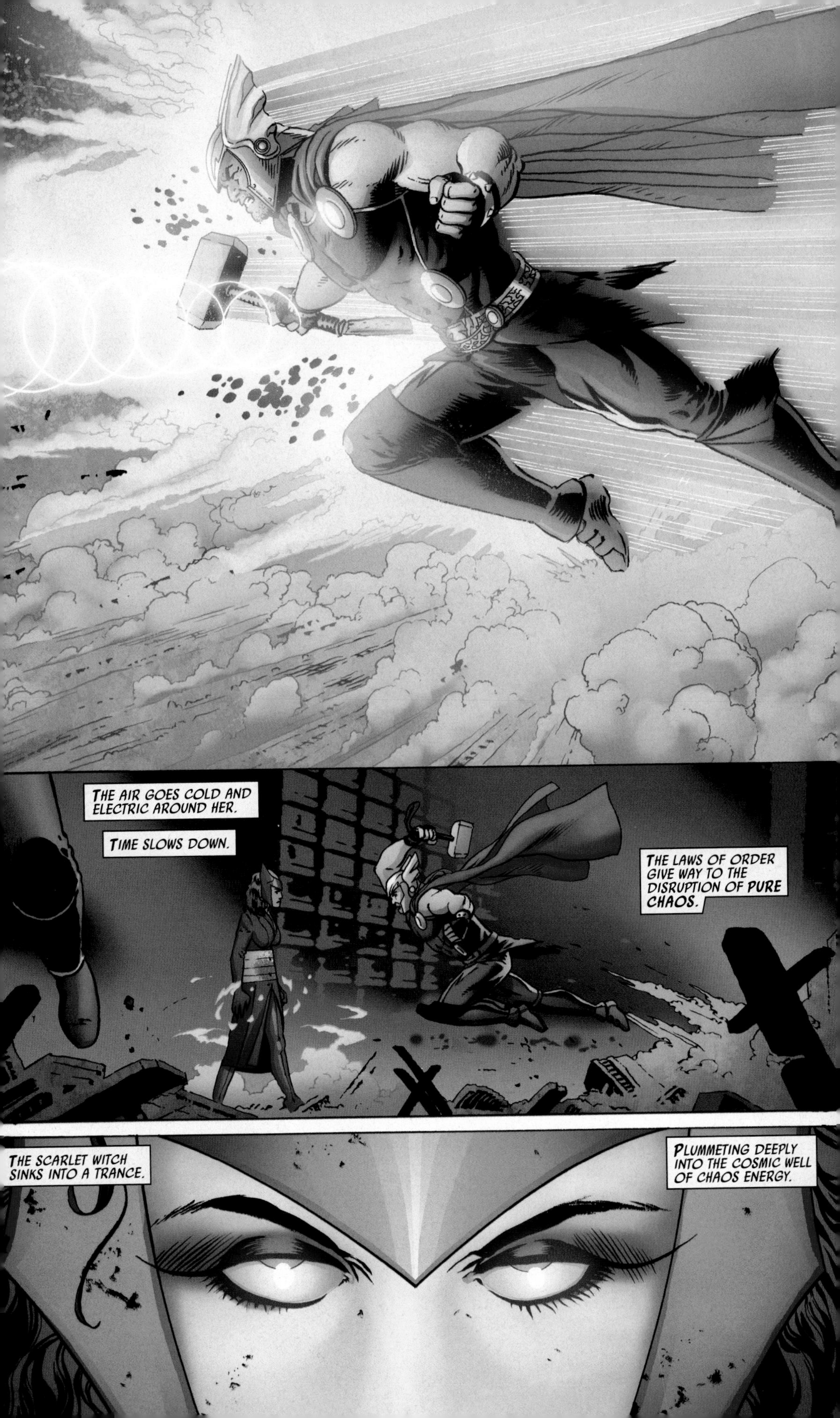
THE AIR GOES COLD AND ELECTRIC AROUND HER.
TIME SLOWS DOWN.
THE LAWS OF ORDER GIVE WAY TO THE DISRUPTION OF PURE CHAOS.
THE SCARLET WITCH SINKS INTO A TRANCE.
PLUMMETING DEEPLY INTO THE COSMIC WELL OF CHAOS ENERGY.

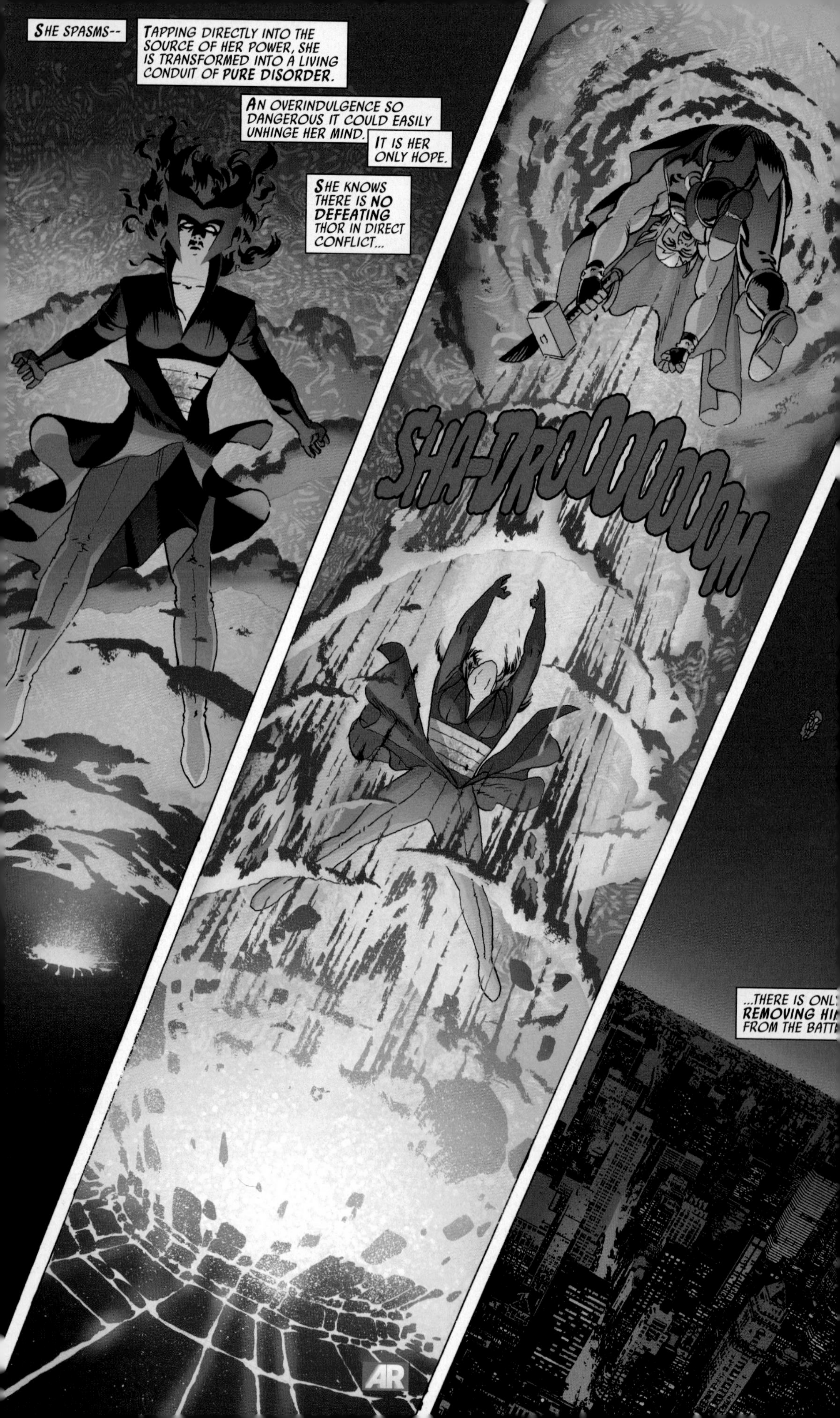
SHE SPASMS--
TAPPING DIRECTLY INTO THE SOURCE OF HER POWER, SHE IS TRANSFORMED INTO A LIVING CONDUIT OF PURE DISORDER.
AN OVERINDULGENCE SO DANGEROUS IT COULD EASILY UNHINGE HER MIND.
IT IS HER ONLY HOPE.
SHE KNOWS THERE IS NO DEFEATING THOR IN DIRECT CONFLICT...
SHA-DROOOOOOOM
...THERE IS ONLY
REMOVING HI
FROM THE BATT

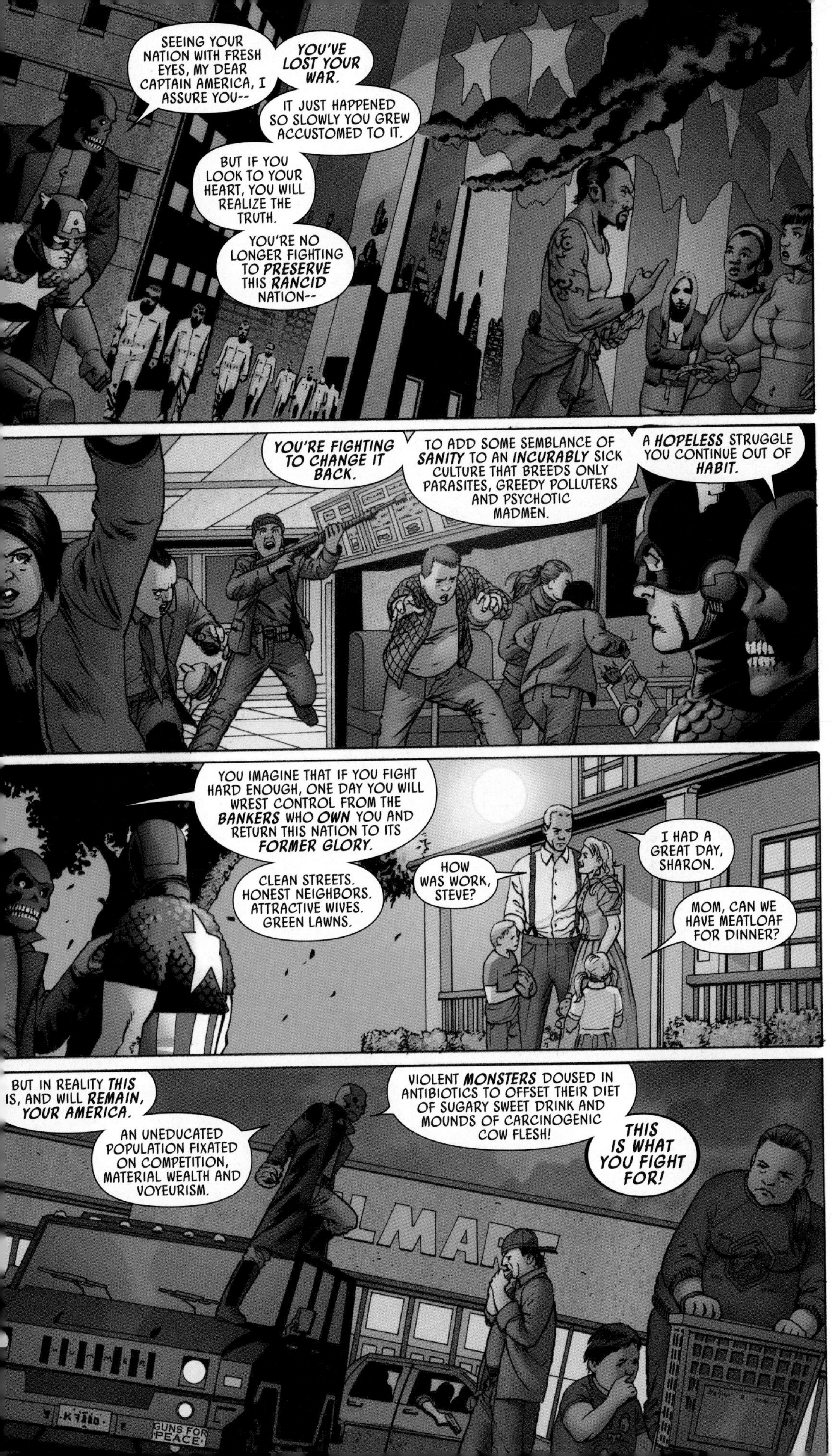
SEEING YOUR NATION WITH FRESH EYES, MY DEAR CAPTAIN AMERICA, I ASSURE YOU--
YOU'VE LOST YOUR WAR.
IT JUST HAPPENED SO SLOWLY YOU GREW ACCUSTOMED TO IT.
BUT IF YOU LOOK TO YOUR HEART, YOU WILL REALIZE THE TRUTH.
YOU'RE NO LONGER FIGHTING TO PRESERVE THIS RANCID NATION--
YOU'RE FIGHTING TO CHANGE IT BACK.
TO ADD SOME SEMBLANCE OF SANITY TO AN INCURABLY SICK CULTURE THAT BREEDS ONLY PARASITES, GREEDY POLLUTERS AND PSYCHOTIC MADMEN.
A HOPELESS STRUGGLE YOU CONTINUE OUT OF HABIT.
YOU IMAGINE THAT IF YOU FIGHT HARD ENOUGH, ONE DAY YOU WILL WREST CONTROL FROM THE BANKERS WHO OWN YOU AND RETURN THIS NATION TO ITS FORMER GLORY.
CLEAN STREETS. HONEST NEIGHBORS. ATTRACTIVE WIVES. GREEN LAWNS.
HOW WAS WORK, STEVE?
I HAD A GREAT DAY, SHARON.
MOM, CAN WE HAVE MEATLOAF FOR DINNER?
BUT IN REALITY THIS IS, AND WILL REMAIN, YOUR AMERICA.
AN UNEDUCATED POPULATION FIXATED ON COMPETITION, MATERIAL WEALTH AND VOYEURISM.
VIOLENT MONSTERS DOUSED IN ANTIBIOTICS TO OFFSET THEIR DIET OF SUGARY SWEET DRINK AND MOUNDS OF CARCINOGENIC COW FLESH!
THIS IS WHAT YOU FIGHT FOR!
GUNS FOR PEACE

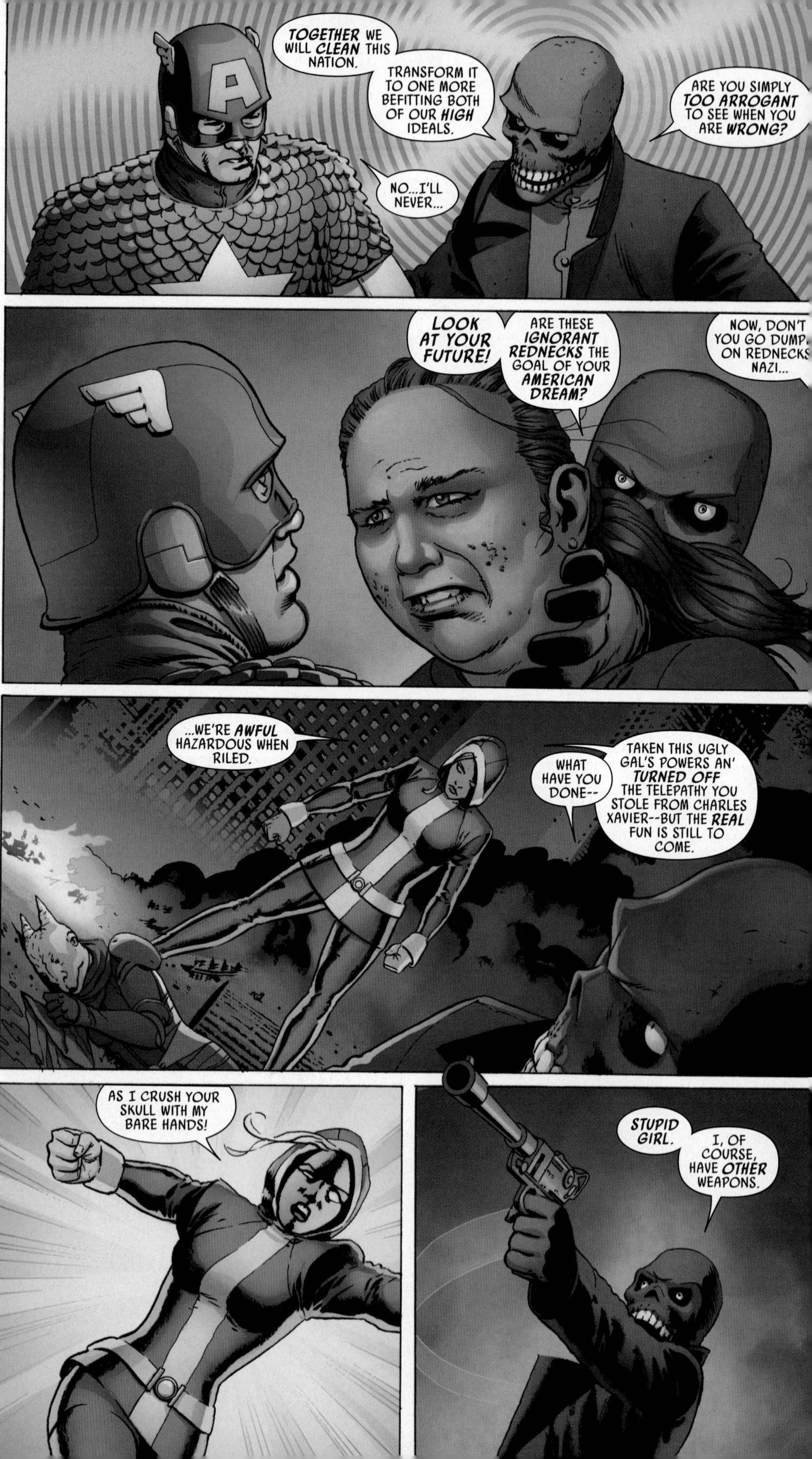
TOGETHER WE WILL CLEAN THIS NATION.
TRANSFORM IT TO ONE MORE BEFITTING BOTH OF OUR HIGH IDEALS.
NO...I'LL NEVER...
ARE YOU SIMPLY TOO ARROGANT TO SEE WHEN YOU ARE WRONG?
LOOK AT YOUR FUTURE!
ARE THESE IGNORANT REDNECKS THE GOAL OF YOUR AMERICAN DREAM?
NOW, DON'T YOU GO DUMP ON REDNECKS NAZI...
...WE'RE AWFUL HAZARDOUS WHEN RILED.
WHAT HAVE YOU DONE--
TAKEN THIS UGLY GAL'S POWERS AN' TURNED OFF THE TELEPATHY YOU STOLE FROM CHARLES XAVIER--BUT THE REAL FUN IS STILL TO COME.
AS I CRUSH YOUR SKULL WITH MY BARE HANDS!
STUPID GIRL.
I, OF COURSE, HAVE OTHER WEAPONS.

...OSMIC ENERGY EARS THE RED ULL'S FLESH--THE OT GOES WIDE.

BLAM!

ROGUE'S INJURY S NOT FATAL...

...HAVOK'S PLANS FOR JOHANN SHMIDT ARE.

TWUKK

OOF--!

HIS ENERGY SPENT, HAVOK IS LEFT WITH A MORE PRIMAL METHOD OF ATTACK--

--AND THAT SUITS HIM JUST FINE.

YOU'RE LIKE THE CLOSETED JOCK WHO BEATS ON GAY KIDS! YOU DON'T HATE MUTANTS--

PLOKK

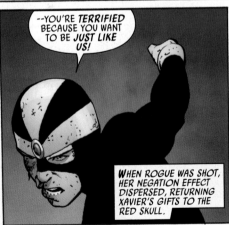

--YOU'RE TERRIFIED BECAUSE YOU WANT TO BE JUST LIKE US!

WHEN ROGUE WAS SHOT, HER NEGATION EFFECT DISPERSED, RETURNING XAVIER'S GIFTS TO THE RED SKULL.

OBLIVIOUS, HAVOK BEATS ROGUE MERCILESS, SEEING IN HER THE FACE OF HIS FOE.

KROKK

FIGHT! PUNCH! ZAP! POOR MUTANT FOOL-- YOU HAVE NO HOPE OF TURNING BACK THIS TIDE.

IT'S LIKE THEY SAY, THE BEST WAY TO SELL A LIE--

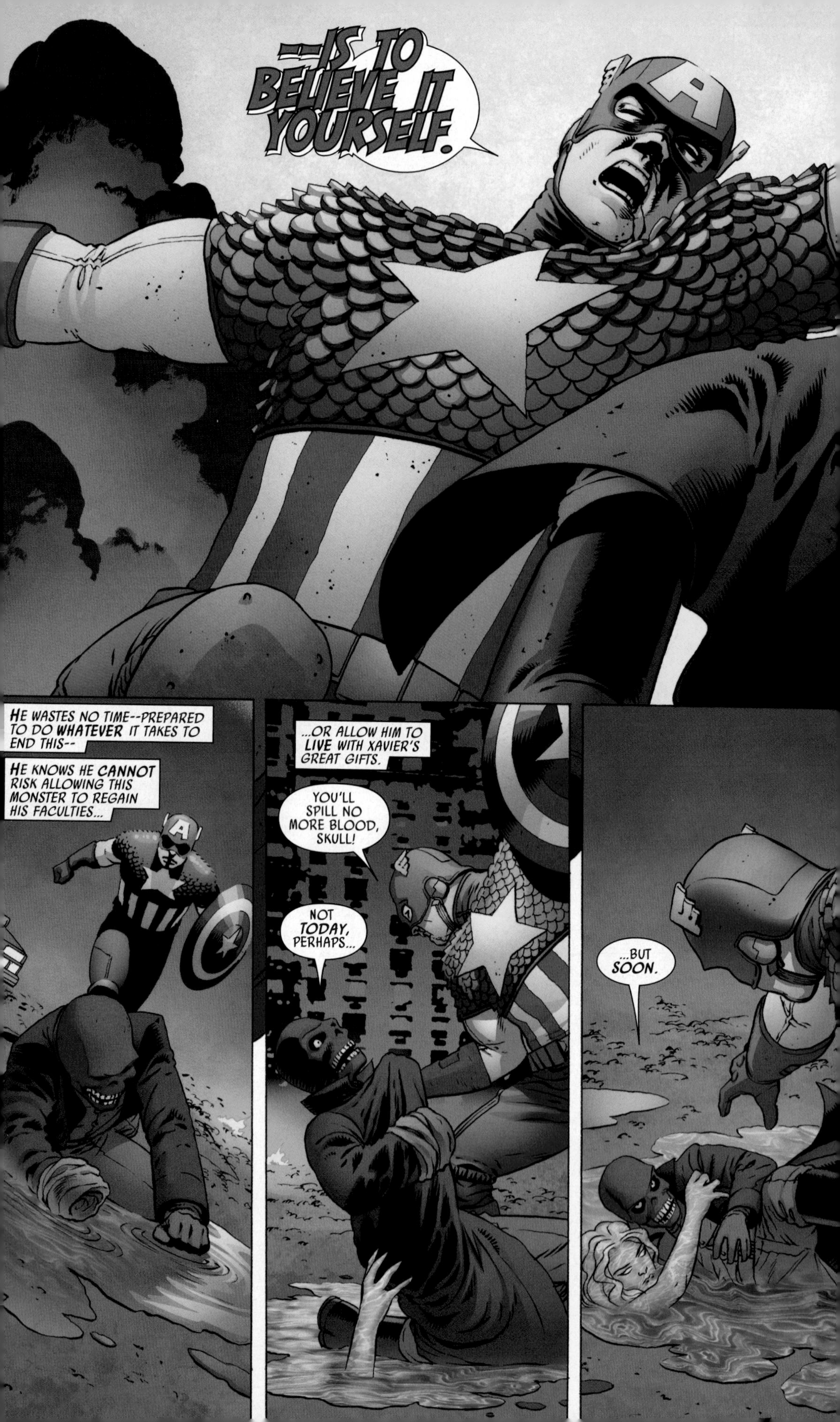

--IS TO BELIEVE IT YOURSELF.
HE WASTES NO TIME--PREPARED TO DO WHATEVER IT TAKES TO END THIS--
HE KNOWS HE CANNOT RISK ALLOWING THIS MONSTER TO REGAIN HIS FACULTIES...
...OR ALLOW HIM TO LIVE WITH XAVIER'S GREAT GIFTS.
YOU'LL SPILL NO MORE BLOOD, SKULL!
NOT TODAY, PERHAPS...
...BUT SOON.

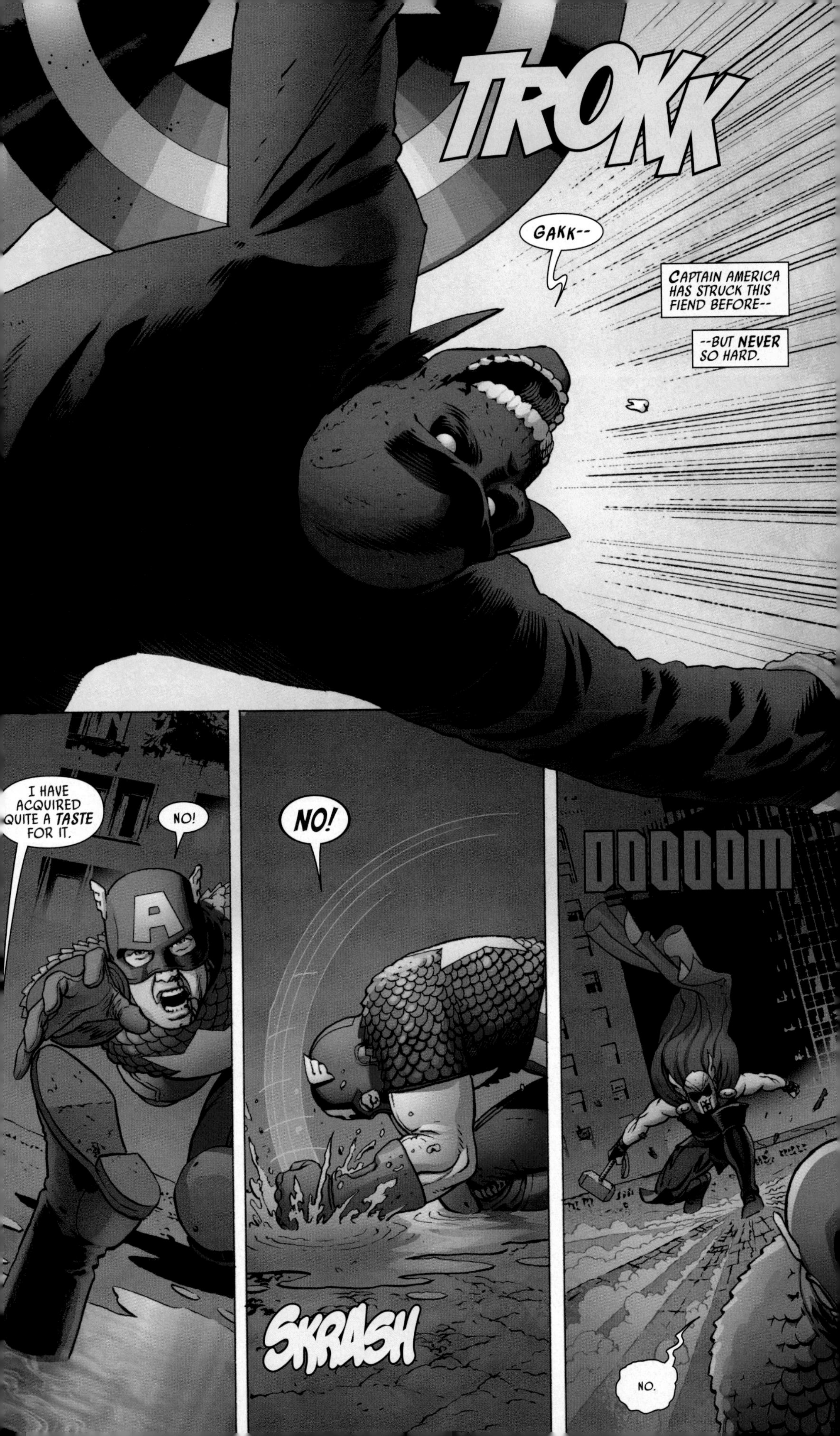
TROKK
GAKK--
CAPTAIN AMERICA HAS STRUCK THIS FIEND BEFORE--
--BUT NEVER SO HARD.
I HAVE ACQUIRED QUITE A TASTE FOR IT.
NO!
NO!
SKRASH
DOOOOM
NO.

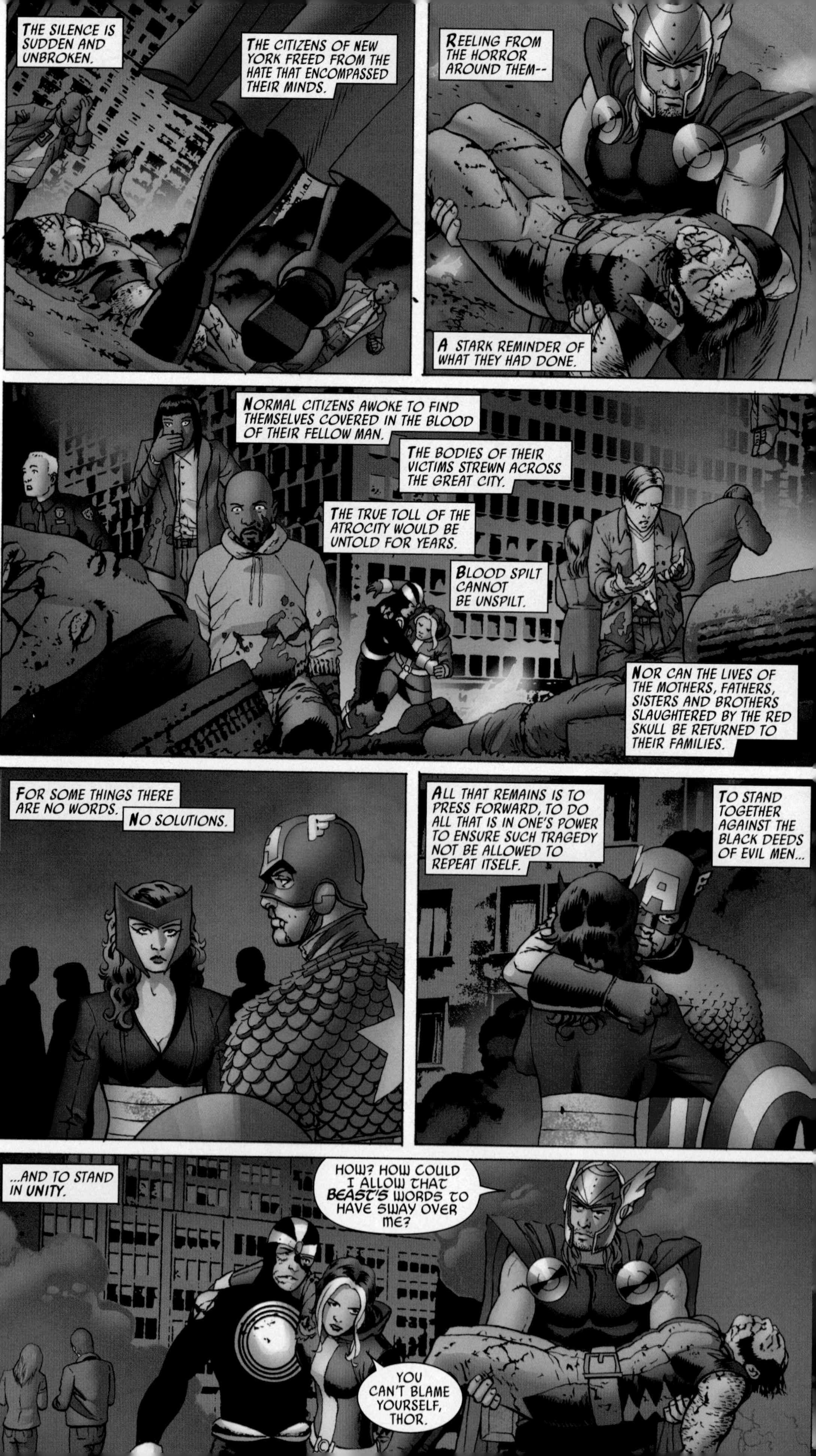
THE SILENCE IS SUDDEN AND UNBROKEN.
THE CITIZENS OF NEW YORK FREED FROM THE HATE THAT ENCOMPASSED THEIR MINDS.
REELING FROM THE HORROR AROUND THEM--
A STARK REMINDER OF WHAT THEY HAD DONE.
NORMAL CITIZENS AWOKE TO FIND THEMSELVES COVERED IN THE BLOOD OF THEIR FELLOW MAN.
THE BODIES OF THEIR VICTIMS STREWN ACROSS THE GREAT CITY.
THE TRUE TOLL OF THE ATROCITY WOULD BE UNTOLD FOR YEARS.
BLOOD SPILT CANNOT BE UNSPILT.
NOR CAN THE LIVES OF THE MOTHERS, FATHERS, SISTERS AND BROTHERS SLAUGHTERED BY THE RED SKULL BE RETURNED TO THEIR FAMILIES.
FOR SOME THINGS THERE ARE NO WORDS.
NO SOLUTIONS.
ALL THAT REMAINS IS TO PRESS FORWARD, TO DO ALL THAT IS IN ONE'S POWER TO ENSURE SUCH TRAGEDY NOT BE ALLOWED TO REPEAT ITSELF.
TO STAND TOGETHER AGAINST THE BLACK DEEDS OF EVIL MEN...
...AND TO STAND IN UNITY.
HOW? HOW COULD I ALLOW THAT BEAST'S WORDS TO HAVE SWAY OVER ME?
YOU CAN'T BLAME YOURSELF, THOR.

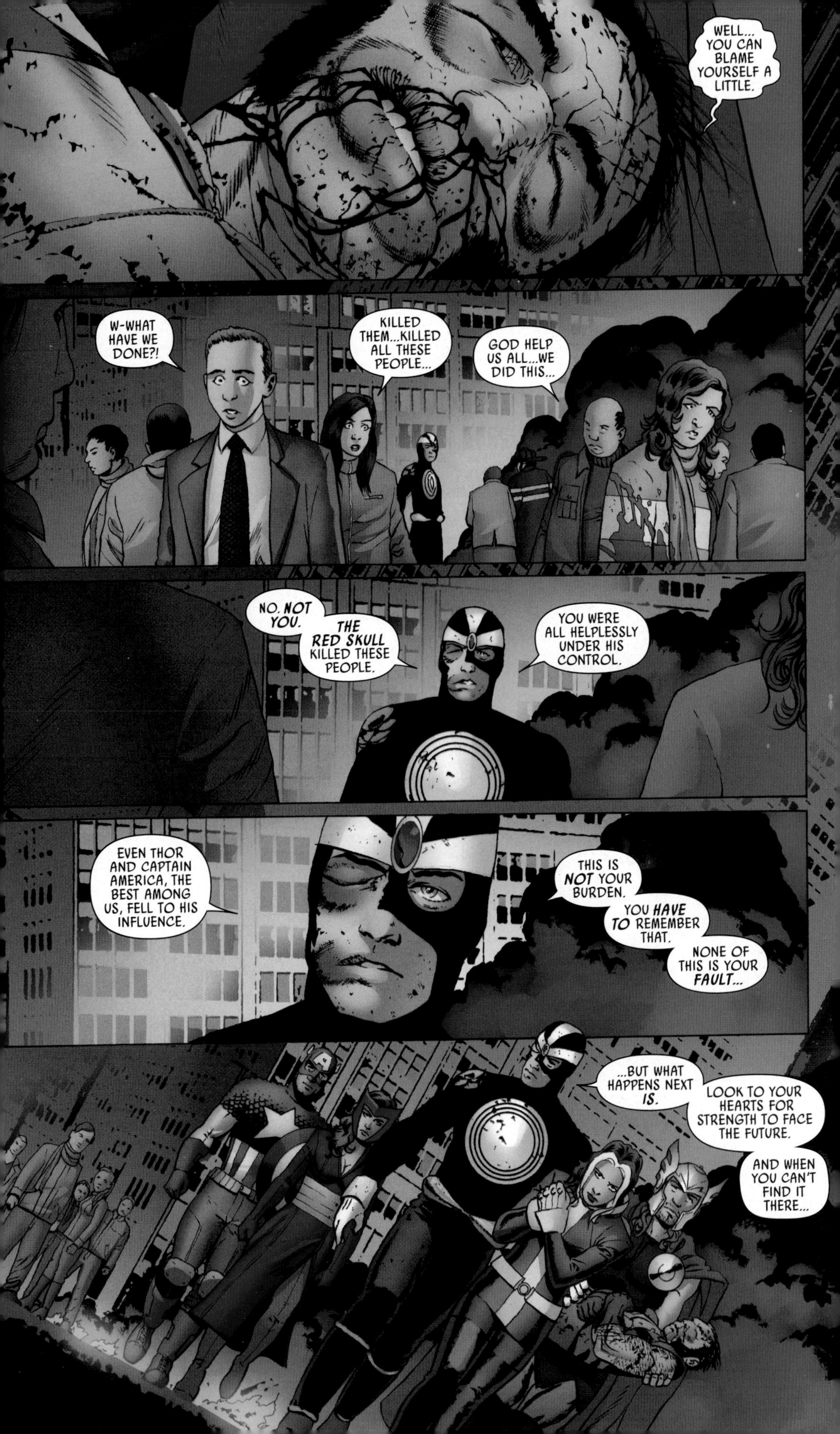
WELL... YOU CAN BLAME YOURSELF A LITTLE.
W-WHAT HAVE WE DONE?!
KILLED THEM...KILLED ALL THESE PEOPLE...
GOD HELP US ALL...WE DID THIS...
NO. NOT YOU.
THE RED SKULL KILLED THESE PEOPLE.
YOU WERE ALL HELPLESSLY UNDER HIS CONTROL.
EVEN THOR AND CAPTAIN AMERICA, THE BEST AMONG US, FELL TO HIS INFLUENCE.
THIS IS NOT YOUR BURDEN.
YOU HAVE TO REMEMBER THAT.
NONE OF THIS IS YOUR FAULT...
...BUT WHAT HAPPENS NEXT IS.
LOOK TO YOUR HEARTS FOR STRENGTH TO FACE THE FUTURE.
AND WHEN YOU CAN'T FIND IT THERE...

"...LOOK TO *EACH OTHER.*"

WE SCOURED THE CITY FOR THEM...

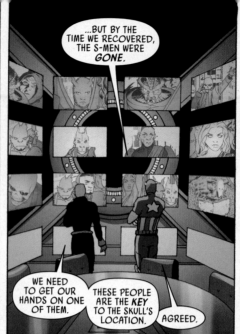

...BUT BY THE TIME WE RECOVERED, THE S-MEN WERE *GONE.*

WE NEED TO GET OUR HANDS ON ONE OF THEM.

THESE PEOPLE ARE THE *KEY* TO THE SKULL'S LOCATION.

AGREED.

GRADE-A *BAD TIMES,* STEVE.

YOU KNOW, GIVEN *WHO* WE'RE UP AGAINST HERE, IF YOU WANT TO TAKE THE CHAIR ON THIS, I *WOULDN'T* BE OFFENDED--

NO.

THE AVENGERS *UNITY SQUAD* IS IN EXCELLENT HANDS WITH YOU IN CHARGE, ALEX.

I'M *ALWAYS RIGHT* ABOUT ONE THING--WHEN SOMEONE HAS *WHAT IT TAKES.*

HEH--WELL, TO BE FAIR, I DON'T THINK YOU CAN SELF-APPLY *"ALWAYS RIGHT",* CAP, BUT THANK YOU...

"...I'LL TRY NOT TO LET YOU DOWN."

ANNA MARIE, I ONLY NEED A MINUTE.

TIMER'S STARTED.

I WANTED YOU TO KNOW...I UNDERSTAND YOUR *TREPIDATION* ABOUT ME.

BUT I NEED YOU TO BELIEVE ME-- I'LL *NEVER AGAIN* BE WIELDED AS A MADMAN'S WEAPON.

EVEN WITH THE POWER OF CHARLES XAVIER, THE RED SKULL COULDN'T MAKE ME CAST THAT SPELL.

IF YOU DECIDE TO STAY ON, I'D LIKE TO START OVER.

I'D LIKE US TO BE *FRIENDS.*

I'M SORRY, WANDA.

I DON'T CARE *WHAT* YOU SAY--I THINK YOU'RE A *DANGEROUS MESS.*

I'M STICKING AROUND FOR TWO REASONS: BECAUSE IT'S WHAT *CHARLES* WOULD *WANT...*

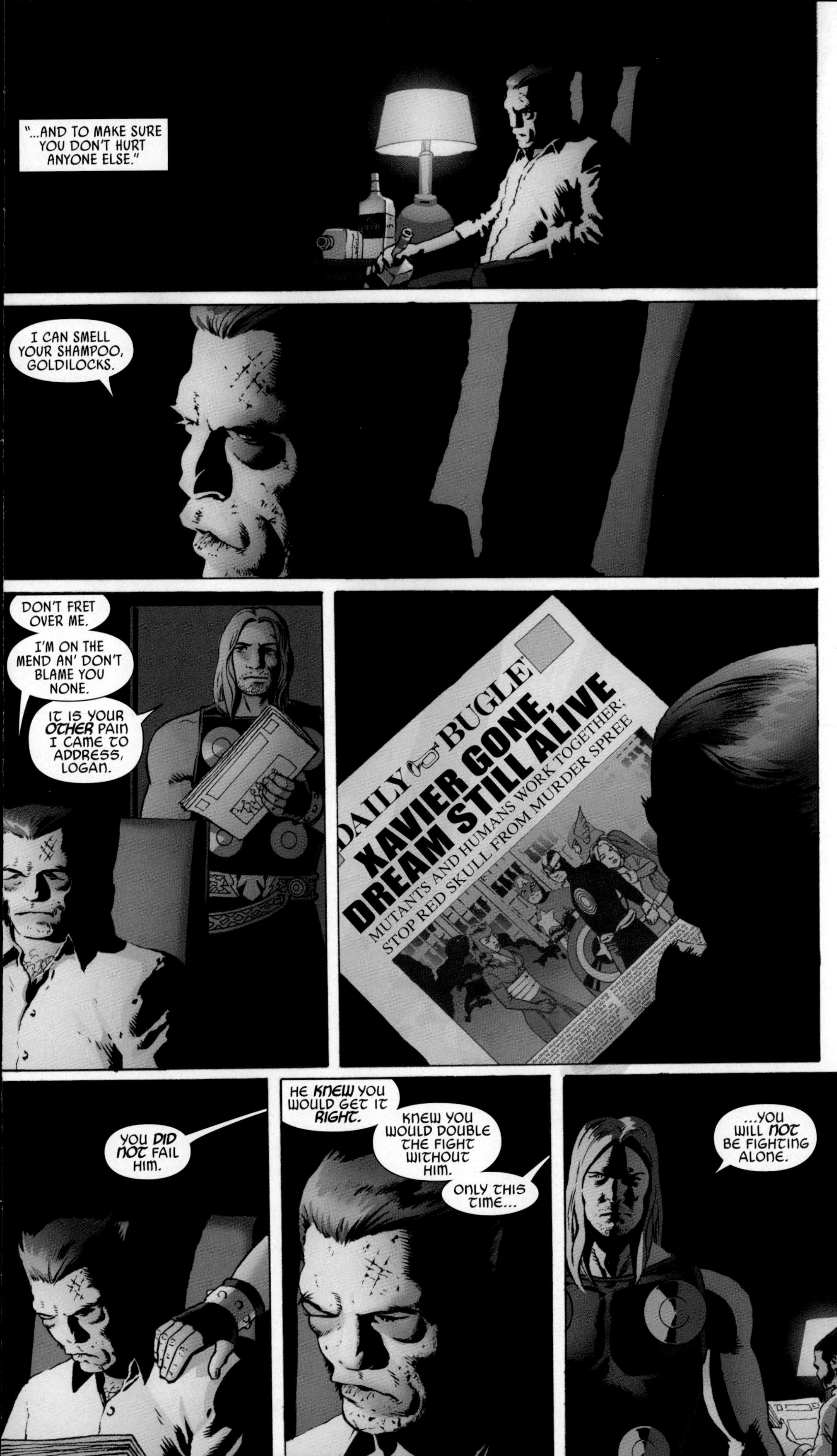
"...AND TO MAKE SURE YOU DON'T HURT ANYONE ELSE."
I CAN SMELL YOUR SHAMPOO, GOLDILOCKS.
DON'T FRET OVER ME.
I'M ON THE MEND AN' DON'T BLAME YOU NONE.
IT IS YOUR OTHER PAIN I CAME TO ADDRESS, LOGAN.
DAILY BUGLE
XAVIER GONE, DREAM STILL ALIVE
MUTANTS AND HUMANS WORK TOGETHER; STOP RED SKULL FROM MURDER SPREE
YOU DID NOT FAIL HIM.
HE KNEW YOU WOULD GET IT RIGHT.
KNEW YOU WOULD DOUBLE THE FIGHT WITHOUT HIM.
ONLY THIS TIME...
...YOU WILL NOT BE FIGHTING ALONE.

THREE MONTHS FROM NOW

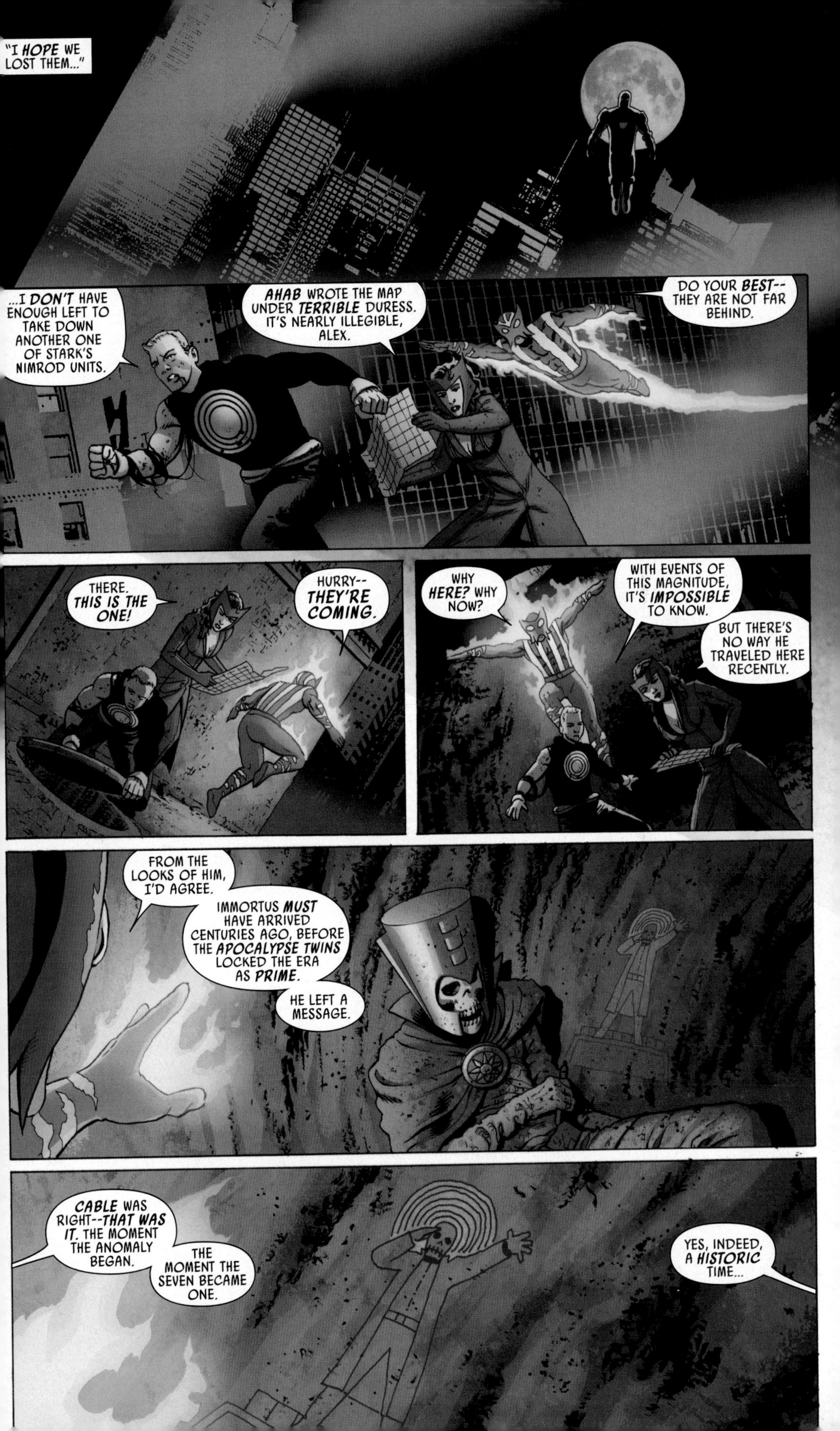
"I HOPE WE LOST THEM..."
...I DON'T HAVE ENOUGH LEFT TO TAKE DOWN ANOTHER ONE OF STARK'S NIMROD UNITS.
AHAB WROTE THE MAP UNDER TERRIBLE DURESS. IT'S NEARLY ILLEGIBLE, ALEX.
DO YOUR BEST-- THEY ARE NOT FAR BEHIND.
THERE. THIS IS THE ONE!
HURRY-- THEY'RE COMING.
WHY HERE? WHY NOW?
WITH EVENTS OF THIS MAGNITUDE, IT'S IMPOSSIBLE TO KNOW.
BUT THERE'S NO WAY HE TRAVELED HERE RECENTLY.
FROM THE LOOKS OF HIM, I'D AGREE.
IMMORTUS MUST HAVE ARRIVED CENTURIES AGO, BEFORE THE APOCALYPSE TWINS LOCKED THE ERA AS PRIME.
HE LEFT A MESSAGE.
CABLE WAS RIGHT--THAT WAS IT. THE MOMENT THE ANOMALY BEGAN.
THE MOMENT THE SEVEN BECAME ONE.
YES, INDEED, A HISTORIC TIME...

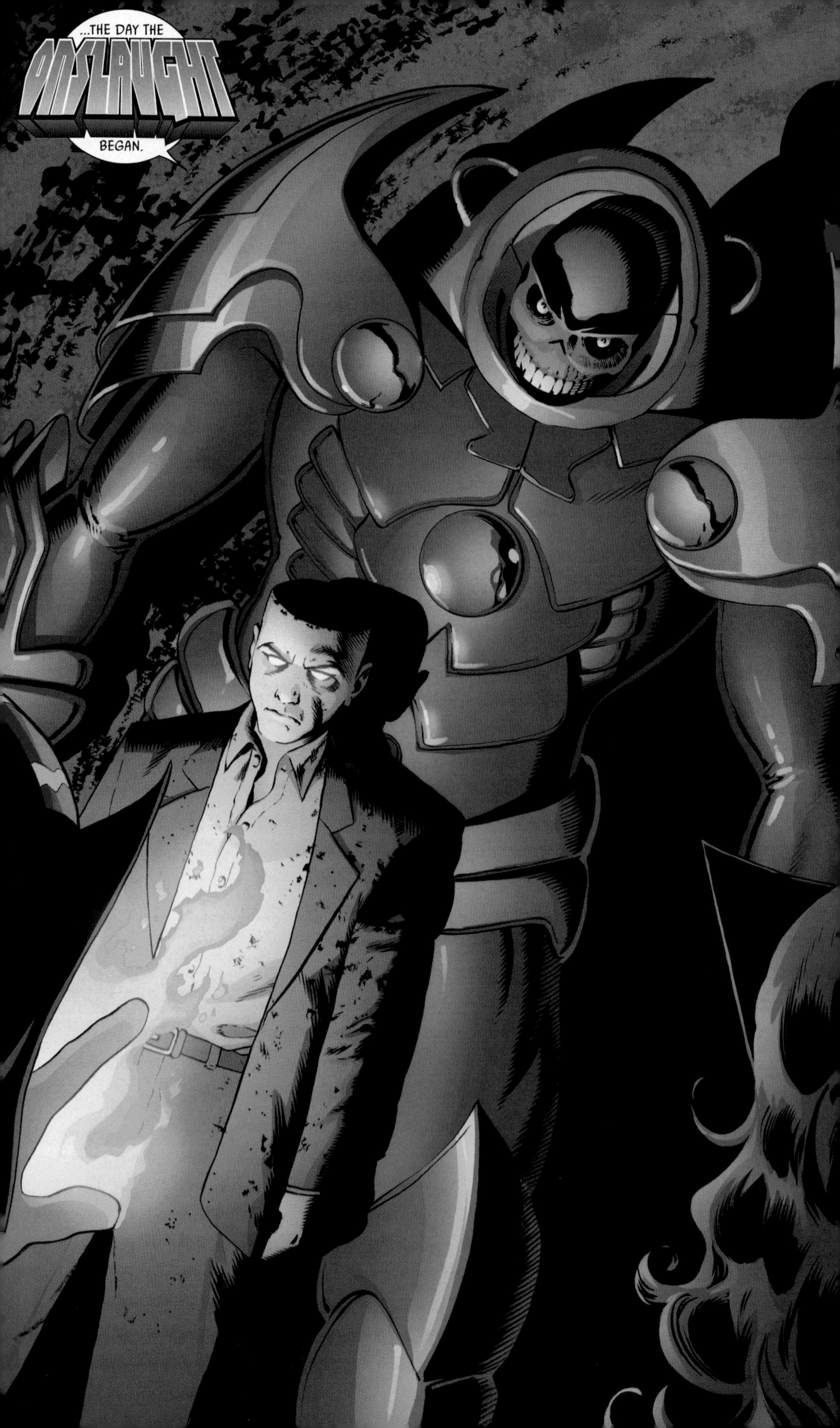
...THE DAY THE
ONSLAUGHT
BEGAN.

NCANNY AVENGERS #1 DETROIT FANFARE VARIANT BY RYAN STEGMAN & MATTHEW WILSON

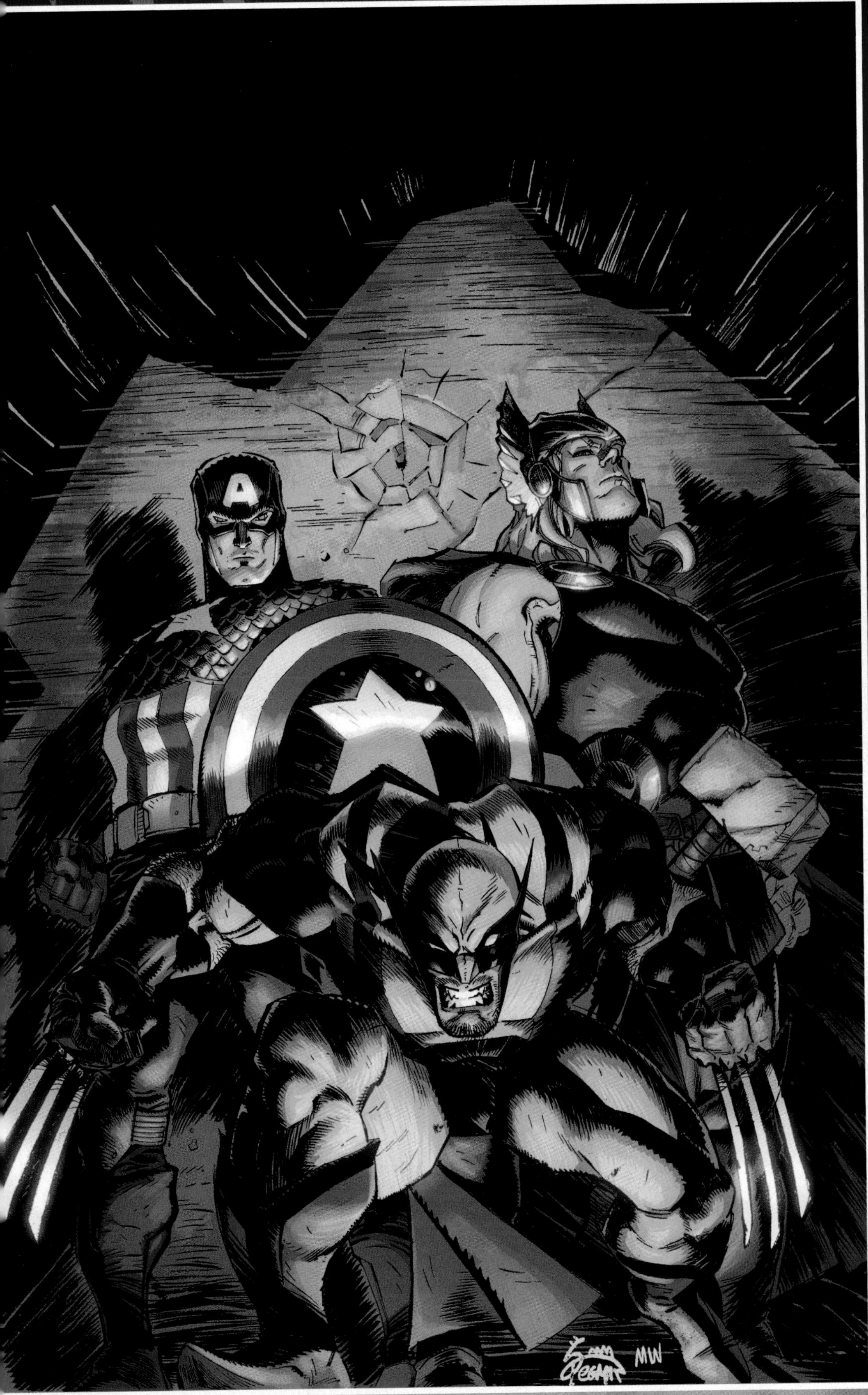
MW

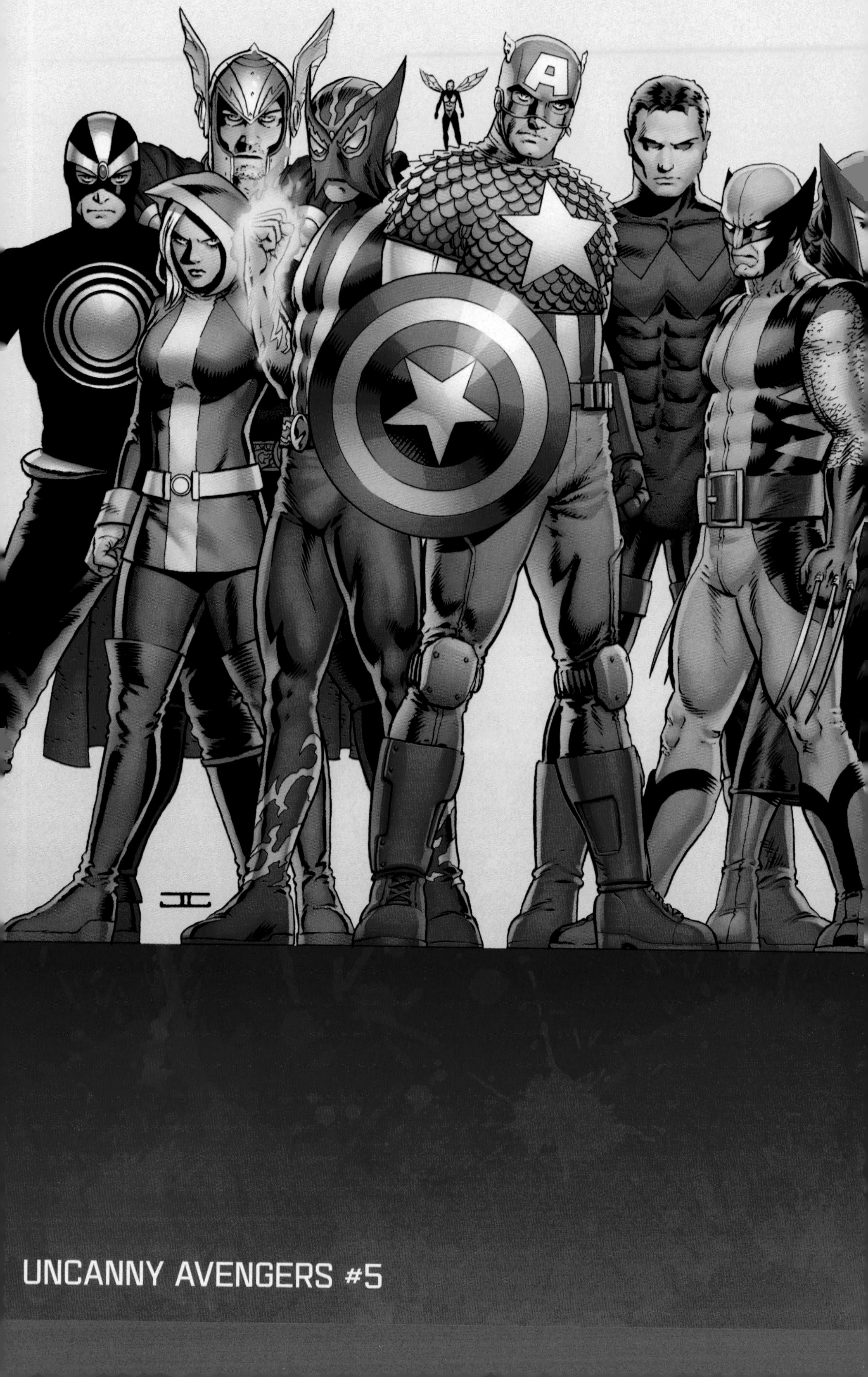

UNCANNY AVENGERS #5

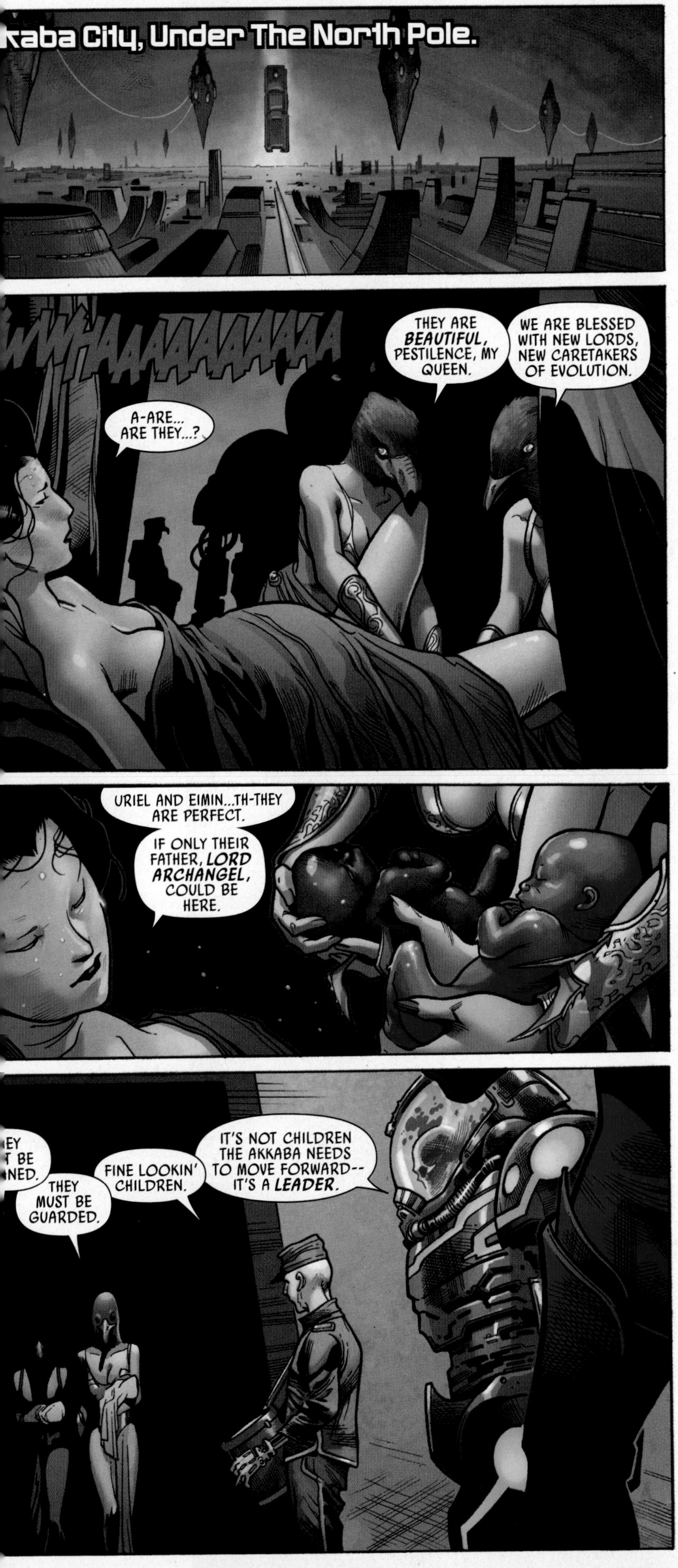

kaba City, Under The North Pole.
WWHAAAAAAAAAAA
A-ARE... ARE THEY...?
THEY ARE BEAUTIFUL, PESTILENCE, MY QUEEN.
WE ARE BLESSED WITH NEW LORDS, NEW CARETAKERS OF EVOLUTION.
URIEL AND EIMIN...TH-THEY ARE PERFECT.
IF ONLY THEIR FATHER, LORD ARCHANGEL, COULD BE HERE.
THEY MUST BE GUARDED.
FINE LOOKIN' CHILDREN.
IT'S NOT CHILDREN THE AKKABA NEEDS TO MOVE FORWARD--IT'S A LEADER.

I HAVE STRUGGLED SINCE THE DAYS OF THE PHARAOHS TO STOP THIS CELESTIAL ***MANIPULATION.***

HAVING EXPLOITED ***ALL*** THE MYRIAD POWERS AT MY DISPOSAL AND GREAT SWATHS OF TIME TO THE ENDEAVOR.

BUT IT HAPPENS ***REGARDLESS--***

THE APOCALYPSE TWINS, RAVAGERS OF MANKIND, ARRIVE WITH LITTLE FANFARE.

YET THEIR INFLUENCE INFECTS ***ALL*** FUTURES.

AND THERE IS ***NO*** SIMPLE WAY OF UNDOING IT.

THEIR INCEPTION AND TIME IN UTERO--ALL OF IT ***SAFEGUARDED.***

THIS ENTIRE ERA NOW ENCLOSED IN A CHRONOS DAM OF ADAPTABLE TACHYONS.

SOME UNSEEN HAND IS ***GUARDING*** THE BIRTH OF THESE TWINS.

NARROWING THE SPECTRUM OF POSSIBLE OUTCOMES.

FEW OF THEM TO ***MY*** SUITING.

TO STOP THESE VERMIN, ALTERATIONS TO HISTORY MUST BE MORE ***SEVERE.***

REARRANGING EVENTS IN A MANNER THAT SUITS ***MY*** PURPOSE, SECURING ***MY*** FUTURE.

I HAVE REORGANIZED THE BOARD IN INCALCULABLE PERMUTATIONS.

IF TIME COULD BE MEASURED WHILE OUTSIDE THE STREAM, I WOULD HAVE AGED ***HUNDREDS*** OF YEARS.

THIS IS WRONG. WHY AM I BEING OVERLOOKED?

I'M THE HEIR OF APOCALYPSE!

THEY'LL BURY YA NEXT TO 'IM IF YOU DON'T WATCH YER MOUTH, GENOCIDE.

NO MATTER MY EFFORTS THE CONTRARY, I LEAR[NED] TO ACCEPT THAT PREVEN[TING] URIEL'S RULE IS FUTIL[E]

OTHERS QUICKLY STO[OD] TO FILL HIS PLACE.

THE CLONED BOY.

THE TRUE SON.

THE SISTER.

THIS WORLD WILL NEVE[R] BE FREE OF THESE EVOLUTIONARY CARETAKE[RS] THESE CELESTIAL PAWNS[.]

AN UNSTOPPABLE TSUNA[MI] INSTIGATED BY A COSM[IC] WILL FAR TOO GREAT T[O] TRULY COMPREHEND, A W[ILL] DEMANDING FORWARD MOTION OF GENETIC PROGRESS.

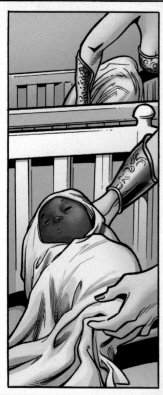

BUT I WILL NOT BE CORRALLED.

MY FATE IS MY OWN.

I WILL STAND AGAINST THIS EVOLUTIONARY WILL...

...I HAVE DISCOVERED HOW TO DERAIL THESE TWINS AND THE APOCALYPSE THEY WILL BRING TO MANKIN[D]

AFTER THOUSANDS OF PERMEATIONS, THOUSAN[DS] OF JUMPS BACKWARDS AND FORWARDS--

I HAVE FINALLY SOLVED THIS CONUNDRUM.

BE STILL, LITTLE ONES.

THIS TIME--THIS PRECISE ARRANGEMENT OF THE PIECES WILL LEAD TO A RESOLUTION MUCH MOR[E] TO MY LIKING.

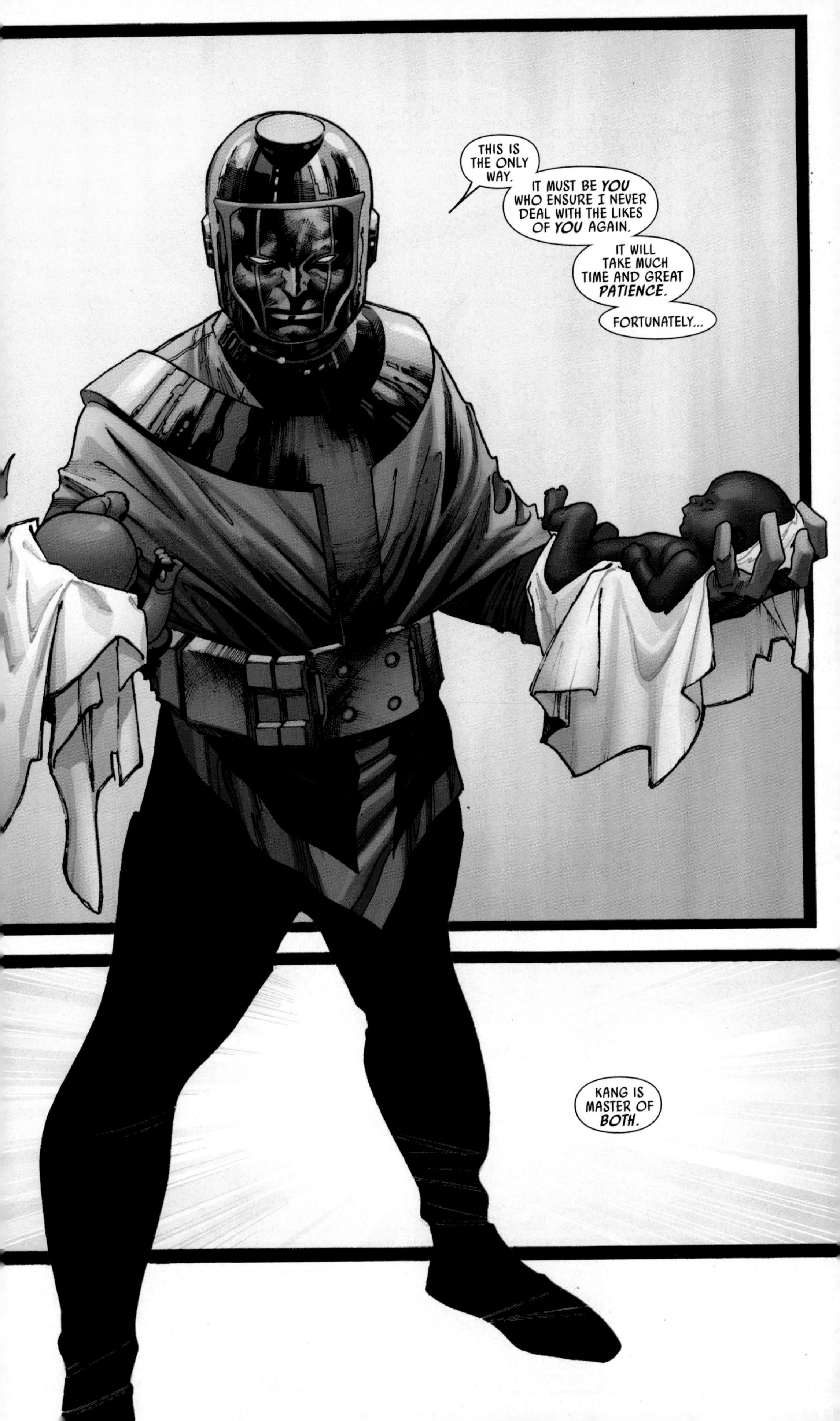

THIS IS THE ONLY WAY.
IT MUST BE YOU WHO ENSURE I NEVER DEAL WITH THE LIKES OF YOU AGAIN.
IT WILL TAKE MUCH TIME AND GREAT PATIENCE.
FORTUNATELY...
KANG IS MASTER OF BOTH.

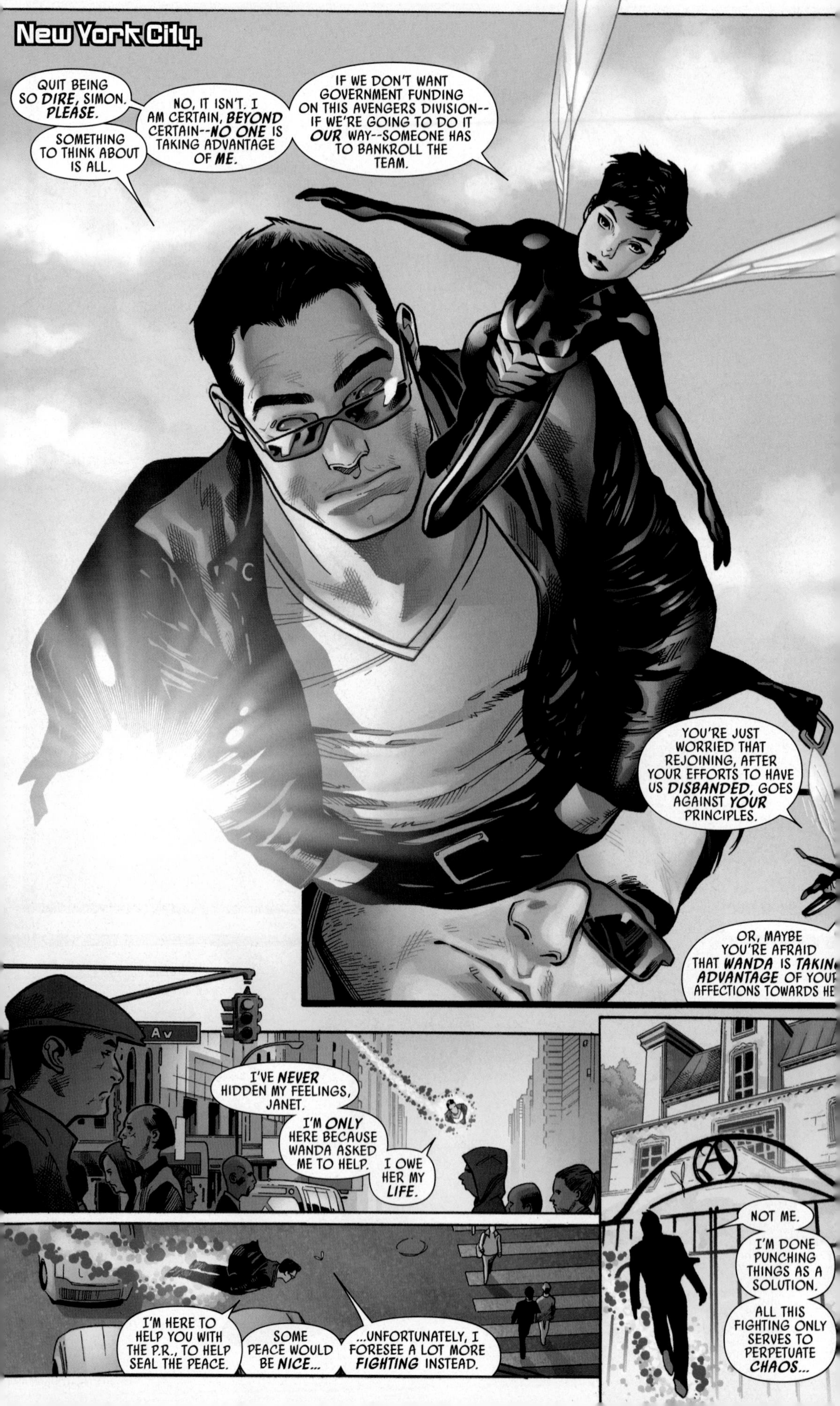
New York City.
QUIT BEING SO DIRE, SIMON. PLEASE.
SOMETHING TO THINK ABOUT IS ALL.
NO, IT ISN'T. I AM CERTAIN, BEYOND CERTAIN--NO ONE IS TAKING ADVANTAGE OF ME.
IF WE DON'T WANT GOVERNMENT FUNDING ON THIS AVENGERS DIVISION--IF WE'RE GOING TO DO IT OUR WAY--SOMEONE HAS TO BANKROLL THE TEAM.
YOU'RE JUST WORRIED THAT REJOINING, AFTER YOUR EFFORTS TO HAVE US DISBANDED, GOES AGAINST YOUR PRINCIPLES.
OR, MAYBE YOU'RE AFRAID THAT WANDA IS TAKIN ADVANTAGE OF YOUR AFFECTIONS TOWARDS HE
I'VE NEVER HIDDEN MY FEELINGS, JANET.
I'M ONLY HERE BECAUSE WANDA ASKED ME TO HELP.
I OWE HER MY LIFE.
I'M HERE TO HELP YOU WITH THE P.R., TO HELP SEAL THE PEACE.
SOME PEACE WOULD BE NICE...
...UNFORTUNATELY, I FORESEE A LOT MORE FIGHTING INSTEAD.
NOT ME.
I'M DONE PUNCHING THINGS AS A SOLUTION.
ALL THIS FIGHTING ONLY SERVES TO PERPETUATE CHAOS...

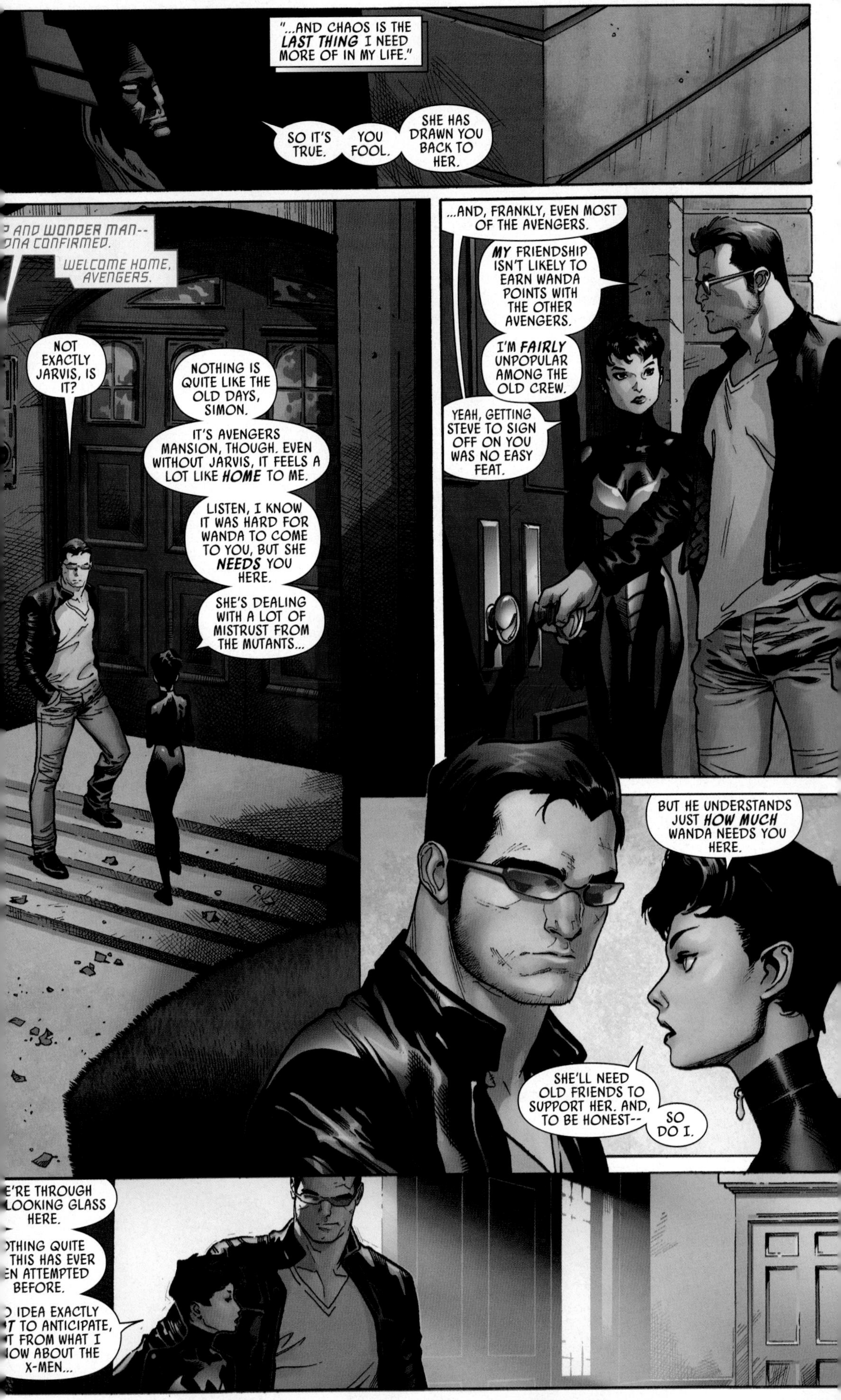
"...AND CHAOS IS THE LAST THING I NEED MORE OF IN MY LIFE."
SO IT'S TRUE.
YOU FOOL.
SHE HAS DRAWN YOU BACK TO HER.
AND WONDER MAN-- DNA CONFIRMED.
WELCOME HOME, AVENGERS.
NOT EXACTLY JARVIS, IS IT?
NOTHING IS QUITE LIKE THE OLD DAYS, SIMON.
IT'S AVENGERS MANSION, THOUGH. EVEN WITHOUT JARVIS, IT FEELS A LOT LIKE HOME TO ME.
LISTEN, I KNOW IT WAS HARD FOR WANDA TO COME TO YOU, BUT SHE NEEDS YOU HERE.
SHE'S DEALING WITH A LOT OF MISTRUST FROM THE MUTANTS...
...AND, FRANKLY, EVEN MOST OF THE AVENGERS.
MY FRIENDSHIP ISN'T LIKELY TO EARN WANDA POINTS WITH THE OTHER AVENGERS.
I'M FAIRLY UNPOPULAR AMONG THE OLD CREW.
YEAH, GETTING STEVE TO SIGN OFF ON YOU WAS NO EASY FEAT.
BUT HE UNDERSTANDS JUST HOW MUCH WANDA NEEDS YOU HERE.
SHE'LL NEED OLD FRIENDS TO SUPPORT HER. AND, TO BE HONEST--
SO DO I.
'RE THROUGH LOOKING GLASS HERE.
OTHING QUITE THIS HAS EVER EN ATTEMPTED BEFORE.
IDEA EXACTLY T TO ANTICIPATE, T FROM WHAT I OW ABOUT THE X-MEN...

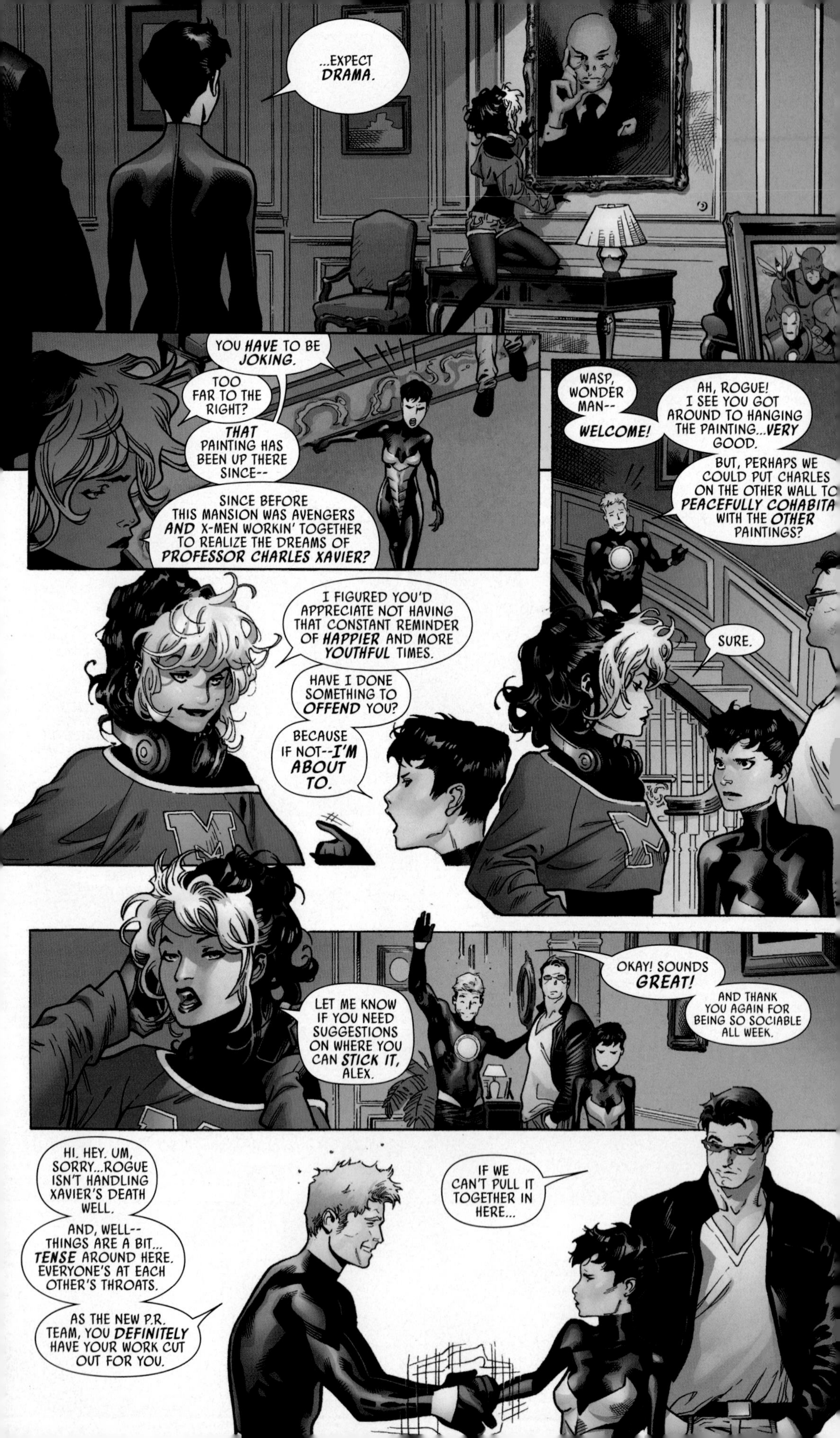
...EXPECT DRAMA.
YOU HAVE TO BE JOKING.
TOO FAR TO THE RIGHT?
THAT PAINTING HAS BEEN UP THERE SINCE--
SINCE BEFORE THIS MANSION WAS AVENGERS AND X-MEN WORKIN' TOGETHER TO REALIZE THE DREAMS OF PROFESSOR CHARLES XAVIER?
WASP, WONDER MAN--
WELCOME!
AH, ROGUE! I SEE YOU GOT AROUND TO HANGING THE PAINTING...VERY GOOD.
BUT, PERHAPS WE COULD PUT CHARLES ON THE OTHER WALL TO PEACEFULLY COHABITA WITH THE OTHER PAINTINGS?
I FIGURED YOU'D APPRECIATE NOT HAVING THAT CONSTANT REMINDER OF HAPPIER AND MORE YOUTHFUL TIMES.
HAVE I DONE SOMETHING TO OFFEND YOU?
BECAUSE IF NOT--I'M ABOUT TO.
SURE.
LET ME KNOW IF YOU NEED SUGGESTIONS ON WHERE YOU CAN STICK IT, ALEX.
OKAY! SOUNDS GREAT!
AND THANK YOU AGAIN FOR BEING SO SOCIABLE ALL WEEK.
HI. HEY. UM, SORRY...ROGUE ISN'T HANDLING XAVIER'S DEATH WELL.
AND, WELL-- THINGS ARE A BIT... TENSE AROUND HERE. EVERYONE'S AT EACH OTHER'S THROATS.
AS THE NEW P.R. TEAM, YOU DEFINITELY HAVE YOUR WORK CUT OUT FOR YOU.
IF WE CAN'T PULL IT TOGETHER IN HERE...

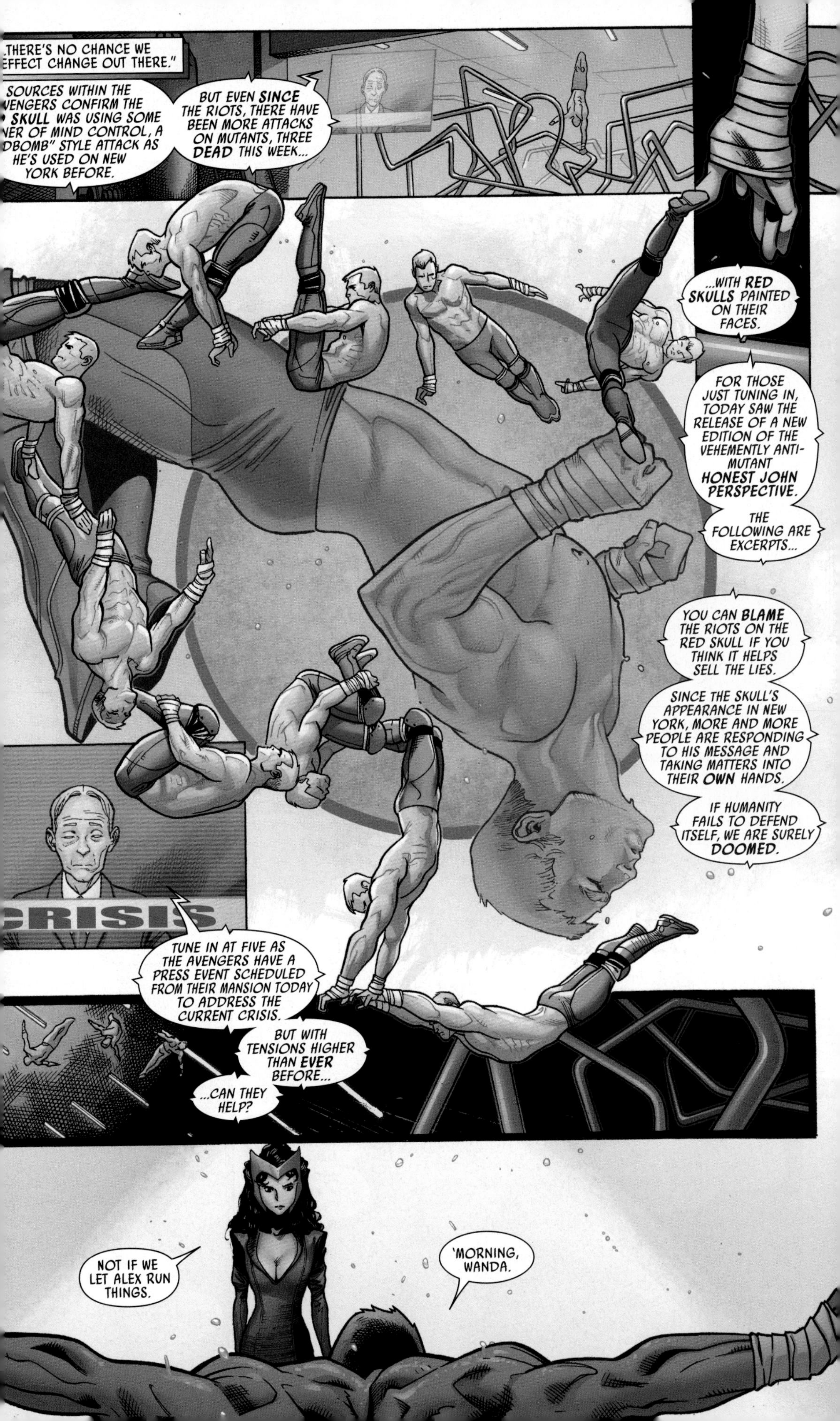

...THERE'S NO CHANCE WE EFFECT CHANGE OUT THERE."
SOURCES WITHIN THE AVENGERS CONFIRM THE SKULL WAS USING SOME ...NER OF MIND CONTROL, A ...DBOMB" STYLE ATTACK AS HE'S USED ON NEW YORK BEFORE.
BUT EVEN SINCE THE RIOTS, THERE HAVE BEEN MORE ATTACKS ON MUTANTS, THREE DEAD THIS WEEK...
...WITH RED SKULLS PAINTED ON THEIR FACES.
FOR THOSE JUST TUNING IN, TODAY SAW THE RELEASE OF A NEW EDITION OF THE VEHEMENTLY ANTI-MUTANT HONEST JOHN PERSPECTIVE.
THE FOLLOWING ARE EXCERPTS...
YOU CAN BLAME THE RIOTS ON THE RED SKULL IF YOU THINK IT HELPS SELL THE LIES.
SINCE THE SKULL'S APPEARANCE IN NEW YORK, MORE AND MORE PEOPLE ARE RESPONDING TO HIS MESSAGE AND TAKING MATTERS INTO THEIR OWN HANDS.
IF HUMANITY FAILS TO DEFEND ITSELF, WE ARE SURELY DOOMED.
CRISIS
TUNE IN AT FIVE AS THE AVENGERS HAVE A PRESS EVENT SCHEDULED FROM THEIR MANSION TODAY TO ADDRESS THE CURRENT CRISIS.
BUT WITH TENSIONS HIGHER THAN EVER BEFORE...
...CAN THEY HELP?
NOT IF WE LET ALEX RUN THINGS.
'MORNING, WANDA.

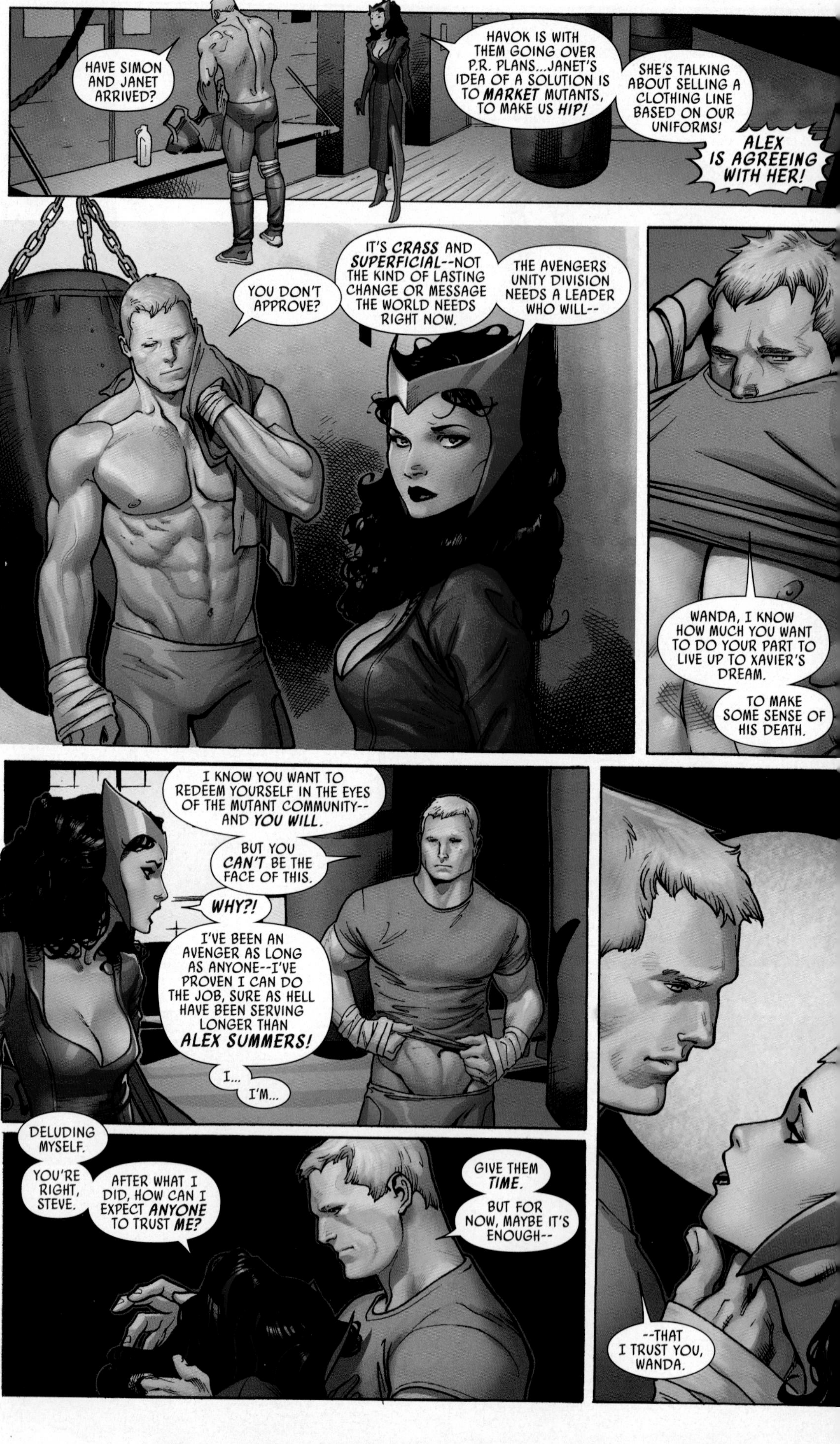

HAVE SIMON AND JANET ARRIVED?
HAVOK IS WITH THEM GOING OVER P.R. PLANS...JANET'S IDEA OF A SOLUTION IS TO MARKET MUTANTS, TO MAKE US HIP!
SHE'S TALKING ABOUT SELLING A CLOTHING LINE BASED ON OUR UNIFORMS!
ALEX IS AGREEING WITH HER!
YOU DON'T APPROVE?
IT'S CRASS AND SUPERFICIAL--NOT THE KIND OF LASTING CHANGE OR MESSAGE THE WORLD NEEDS RIGHT NOW.
THE AVENGERS UNITY DIVISION NEEDS A LEADER WHO WILL--
WANDA, I KNOW HOW MUCH YOU WANT TO DO YOUR PART TO LIVE UP TO XAVIER'S DREAM.
TO MAKE SOME SENSE OF HIS DEATH.
I KNOW YOU WANT TO REDEEM YOURSELF IN THE EYES OF THE MUTANT COMMUNITY--AND YOU WILL.
BUT YOU CAN'T BE THE FACE OF THIS.
WHY?!
I'VE BEEN AN AVENGER AS LONG AS ANYONE--I'VE PROVEN I CAN DO THE JOB, SURE AS HELL HAVE BEEN SERVING LONGER THAN ALEX SUMMERS!
I...
I'M...
DELUDING MYSELF.
YOU'RE RIGHT, STEVE.
AFTER WHAT I DID, HOW CAN I EXPECT ANYONE TO TRUST ME?
GIVE THEM TIME.
BUT FOR NOW, MAYBE IT'S ENOUGH--
--THAT I TRUST YOU, WANDA.

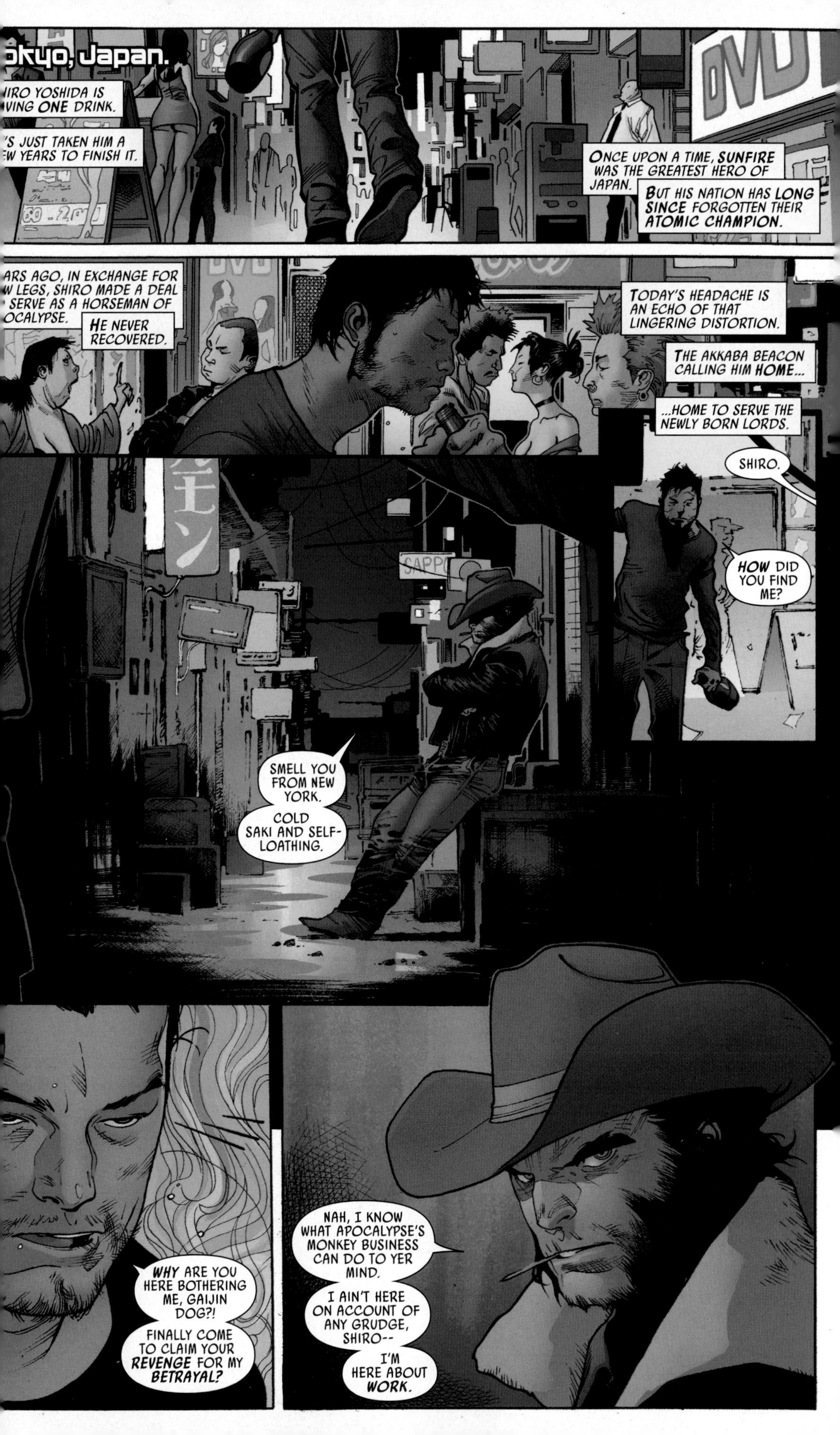
okyo, Japan.
IIRO YOSHIDA IS
VING ONE DRINK.
'S JUST TAKEN HIM A
W YEARS TO FINISH IT.
ONCE UPON A TIME, SUNFIRE WAS THE GREATEST HERO OF JAPAN.
BUT HIS NATION HAS LONG SINCE FORGOTTEN THEIR ATOMIC CHAMPION.
DVD
ARS AGO, IN EXCHANGE FOR
W LEGS, SHIRO MADE A DEAL
SERVE AS A HORSEMAN OF
OCALYPSE.
HE NEVER RECOVERED.
TODAY'S HEADACHE IS AN ECHO OF THAT LINGERING DISTORTION.
THE AKKABA BEACON CALLING HIM HOME...
...HOME TO SERVE THE NEWLY BORN LORDS.
SHIRO.
HOW DID YOU FIND ME?
SMELL YOU FROM NEW YORK.
COLD SAKI AND SELF-LOATHING.
WHY ARE YOU HERE BOTHERING ME, GAIJIN DOG?!
FINALLY COME TO CLAIM YOUR REVENGE FOR MY BETRAYAL?
NAH, I KNOW WHAT APOCALYPSE'S MONKEY BUSINESS CAN DO TO YER MIND.
I AIN'T HERE ON ACCOUNT OF ANY GRUDGE, SHIRO--
I'M HERE ABOUT WORK.

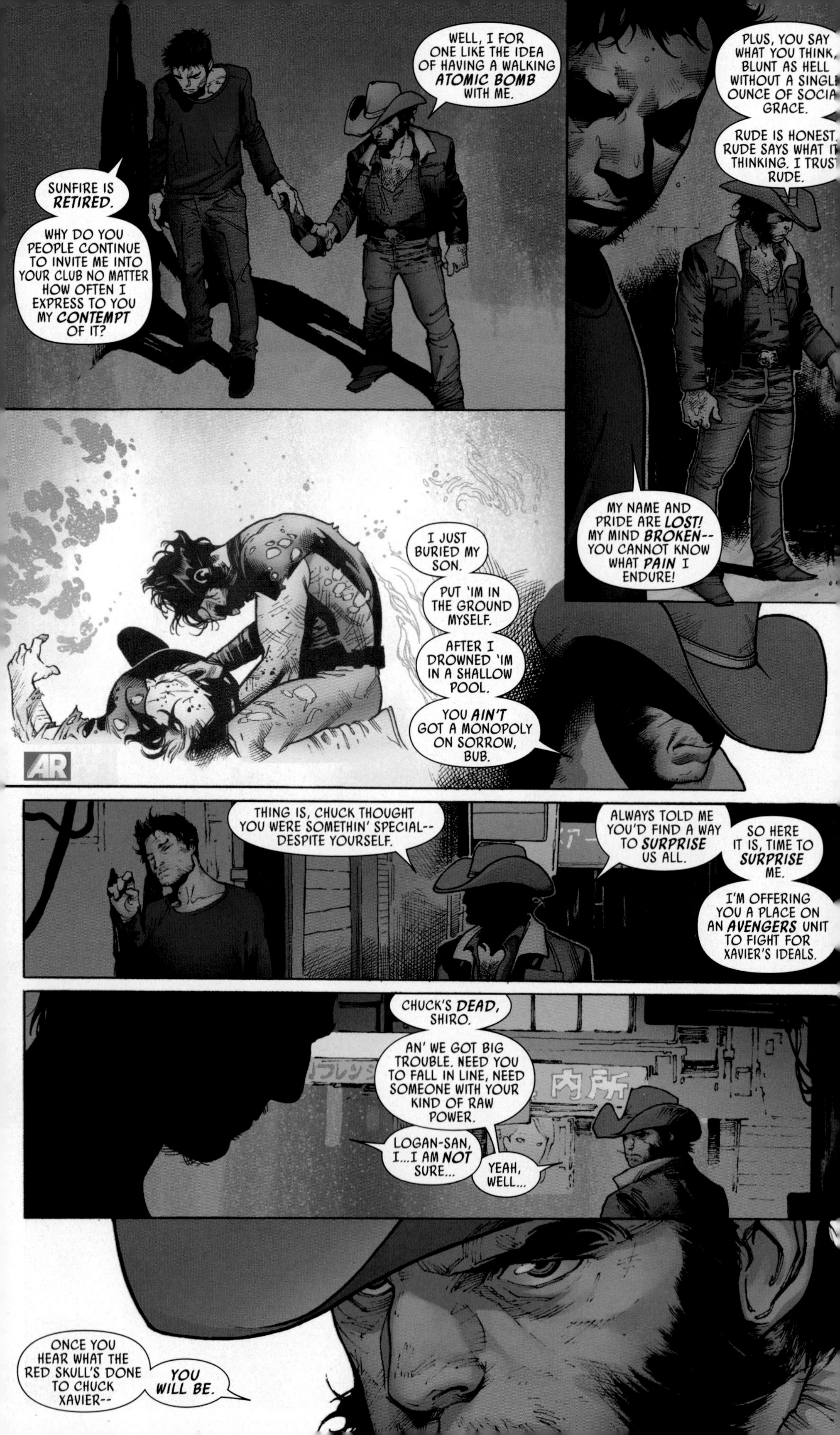

WELL, I FOR ONE LIKE THE IDEA OF HAVING A WALKING ATOMIC BOMB WITH ME.
SUNFIRE IS RETIRED.
WHY DO YOU PEOPLE CONTINUE TO INVITE ME INTO YOUR CLUB NO MATTER HOW OFTEN I EXPRESS TO YOU MY CONTEMPT OF IT?
PLUS, YOU SAY WHAT YOU THINK, BLUNT AS HELL WITHOUT A SINGL OUNCE OF SOCIA GRACE.
RUDE IS HONEST. RUDE SAYS WHAT IT THINKING. I TRUS RUDE.
MY NAME AND PRIDE ARE LOST! MY MIND BROKEN-- YOU CANNOT KNOW WHAT PAIN I ENDURE!
I JUST BURIED MY SON.
PUT 'IM IN THE GROUND MYSELF.
AFTER I DROWNED 'IM IN A SHALLOW POOL.
YOU AIN'T GOT A MONOPOLY ON SORROW, BUB.
THING IS, CHUCK THOUGHT YOU WERE SOMETHIN' SPECIAL-- DESPITE YOURSELF.
ALWAYS TOLD ME YOU'D FIND A WAY TO SURPRISE US ALL.
SO HERE IT IS, TIME TO SURPRISE ME.
I'M OFFERING YOU A PLACE ON AN AVENGERS UNIT TO FIGHT FOR XAVIER'S IDEALS.
CHUCK'S DEAD, SHIRO.
AN' WE GOT BIG TROUBLE. NEED YOU TO FALL IN LINE, NEED SOMEONE WITH YOUR KIND OF RAW POWER.
LOGAN-SAN, I...I AM NOT SURE...
YEAH, WELL...
ONCE YOU HEAR WHAT THE RED SKULL'S DONE TO CHUCK XAVIER--
YOU WILL BE.

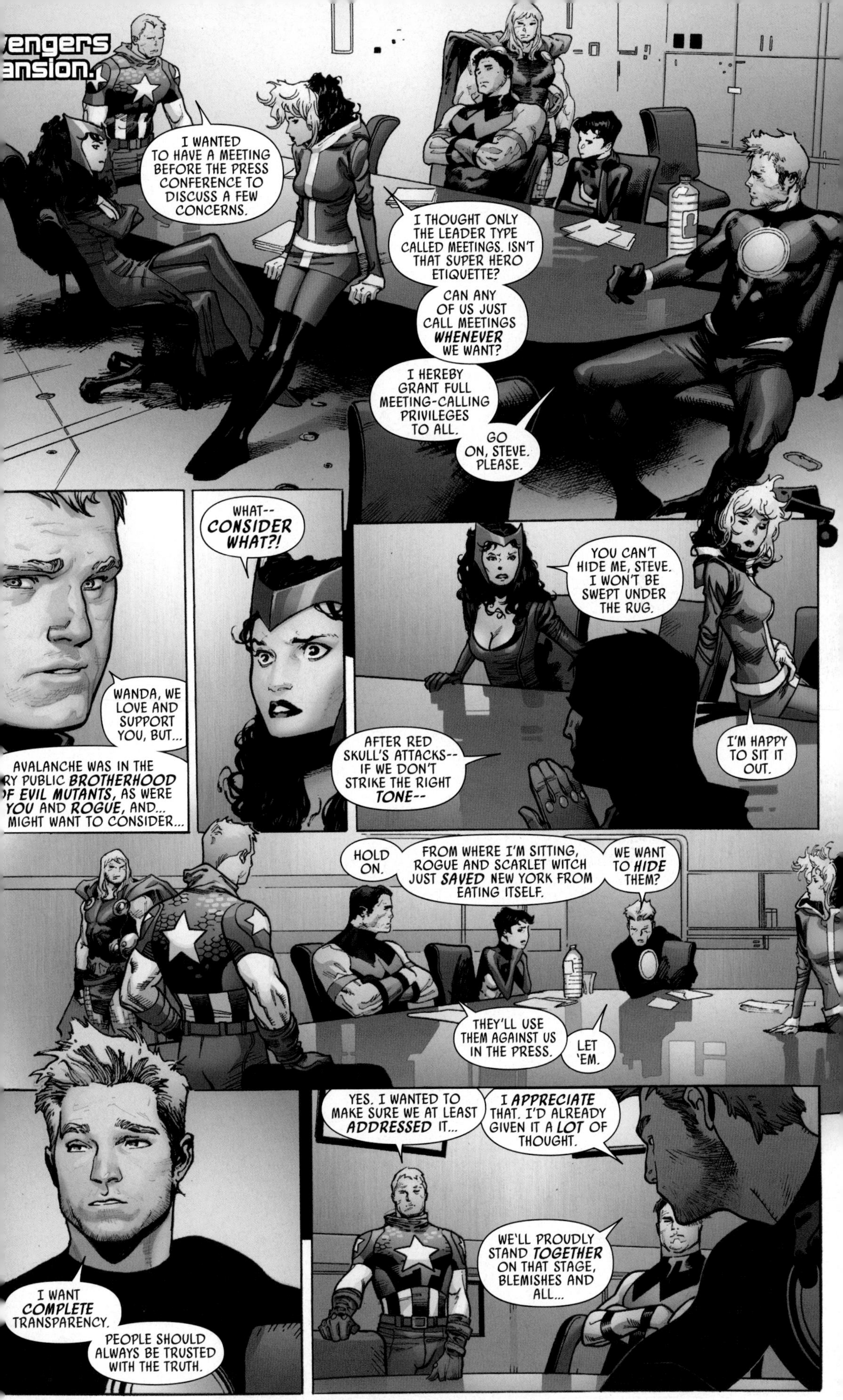

...vengers ...ansion.
I WANTED TO HAVE A MEETING BEFORE THE PRESS CONFERENCE TO DISCUSS A FEW CONCERNS.
I THOUGHT ONLY THE LEADER TYPE CALLED MEETINGS. ISN'T THAT SUPER HERO ETIQUETTE?
CAN ANY OF US JUST CALL MEETINGS WHENEVER WE WANT?
I HEREBY GRANT FULL MEETING-CALLING PRIVILEGES TO ALL.
GO ON, STEVE. PLEASE.
WANDA, WE LOVE AND SUPPORT YOU, BUT...
AVALANCHE WAS IN THE ...RY PUBLIC BROTHERHOOD ...F EVIL MUTANTS, AS WERE YOU AND ROGUE, AND... MIGHT WANT TO CONSIDER...
WHAT-- CONSIDER WHAT?!
YOU CAN'T HIDE ME, STEVE. I WON'T BE SWEPT UNDER THE RUG.
AFTER RED SKULL'S ATTACKS-- IF WE DON'T STRIKE THE RIGHT TONE--
I'M HAPPY TO SIT IT OUT.
HOLD ON.
FROM WHERE I'M SITTING, ROGUE AND SCARLET WITCH JUST SAVED NEW YORK FROM EATING ITSELF.
WE WANT TO HIDE THEM?
THEY'LL USE THEM AGAINST US IN THE PRESS.
LET 'EM.
I WANT COMPLETE TRANSPARENCY.
PEOPLE SHOULD ALWAYS BE TRUSTED WITH THE TRUTH.
YES. I WANTED TO MAKE SURE WE AT LEAST ADDRESSED IT...
I APPRECIATE THAT. I'D ALREADY GIVEN IT A LOT OF THOUGHT.
WE'LL PROUDLY STAND TOGETHER ON THAT STAGE, BLEMISHES AND ALL...

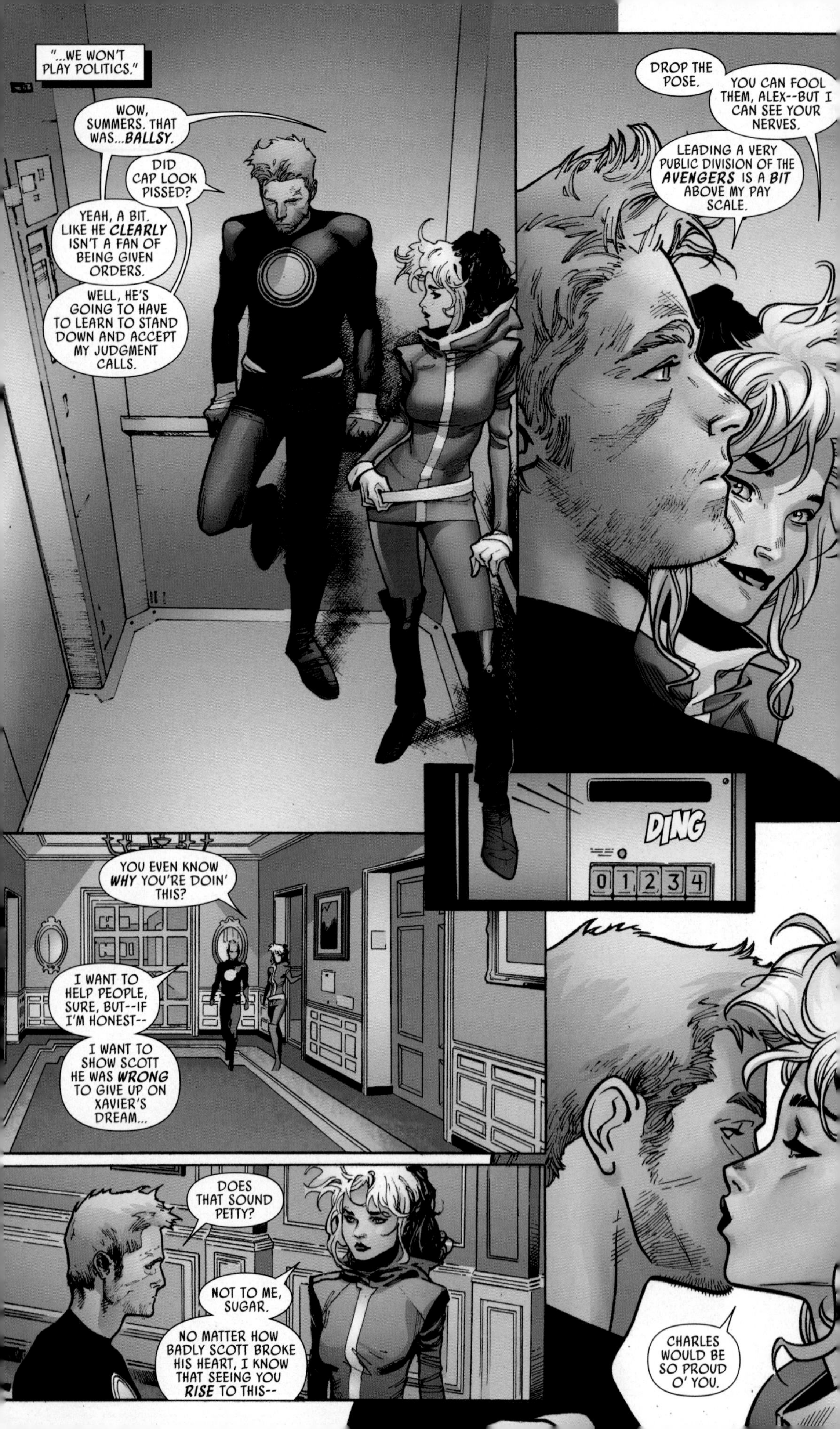
"...WE WON'T PLAY POLITICS."
WOW, SUMMERS. THAT WAS...BALLSY.
DID CAP LOOK PISSED?
YEAH, A BIT. LIKE HE CLEARLY ISN'T A FAN OF BEING GIVEN ORDERS.
WELL, HE'S GOING TO HAVE TO LEARN TO STAND DOWN AND ACCEPT MY JUDGMENT CALLS.
DROP THE POSE.
YOU CAN FOOL THEM, ALEX--BUT I CAN SEE YOUR NERVES.
LEADING A VERY PUBLIC DIVISION OF THE AVENGERS IS A BIT ABOVE MY PAY SCALE.
DING
01234
YOU EVEN KNOW WHY YOU'RE DOIN' THIS?
I WANT TO HELP PEOPLE, SURE, BUT--IF I'M HONEST--
I WANT TO SHOW SCOTT HE WAS WRONG TO GIVE UP ON XAVIER'S DREAM...
DOES THAT SOUND PETTY?
NOT TO ME, SUGAR.
NO MATTER HOW BADLY SCOTT BROKE HIS HEART, I KNOW THAT SEEING YOU RISE TO THIS--
CHARLES WOULD BE SO PROUD O' YOU.

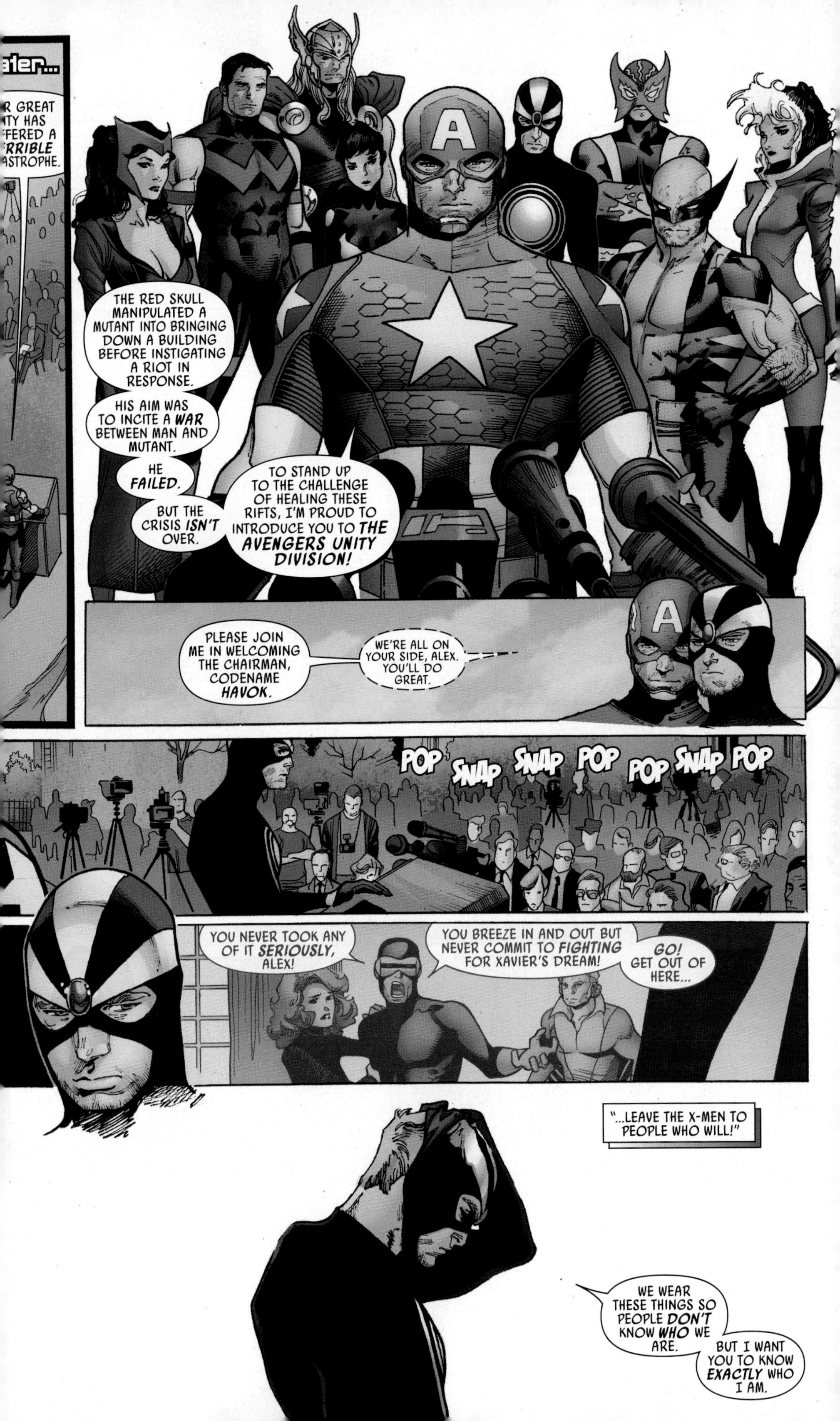
...ater...
...R GREAT ...ITY HAS ...FFERED A ...RRIBLE ...ASTROPHE.
THE RED SKULL MANIPULATED A MUTANT INTO BRINGING DOWN A BUILDING BEFORE INSTIGATING A RIOT IN RESPONSE.
HIS AIM WAS TO INCITE A WAR BETWEEN MAN AND MUTANT.
HE FAILED.
BUT THE CRISIS ISN'T OVER.
TO STAND UP TO THE CHALLENGE OF HEALING THESE RIFTS, I'M PROUD TO INTRODUCE YOU TO THE AVENGERS UNITY DIVISION!
PLEASE JOIN ME IN WELCOMING THE CHAIRMAN, CODENAME HAVOK.
WE'RE ALL ON YOUR SIDE, ALEX. YOU'LL DO GREAT.
POP SNAP SNAP POP POP SNAP POP
YOU NEVER TOOK ANY OF IT SERIOUSLY, ALEX!
YOU BREEZE IN AND OUT BUT NEVER COMMIT TO FIGHTING FOR XAVIER'S DREAM!
GO! GET OUT OF HERE...
"...LEAVE THE X-MEN TO PEOPLE WHO WILL!"
WE WEAR THESE THINGS SO PEOPLE DON'T KNOW WHO WE ARE.
BUT I WANT YOU TO KNOW EXACTLY WHO I AM.

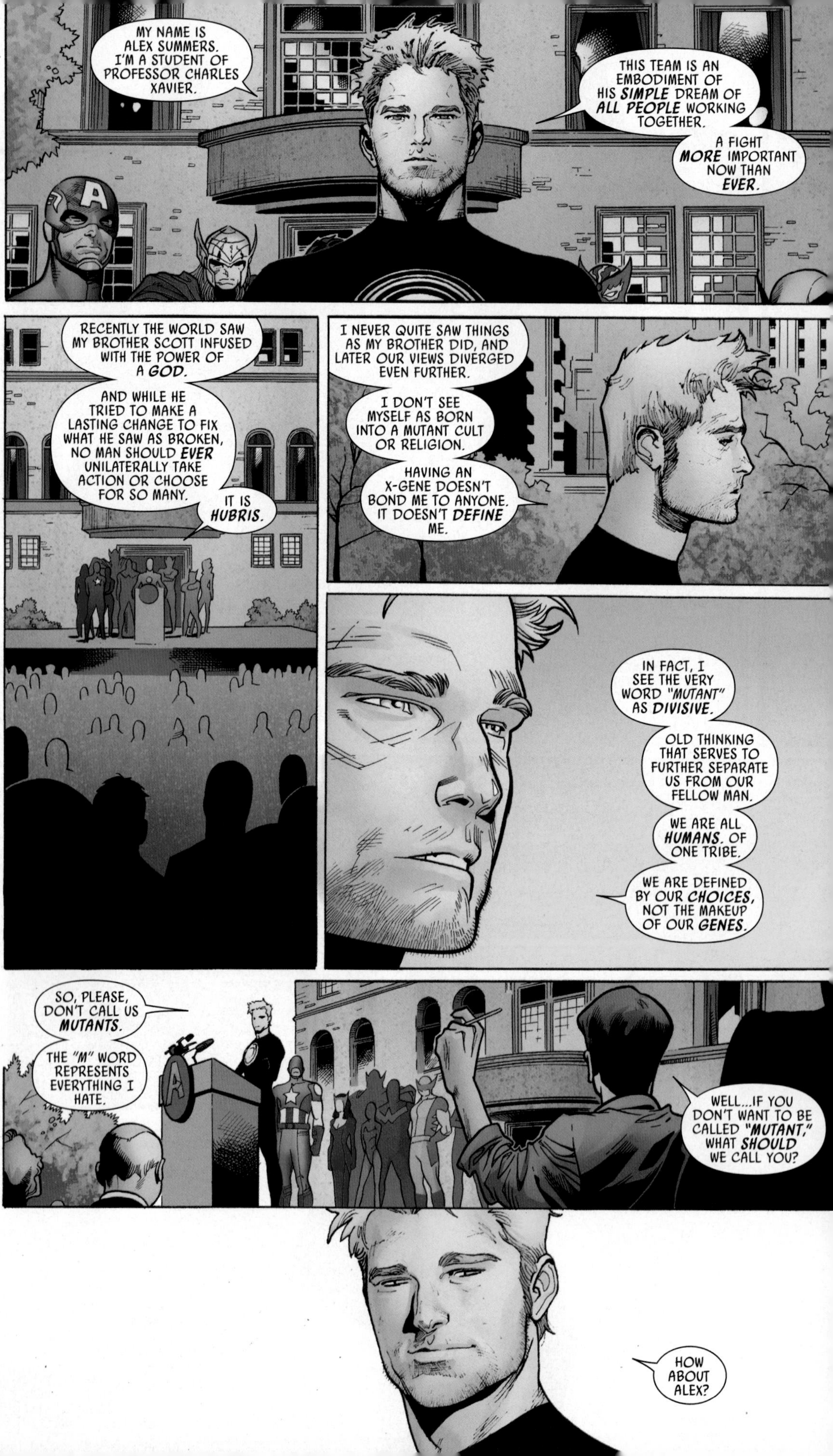
MY NAME IS ALEX SUMMERS. I'M A STUDENT OF PROFESSOR CHARLES XAVIER.
THIS TEAM IS AN EMBODIMENT OF HIS SIMPLE DREAM OF ALL PEOPLE WORKING TOGETHER.
A FIGHT MORE IMPORTANT NOW THAN EVER.
RECENTLY THE WORLD SAW MY BROTHER SCOTT INFUSED WITH THE POWER OF A GOD.
AND WHILE HE TRIED TO MAKE A LASTING CHANGE TO FIX WHAT HE SAW AS BROKEN, NO MAN SHOULD EVER UNILATERALLY TAKE ACTION OR CHOOSE FOR SO MANY.
IT IS HUBRIS.
I NEVER QUITE SAW THINGS AS MY BROTHER DID, AND LATER OUR VIEWS DIVERGED EVEN FURTHER.
I DON'T SEE MYSELF AS BORN INTO A MUTANT CULT OR RELIGION.
HAVING AN X-GENE DOESN'T BOND ME TO ANYONE. IT DOESN'T DEFINE ME.
IN FACT, I SEE THE VERY WORD "MUTANT" AS DIVISIVE.
OLD THINKING THAT SERVES TO FURTHER SEPARATE US FROM OUR FELLOW MAN.
WE ARE ALL HUMANS. OF ONE TRIBE.
WE ARE DEFINED BY OUR CHOICES, NOT THE MAKEUP OF OUR GENES.
SO, PLEASE, DON'T CALL US MUTANTS.
THE "M" WORD REPRESENTS EVERYTHING I HATE.
WELL...IF YOU DON'T WANT TO BE CALLED "MUTANT," WHAT SHOULD WE CALL YOU?
HOW ABOUT ALEX?

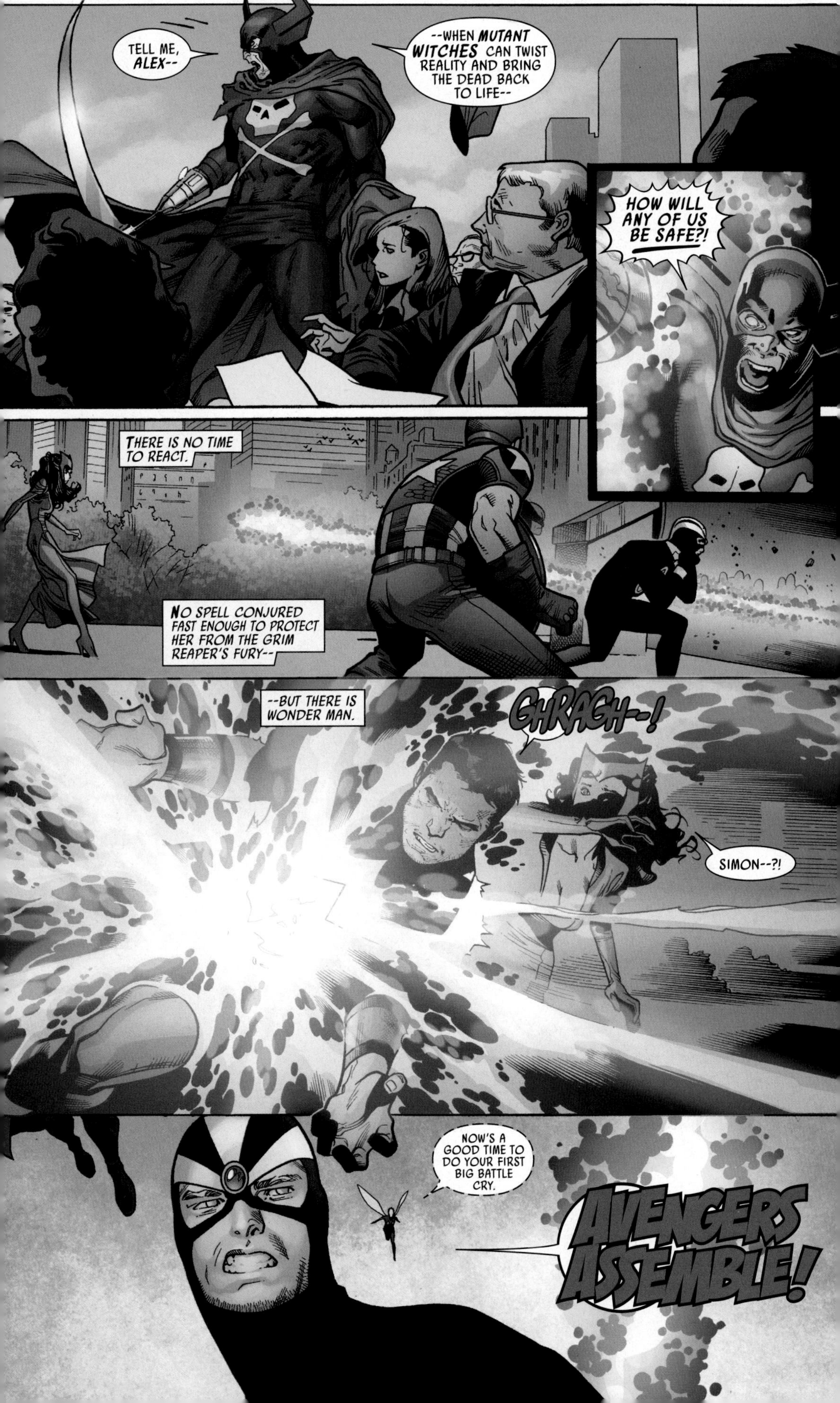
TELL ME, ALEX--
--WHEN MUTANT WITCHES CAN TWIST REALITY AND BRING THE DEAD BACK TO LIFE--
HOW WILL ANY OF US BE SAFE?!
THERE IS NO TIME TO REACT.
NO SPELL CONJURED FAST ENOUGH TO PROTECT HER FROM THE GRIM REAPER'S FURY--
--BUT THERE IS WONDER MAN.
GHRAGH--!
SIMON--?!
NOW'S A GOOD TIME TO DO YOUR FIRST BIG BATTLE CRY.
AVENGERS ASSEMBLE!

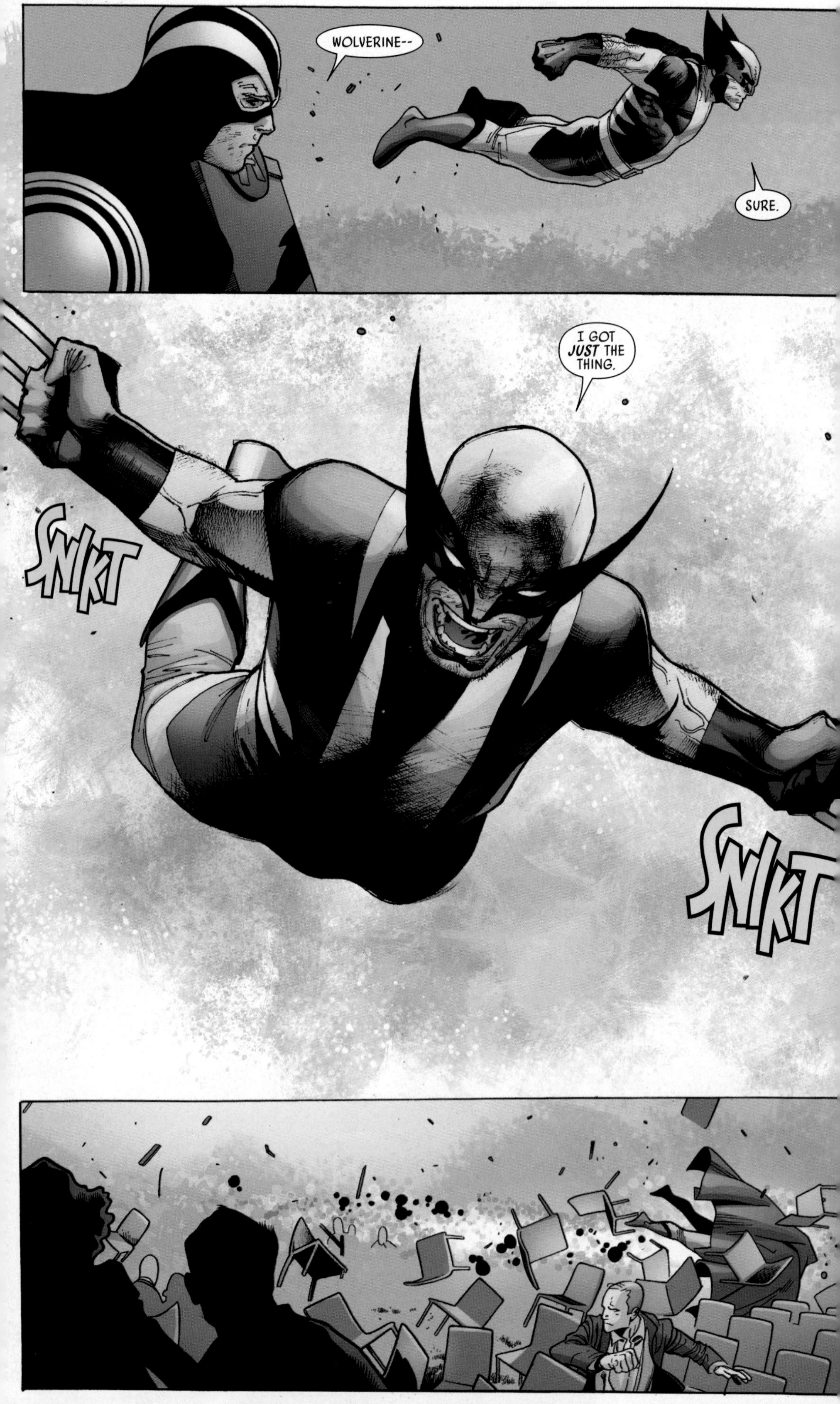
WOLVERINE--
SURE.
I GOT JUST THE THING.
SNIKT
SNIKT

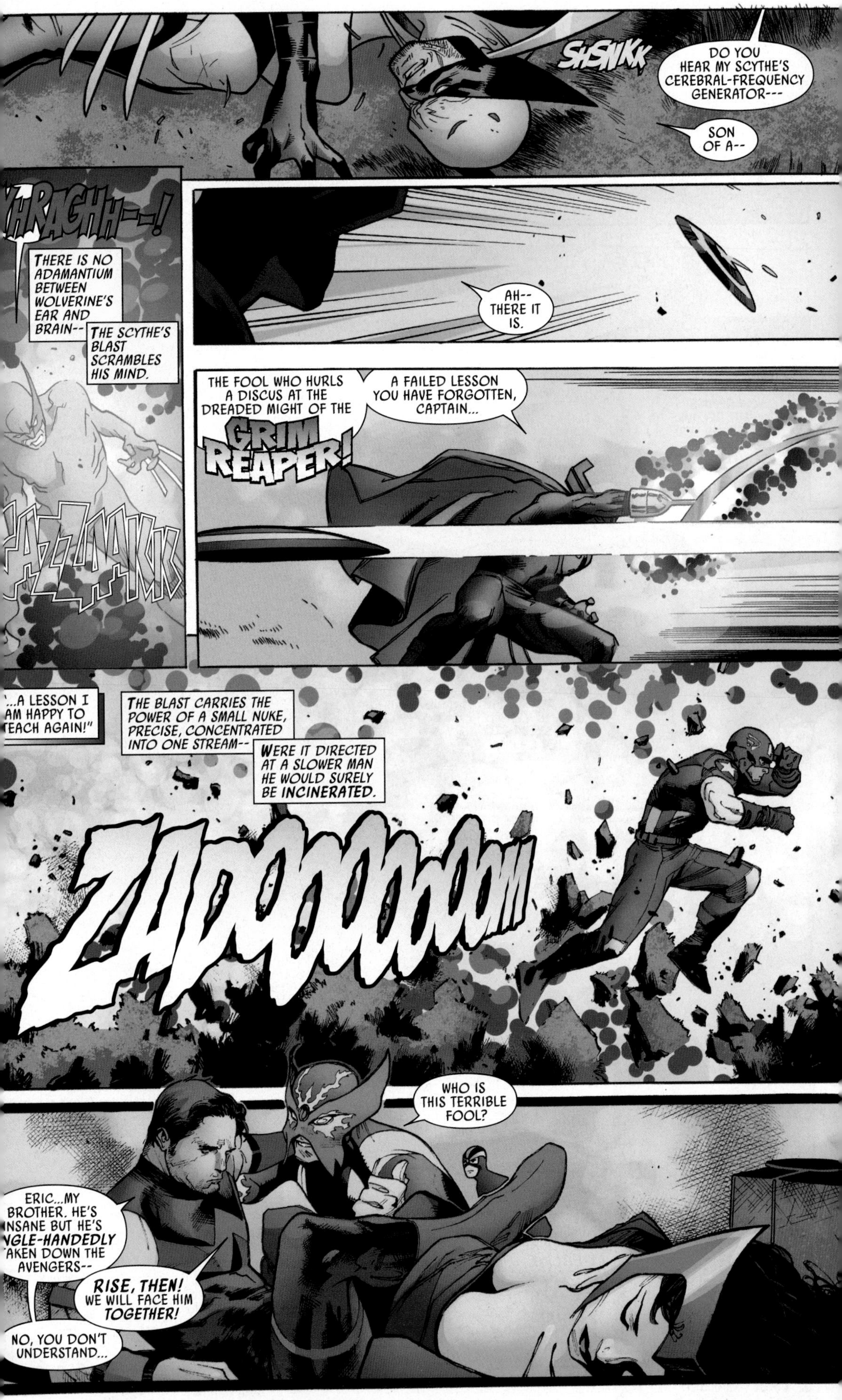
SHSNIKK
DO YOU HEAR MY SCYTHE'S CEREBRAL-FREQUENCY GENERATOR---
SON OF A--
YHRAGHH--!
THERE IS NO ADAMANTIUM BETWEEN WOLVERINE'S EAR AND BRAIN--
THE SCYTHE'S BLAST SCRAMBLES HIS MIND.
AH-- THERE IT IS.
THE FOOL WHO HURLS A DISCUS AT THE DREADED MIGHT OF THE GRIM REAPER!
A FAILED LESSON YOU HAVE FORGOTTEN, CAPTAIN...
"...A LESSON I AM HAPPY TO TEACH AGAIN!"
THE BLAST CARRIES THE POWER OF A SMALL NUKE, PRECISE, CONCENTRATED INTO ONE STREAM--
WERE IT DIRECTED AT A SLOWER MAN HE WOULD SURELY BE INCINERATED.
ZADOOOOOOOM
WHO IS THIS TERRIBLE FOOL?
ERIC...MY BROTHER. HE'S INSANE BUT HE'S SINGLE-HANDEDLY TAKEN DOWN THE AVENGERS--
RISE, THEN! WE WILL FACE HIM TOGETHER!
NO, YOU DON'T UNDERSTAND...

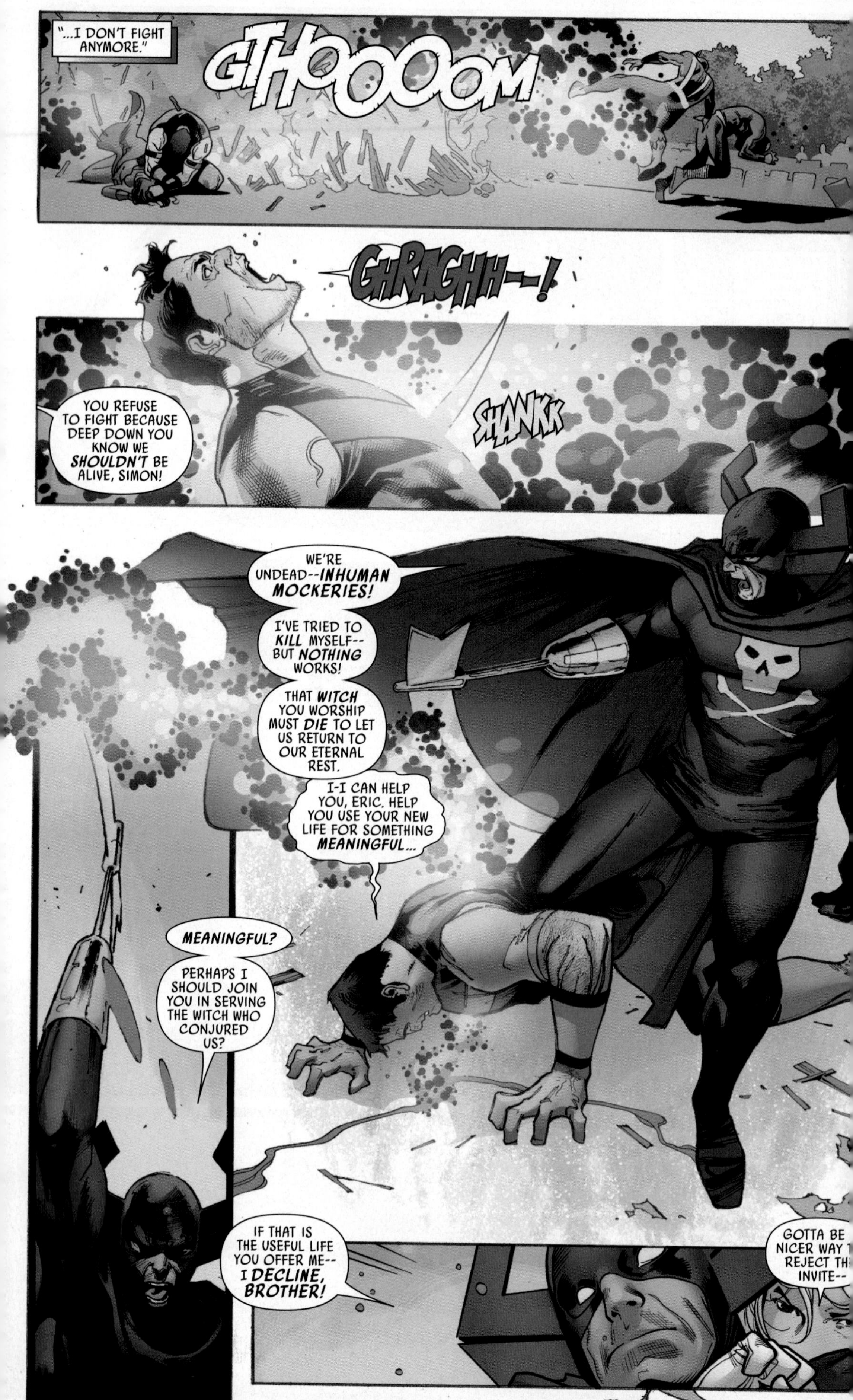
"...I DON'T FIGHT ANYMORE."
GTHOOOOOM
GHRAGHH--!
YOU REFUSE TO FIGHT BECAUSE DEEP DOWN YOU KNOW WE SHOULDN'T BE ALIVE, SIMON!
SHANKK
WE'RE UNDEAD--INHUMAN MOCKERIES!
I'VE TRIED TO KILL MYSELF--BUT NOTHING WORKS!
THAT WITCH YOU WORSHIP MUST DIE TO LET US RETURN TO OUR ETERNAL REST.
I-I CAN HELP YOU, ERIC. HELP YOU USE YOUR NEW LIFE FOR SOMETHING MEANINGFUL...
MEANINGFUL?
PERHAPS I SHOULD JOIN YOU IN SERVING THE WITCH WHO CONJURED US?
IF THAT IS THE USEFUL LIFE YOU OFFER ME--I DECLINE, BROTHER!
GOTTA BE NICER WAY T REJECT TH INVITE--

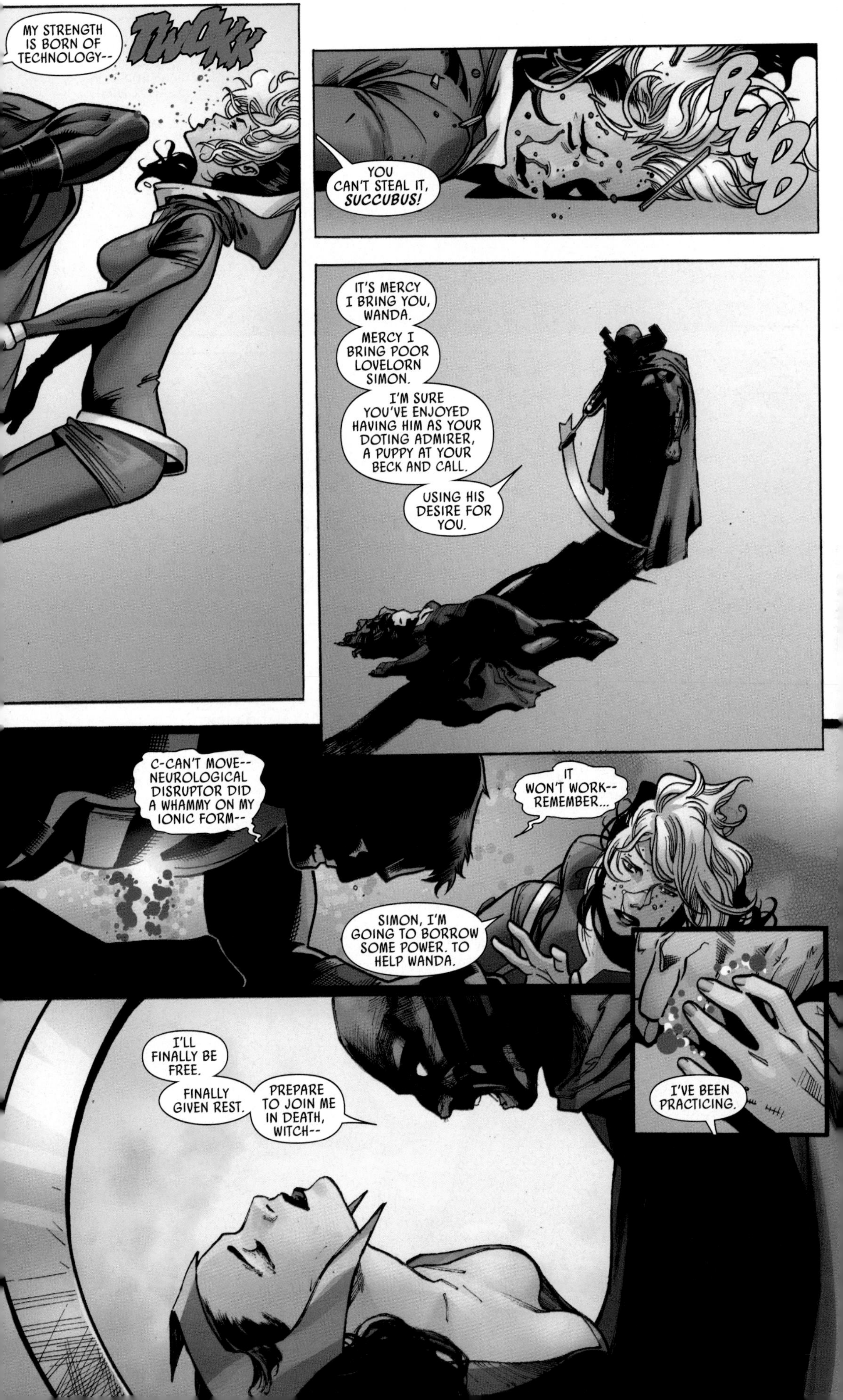
MY STRENGTH IS BORN OF TECHNOLOGY--
TWOKK
YOU CAN'T STEAL IT, SUCCUBUS!
IT'S MERCY I BRING YOU, WANDA.
MERCY I BRING POOR LOVELORN SIMON.
I'M SURE YOU'VE ENJOYED HAVING HIM AS YOUR DOTING ADMIRER, A PUPPY AT YOUR BECK AND CALL.
USING HIS DESIRE FOR YOU.
C-CAN'T MOVE-- NEUROLOGICAL DISRUPTOR DID A WHAMMY ON MY IONIC FORM--
IT WON'T WORK-- REMEMBER...
SIMON, I'M GOING TO BORROW SOME POWER. TO HELP WANDA.
I'VE BEEN PRACTICING.
I'LL FINALLY BE FREE.
FINALLY GIVEN REST.
PREPARE TO JOIN ME IN DEATH, WITCH--

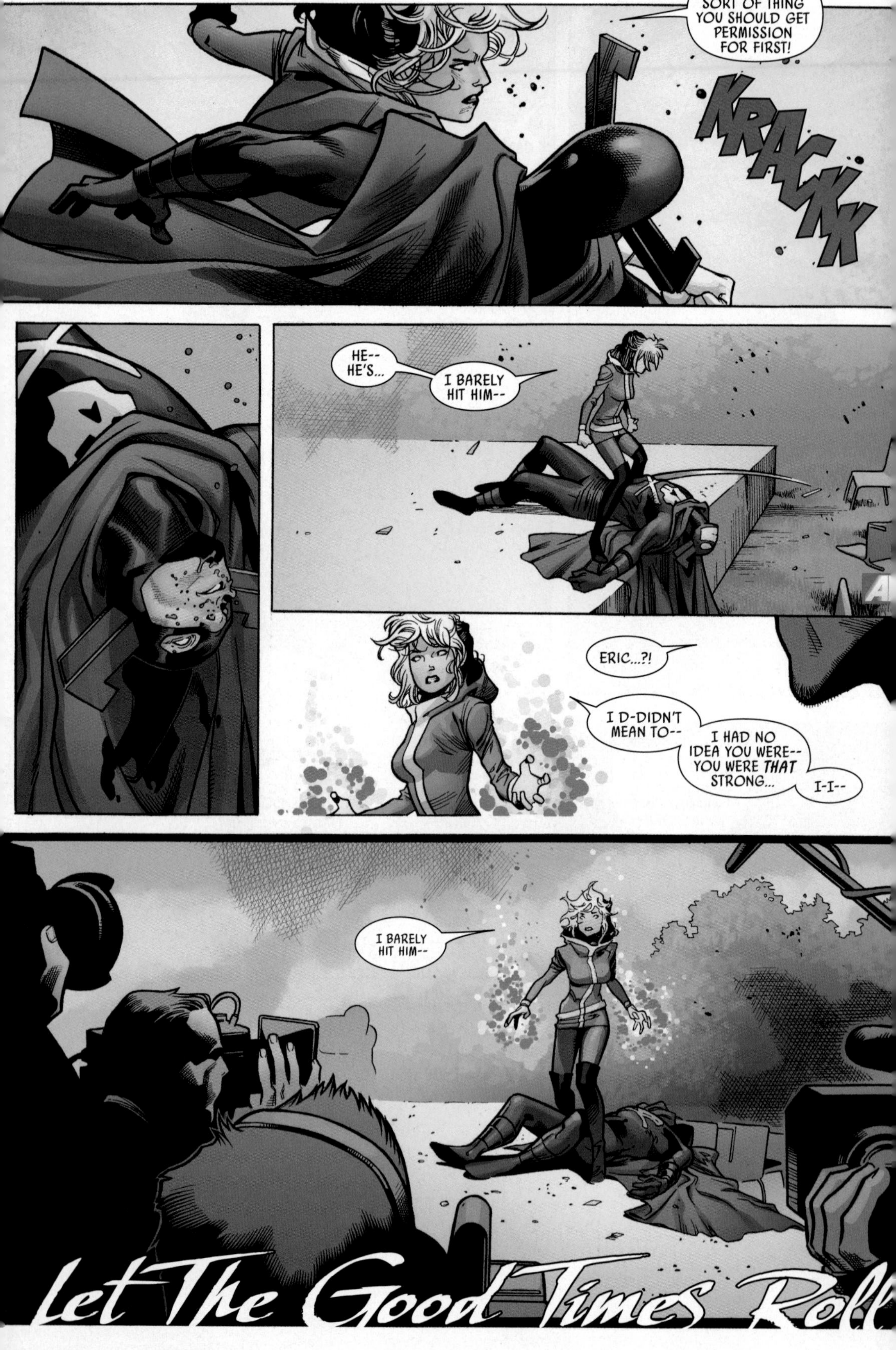
SEEMS LIKE THE SORT OF THING YOU SHOULD GET PERMISSION FOR FIRST!
KRACKK
HE-- HE'S...
I BARELY HIT HIM--
ERIC...?!
I D-DIDN'T MEAN TO--
I HAD NO IDEA YOU WERE-- YOU WERE THAT STRONG...
I-I--
I BARELY HIT HIM--
Let The Good Times Roll

UNCANNY AVENGERS #1 VARIANT BY DANIEL ACUÑA

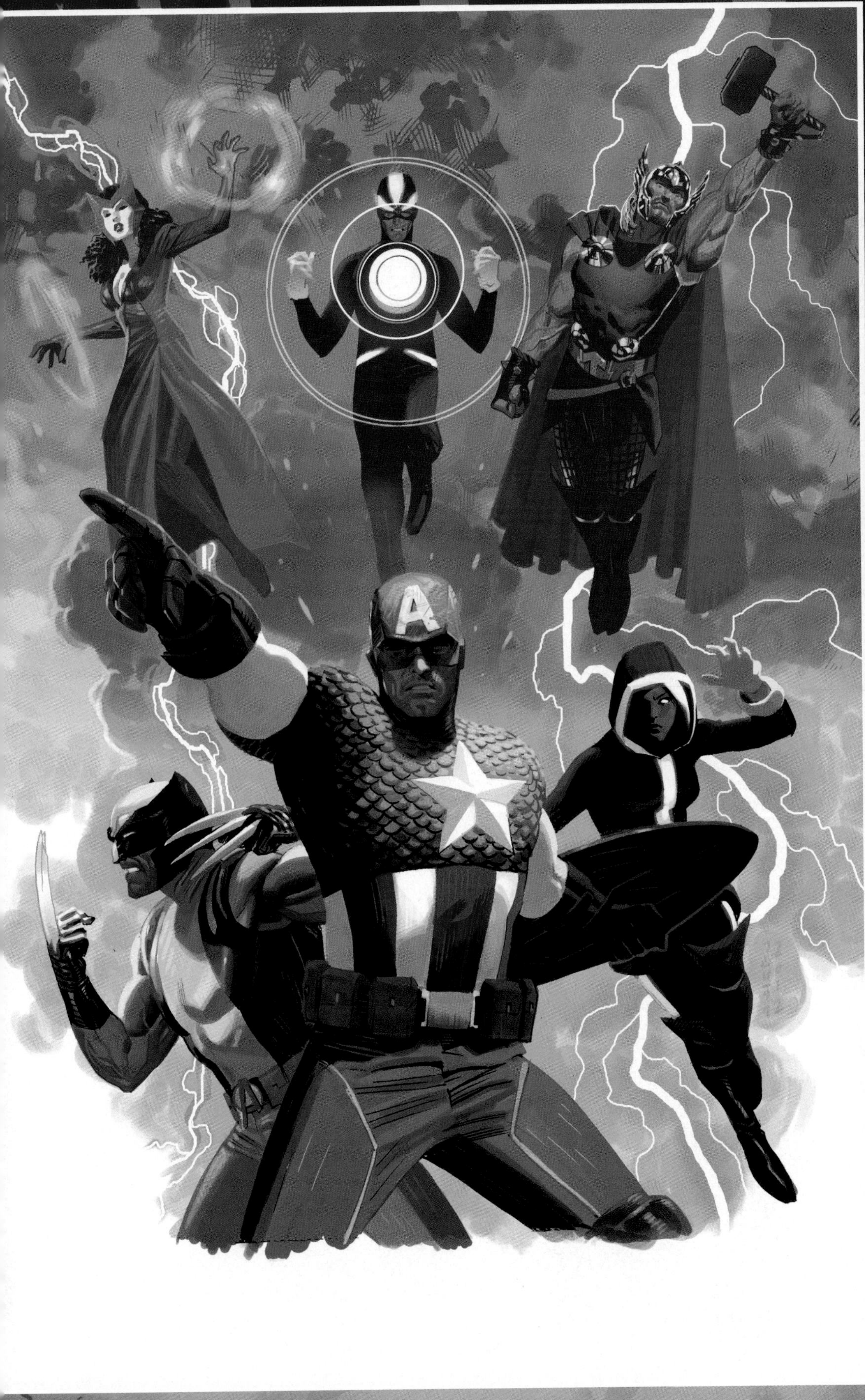

UNCANNY AVENGERS #1 VARIANT BY ADI GRANOV

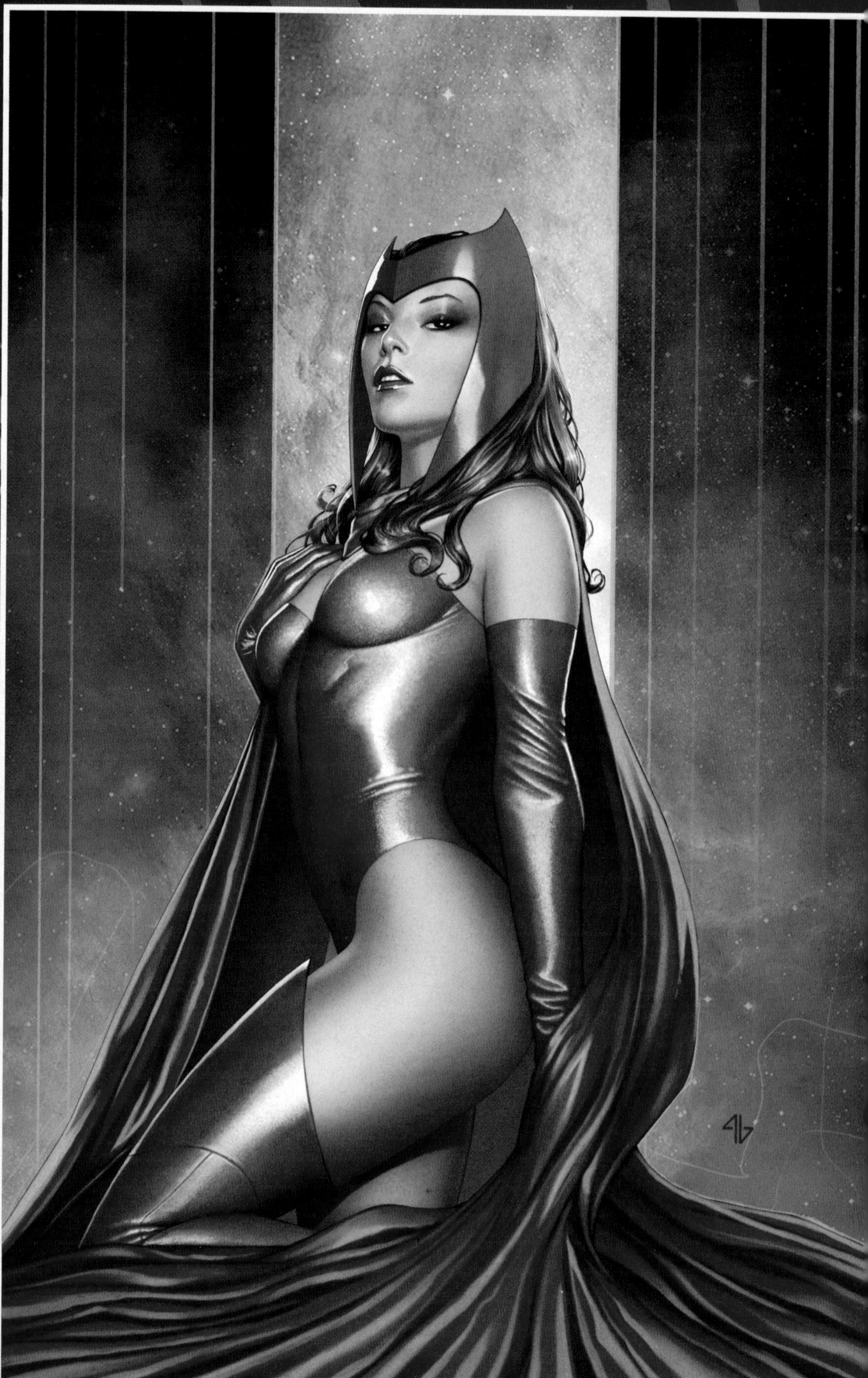

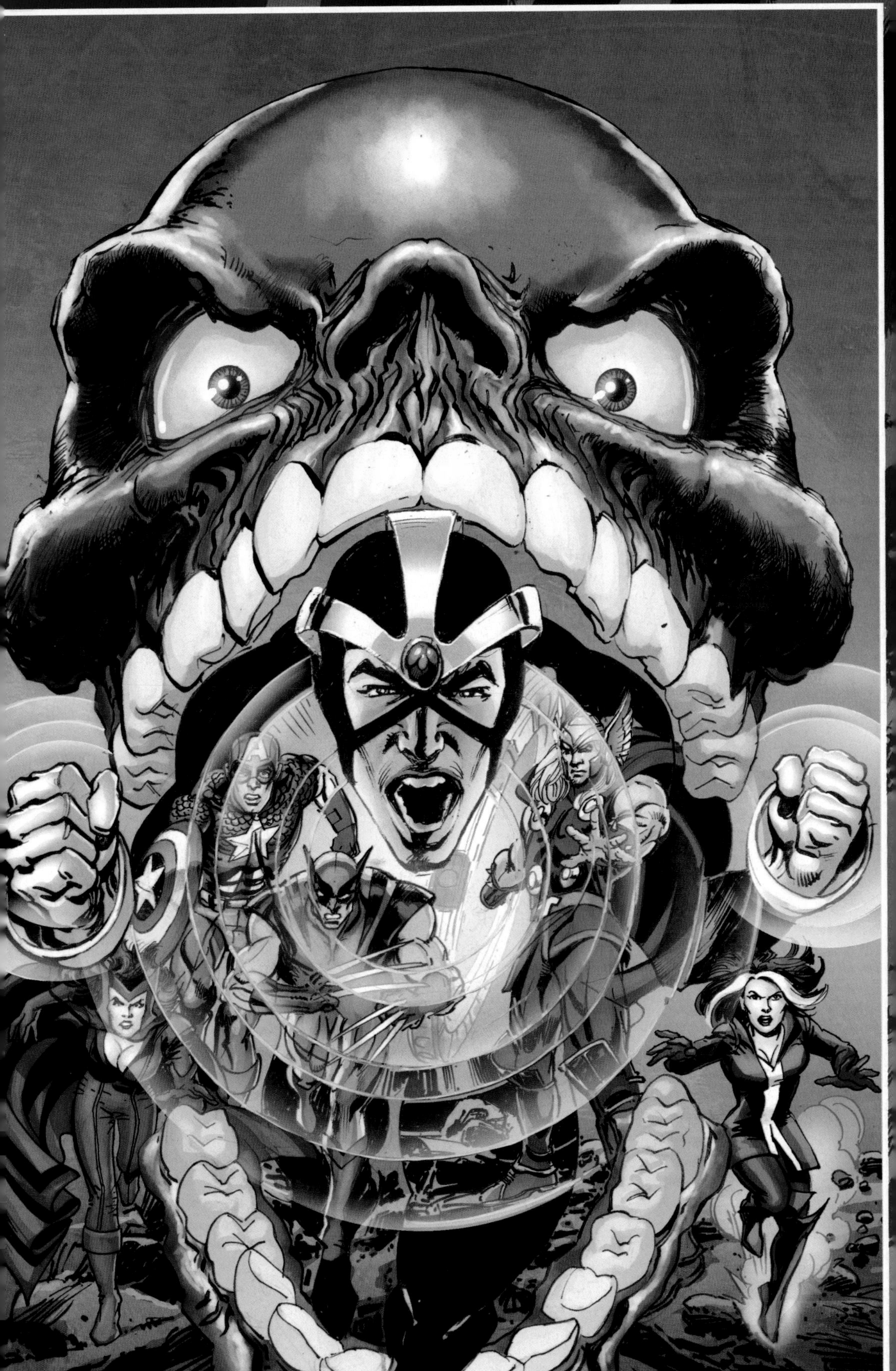

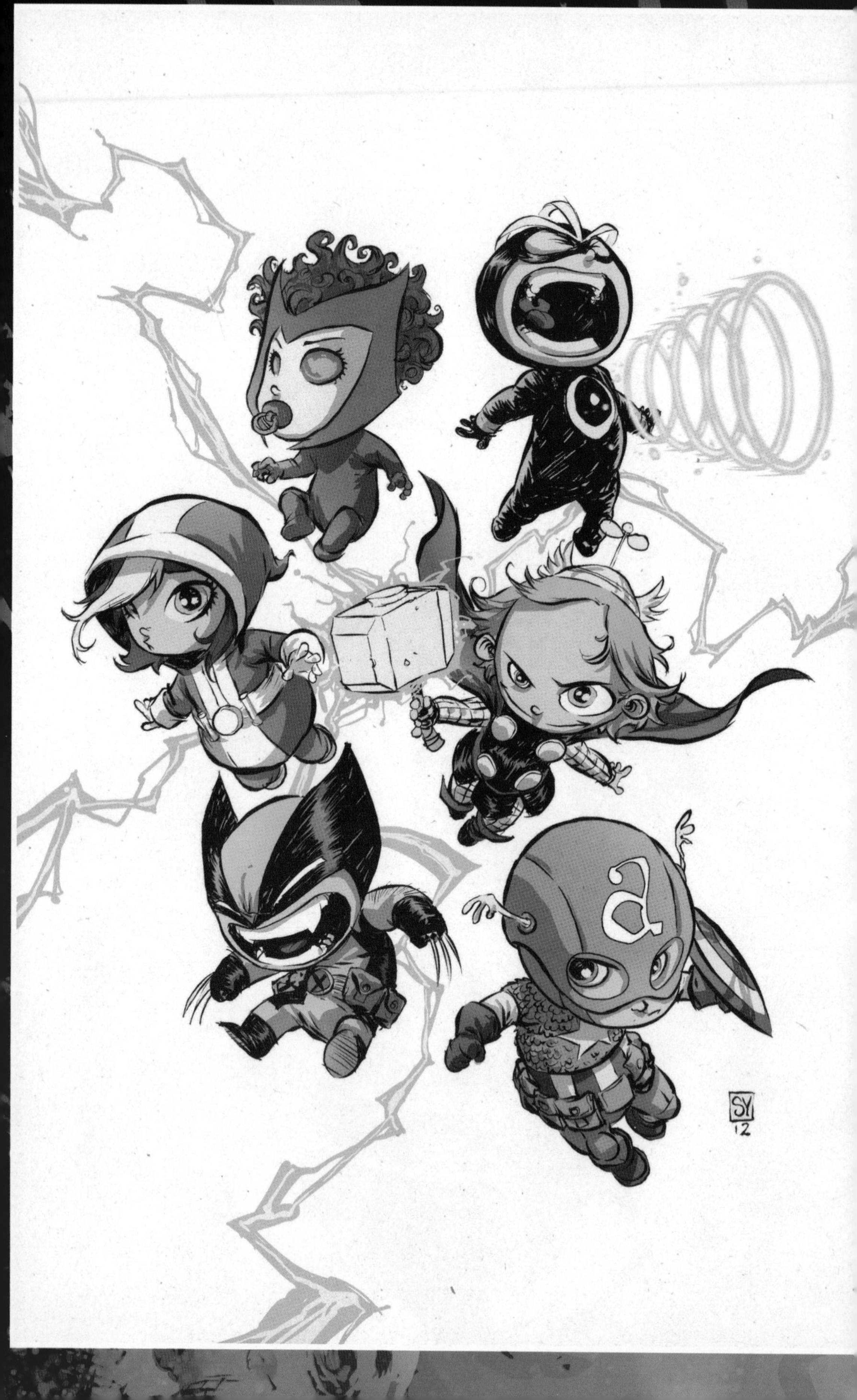
SY
'12

UNCANNY AVENGERS #1 DEADPOOL "CALL ME MAYBE" VARIANT BY MARK BROOKS

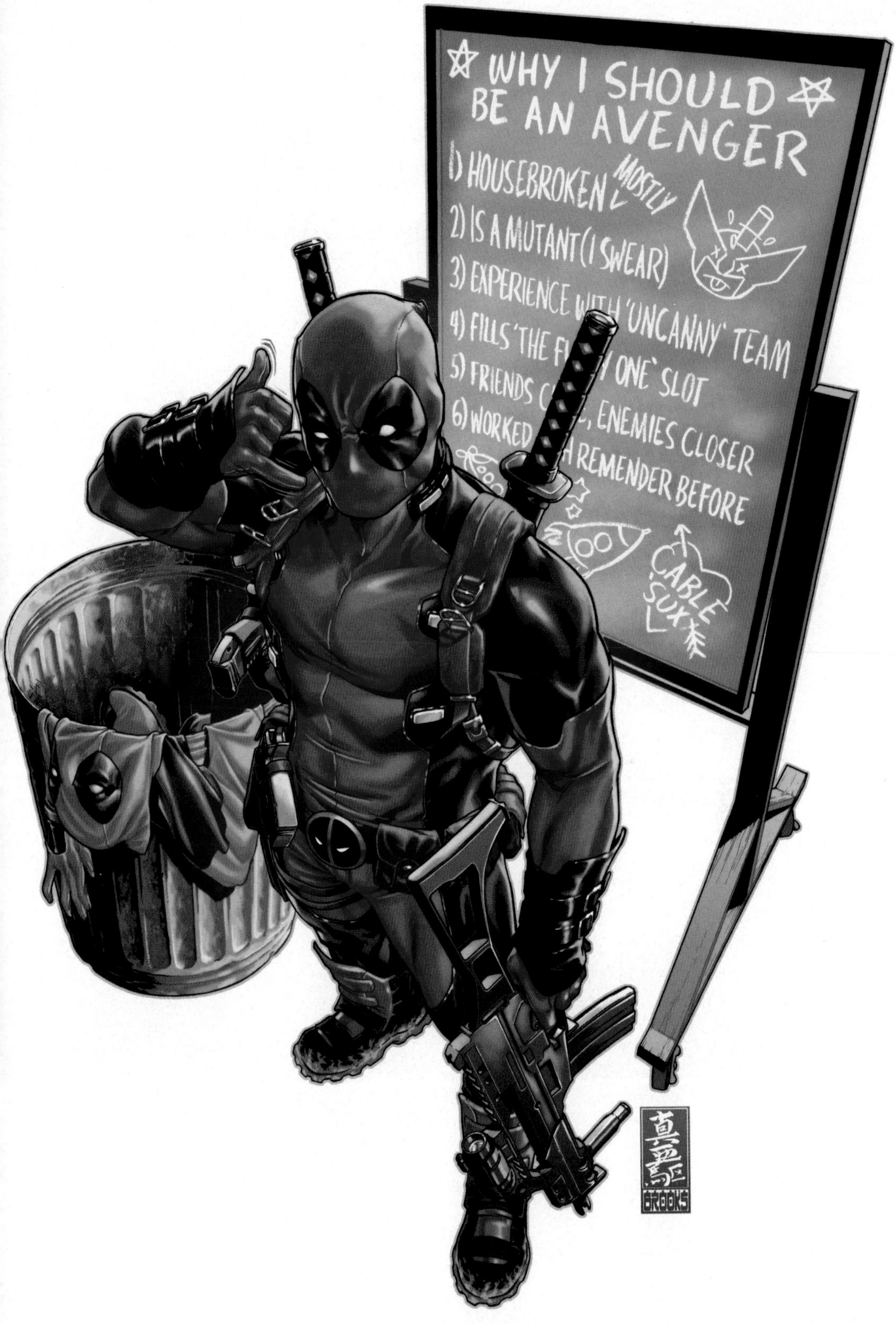
WHY I SHOULD BE AN AVENGER
1) HOUSEBROKEN ✓ MOSTLY
2) IS A MUTANT (I SWEAR)
3) EXPERIENCE WITH 'UNCANNY' TEAM
4) FILLS 'THE F ONE' SLOT
5) FRIENDS C , ENEMIES CLOSER
6) WORKED H REMENDER BEFORE
CABLE SUX
BROOKS

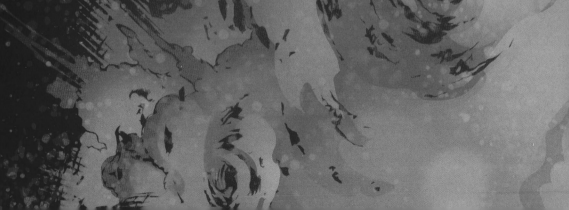

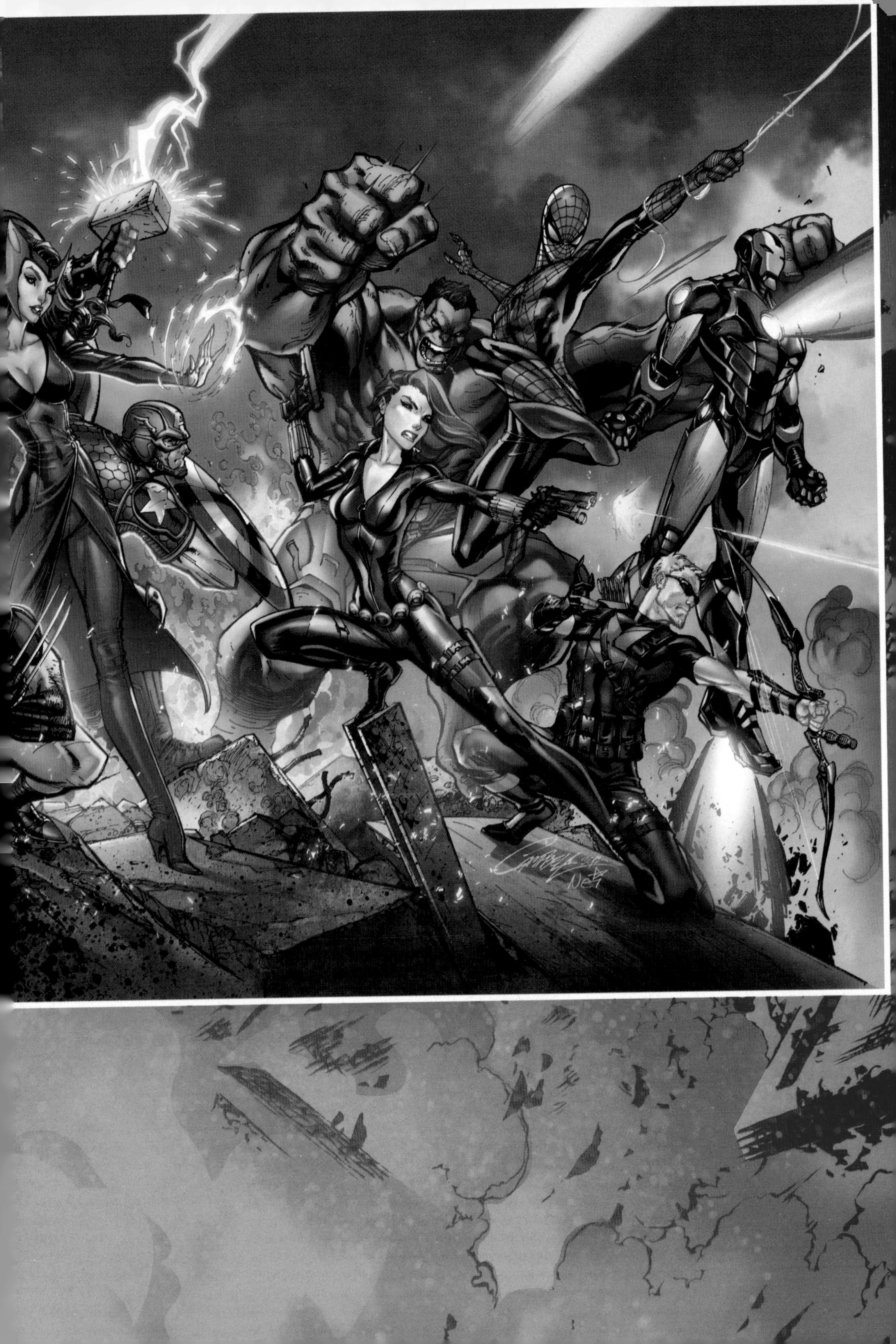

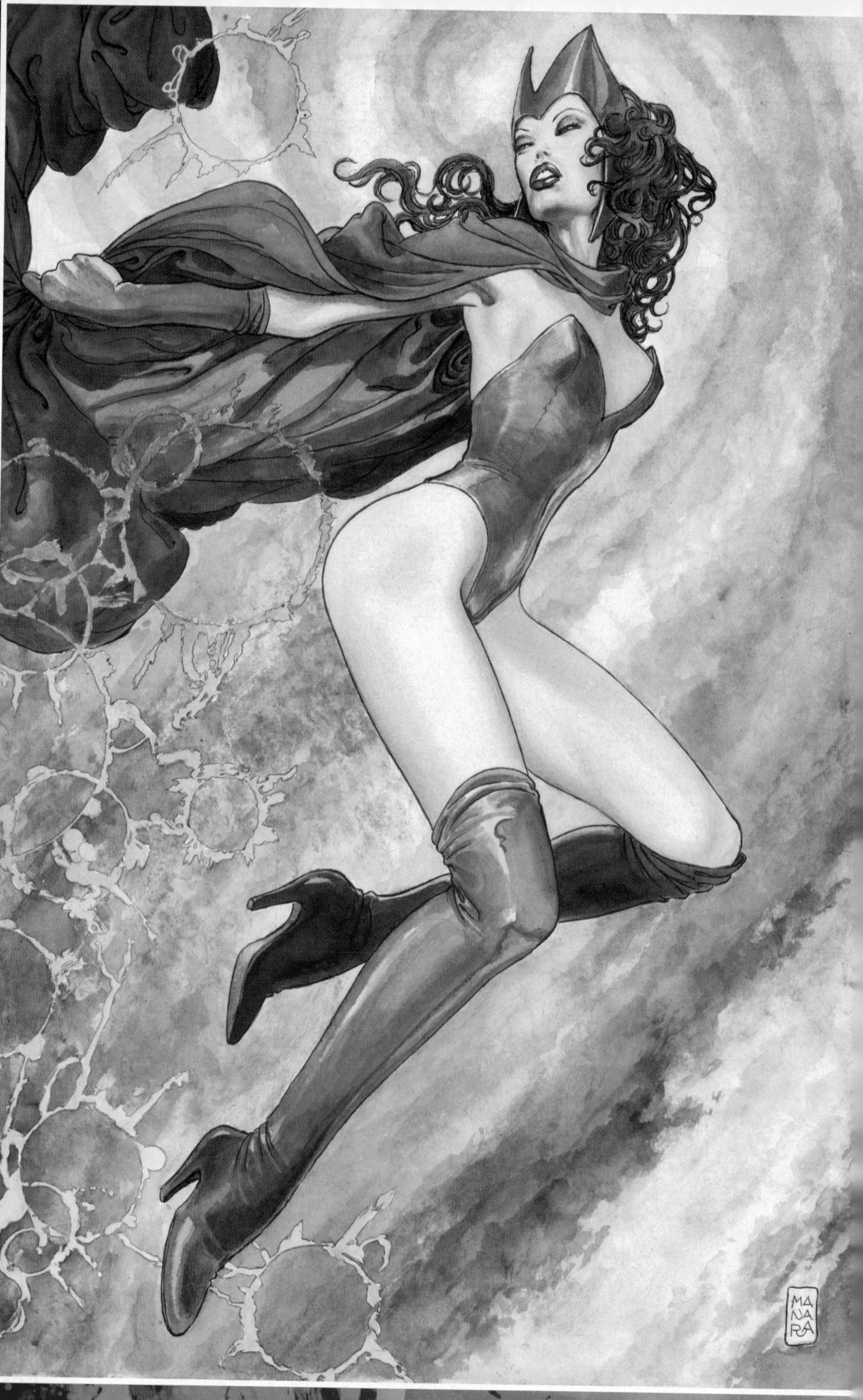
MA
NA
RA

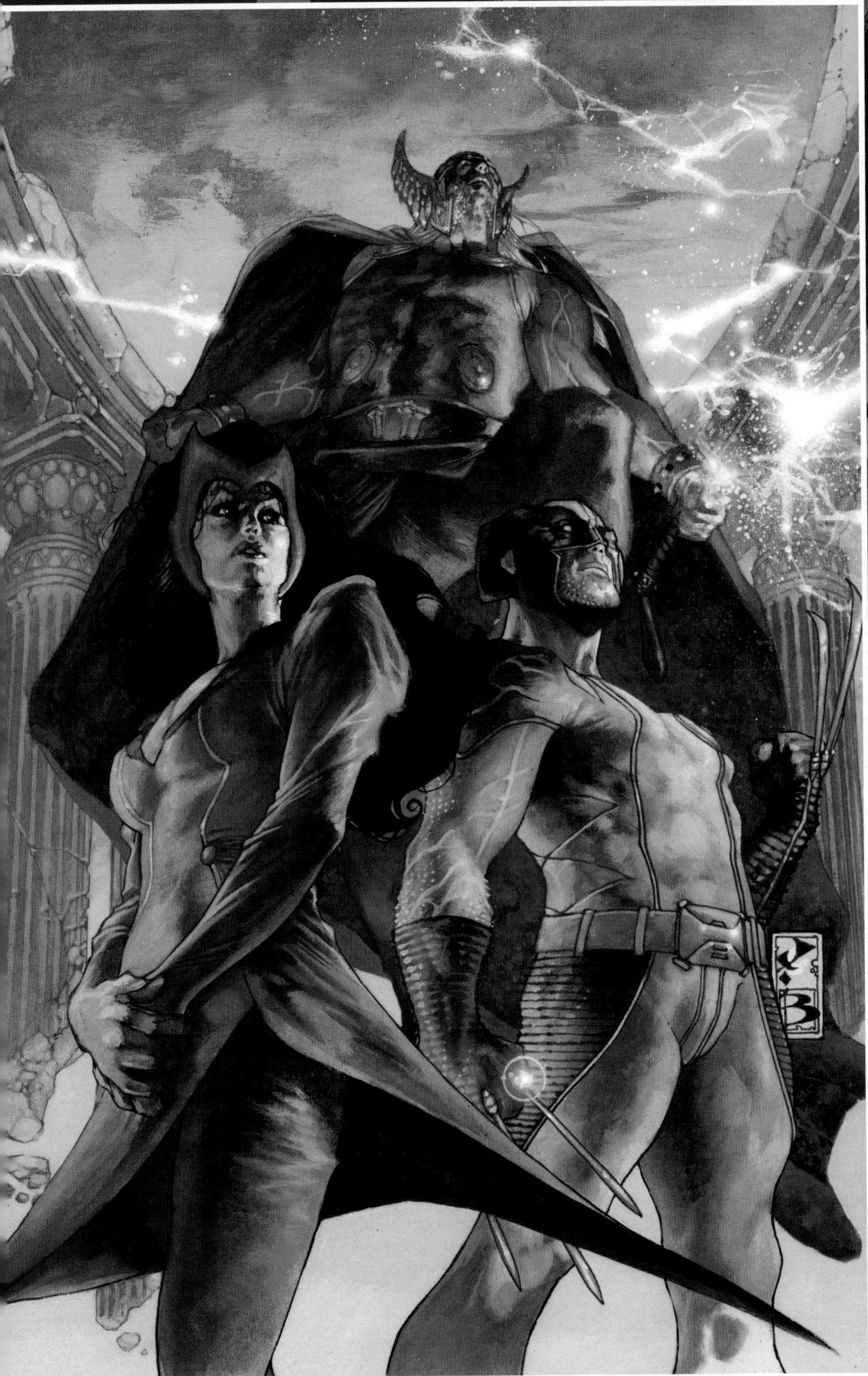

UNCANNY AVENGERS #4 VARIANT BY JOHN CASSADAY & LAURA MARTIN

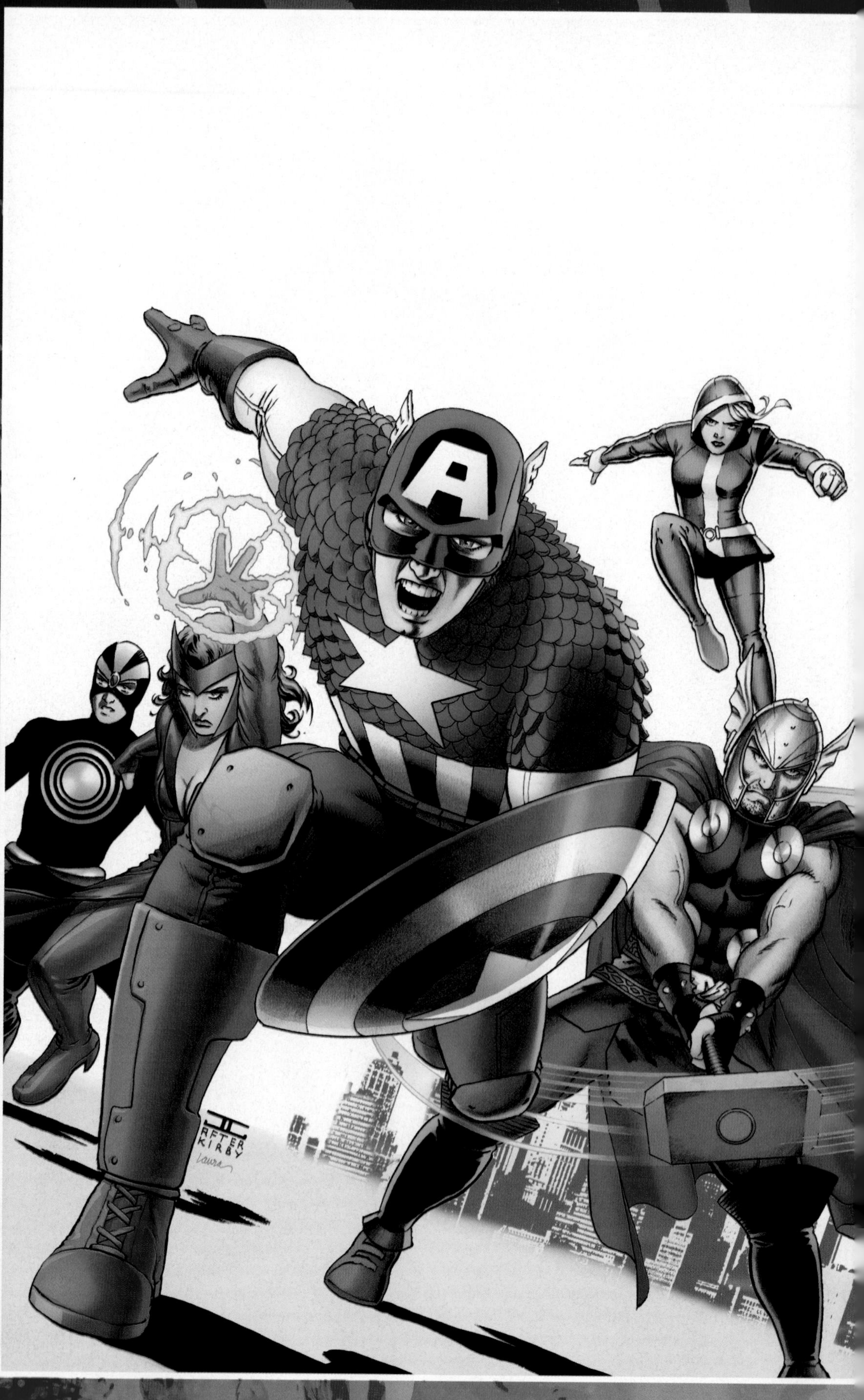
AFTER KIRBY
Laura

UNCANNY AVENGERS #5 VARIANT BY OLIVIER COIPEL & LAURA MARTIN

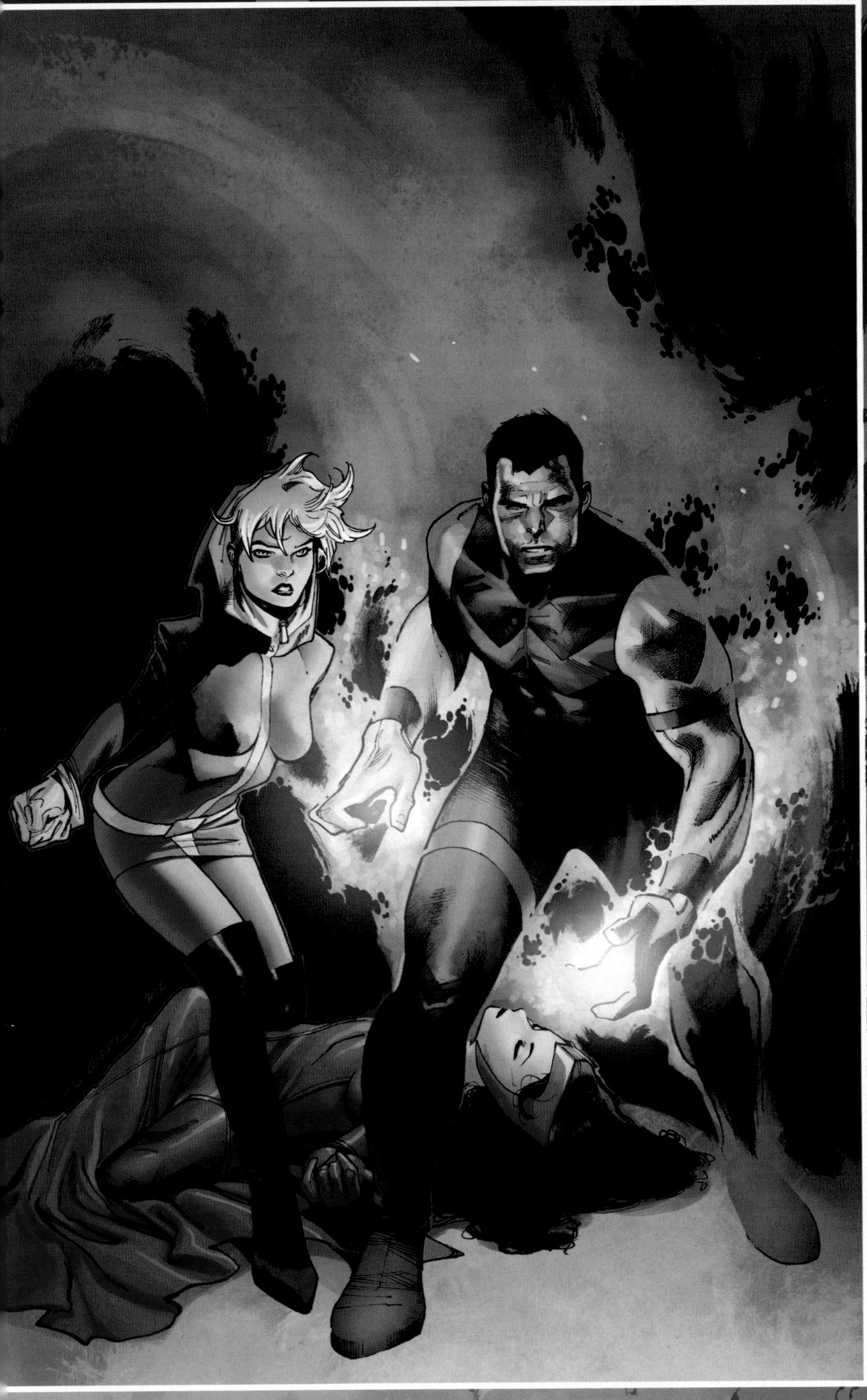

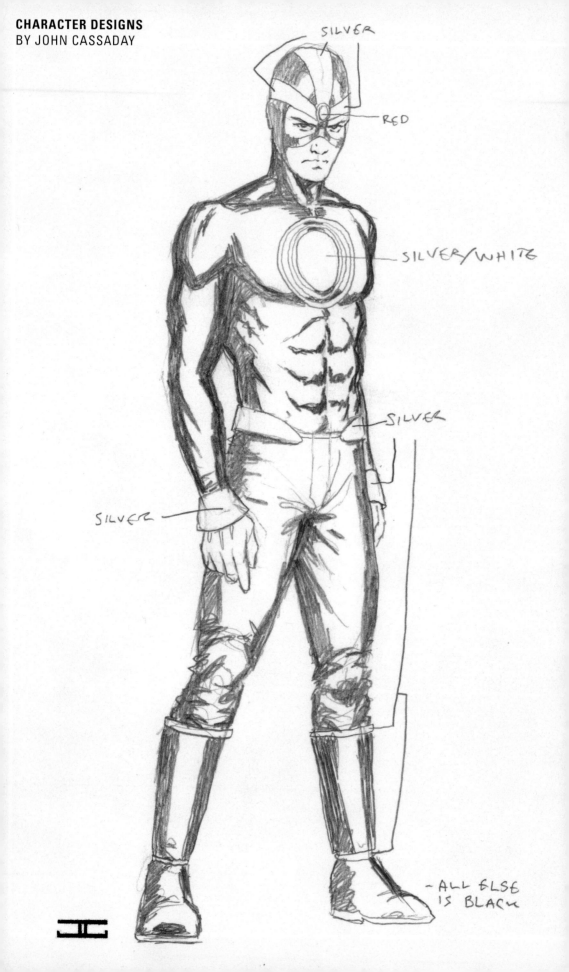

CHARACTER DESIGNS
BY JOHN CASSADAY

SILVER

RED

SILVER/WHITE

SILVER

SILVER

-ALL ELSE
IS BLACK

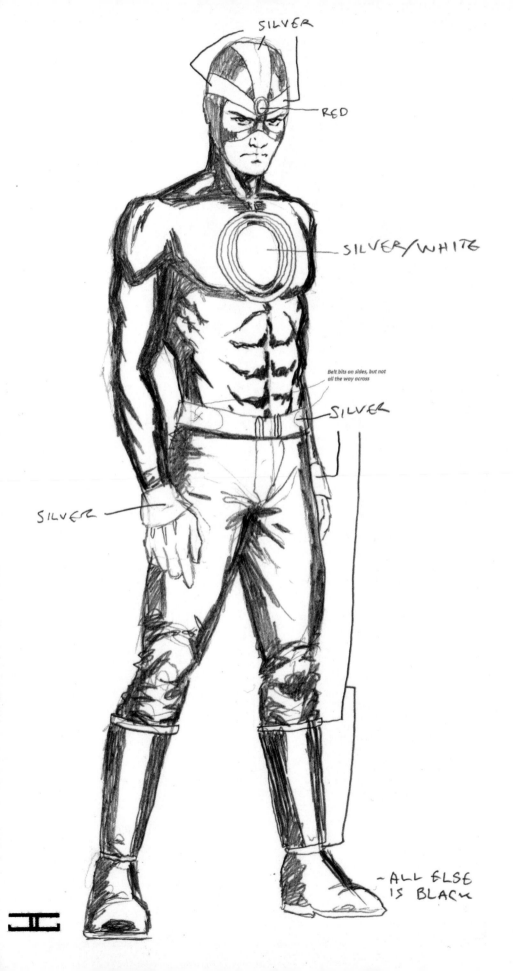

SILVER

RED

SILVER/WHITE

Belt bits on sides, but not
all the way across

SILVER

SILVER

~ALL ELSE
IS BLACK

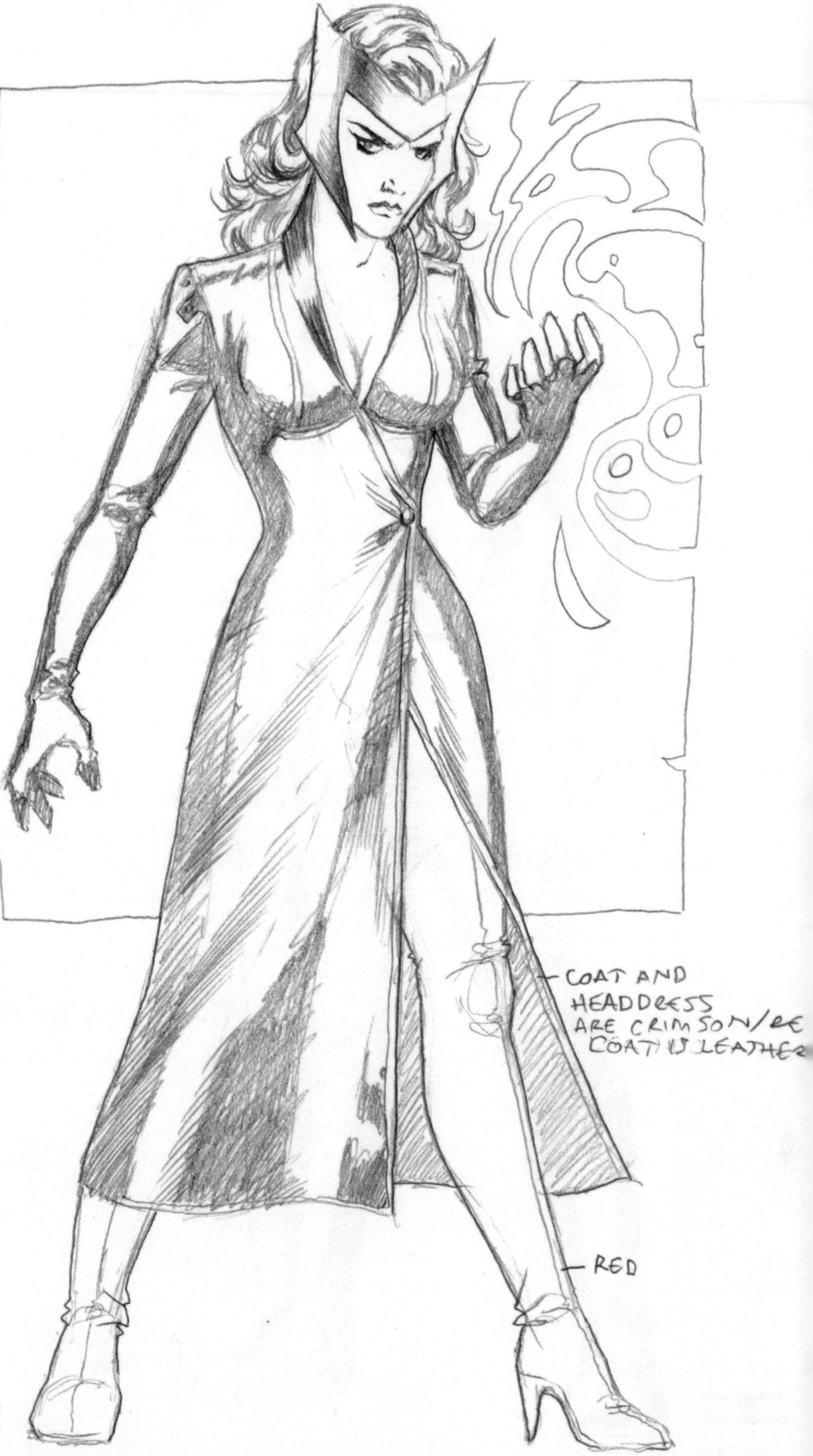
COAT AND
HEADDRESS
ARE CRIMSON/RE
COAT IS LEATHER
RED

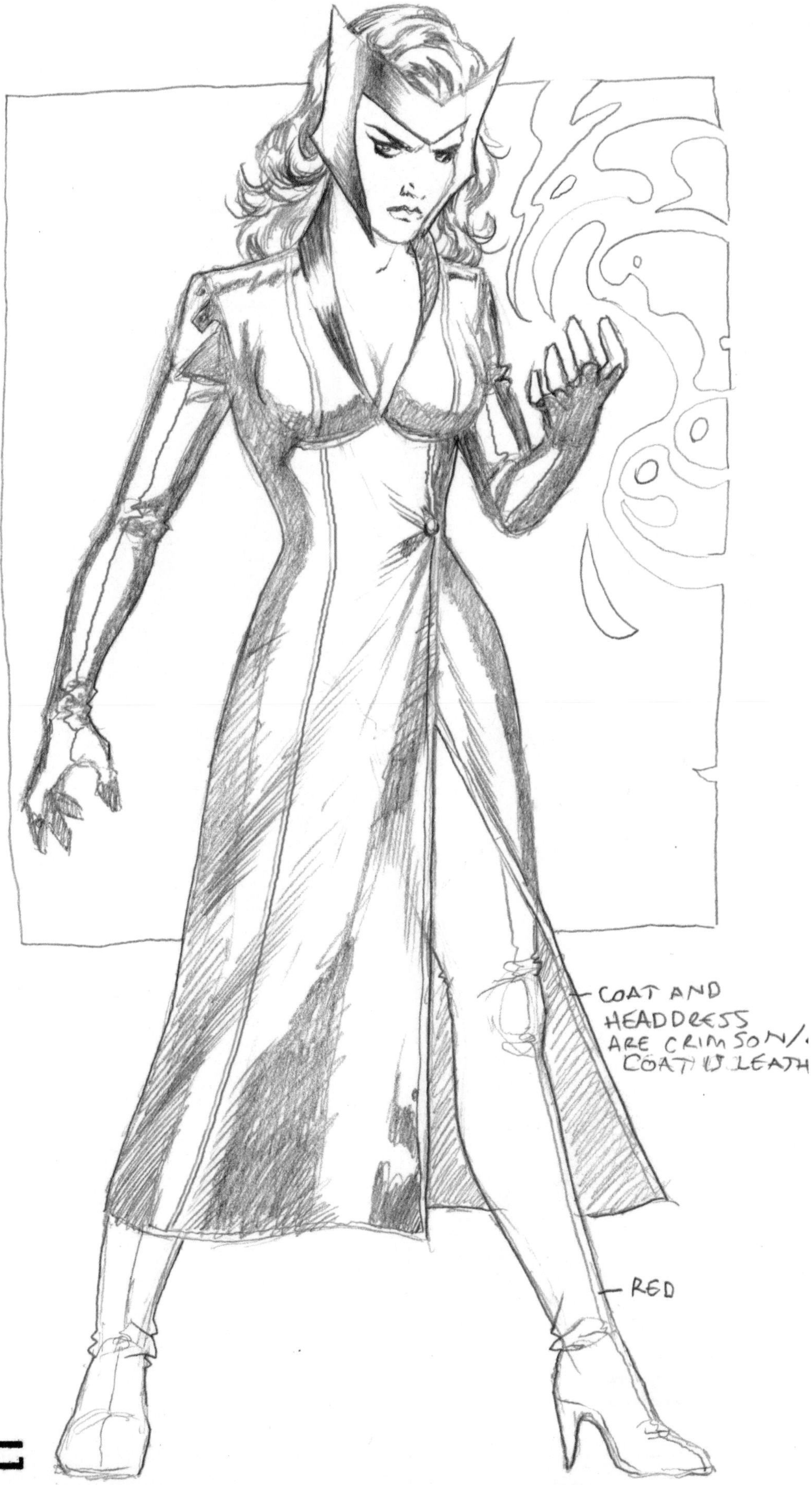
COAT AND
HEADDRESS
ARE CRIMSON/.
COAT IS LEATH
RED

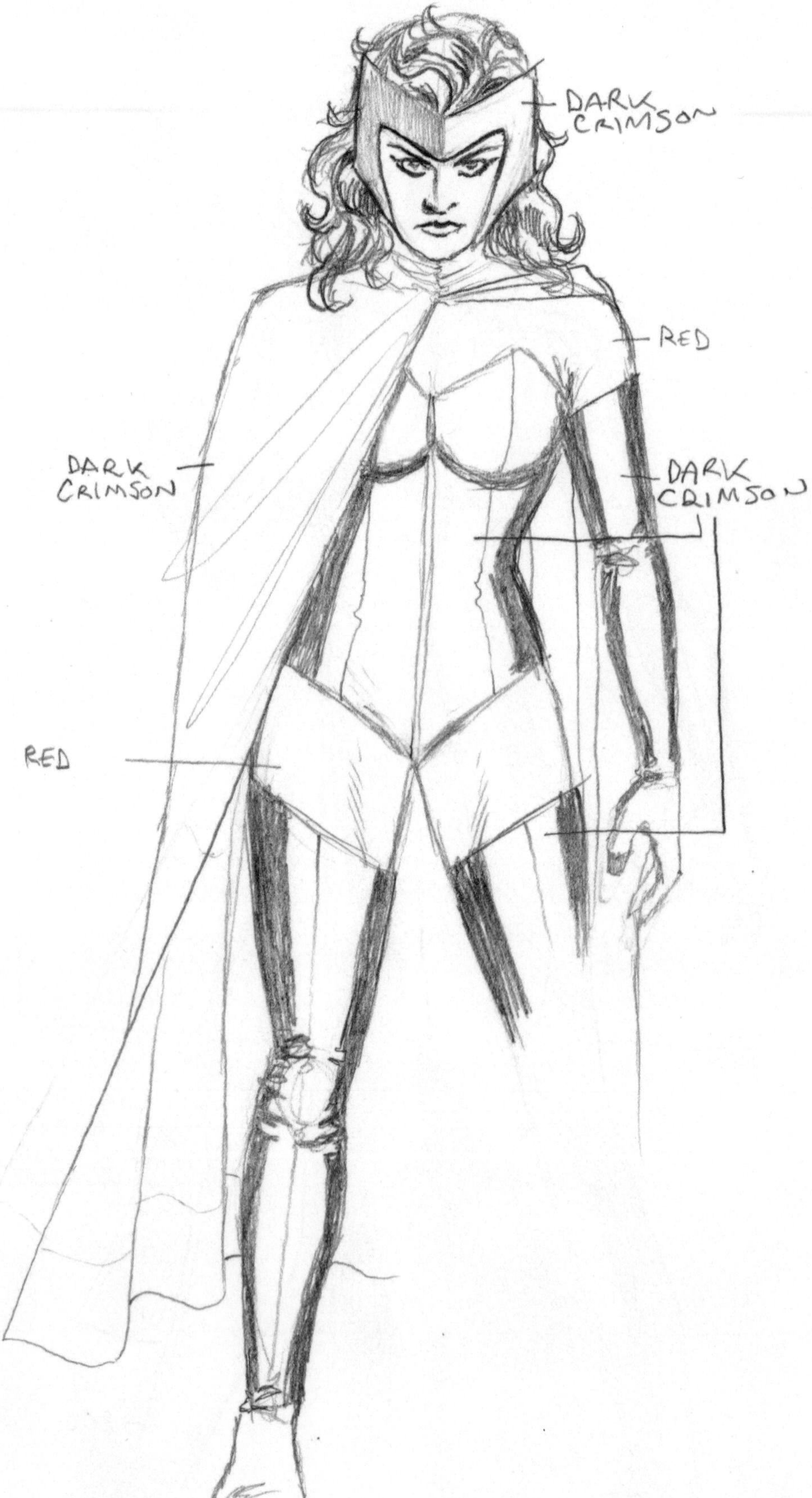
DARK CRIMSON
RED
DARK CRIMSON
DARK CRIMSON
RED

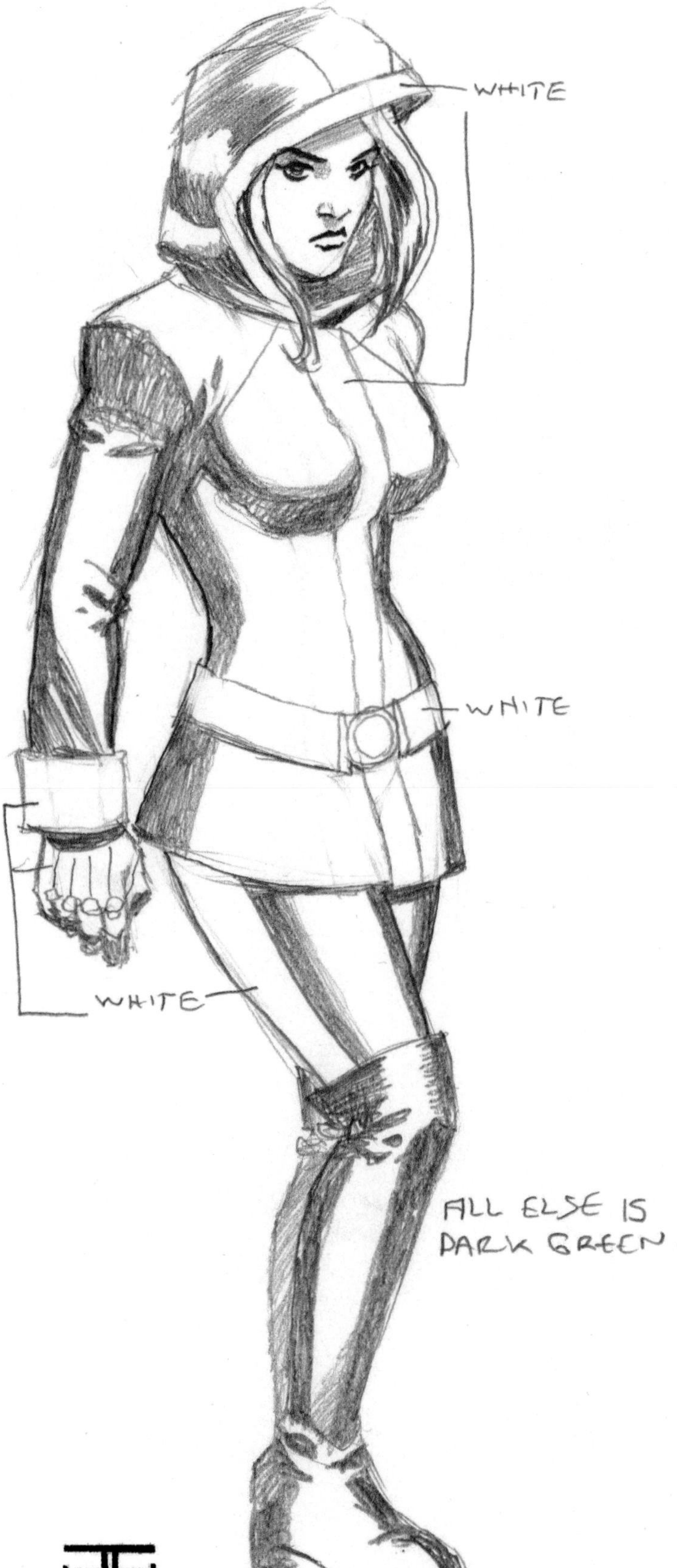
WHITE
WHITE
WHITE
ALL ELSE IS
DARK GREEN.

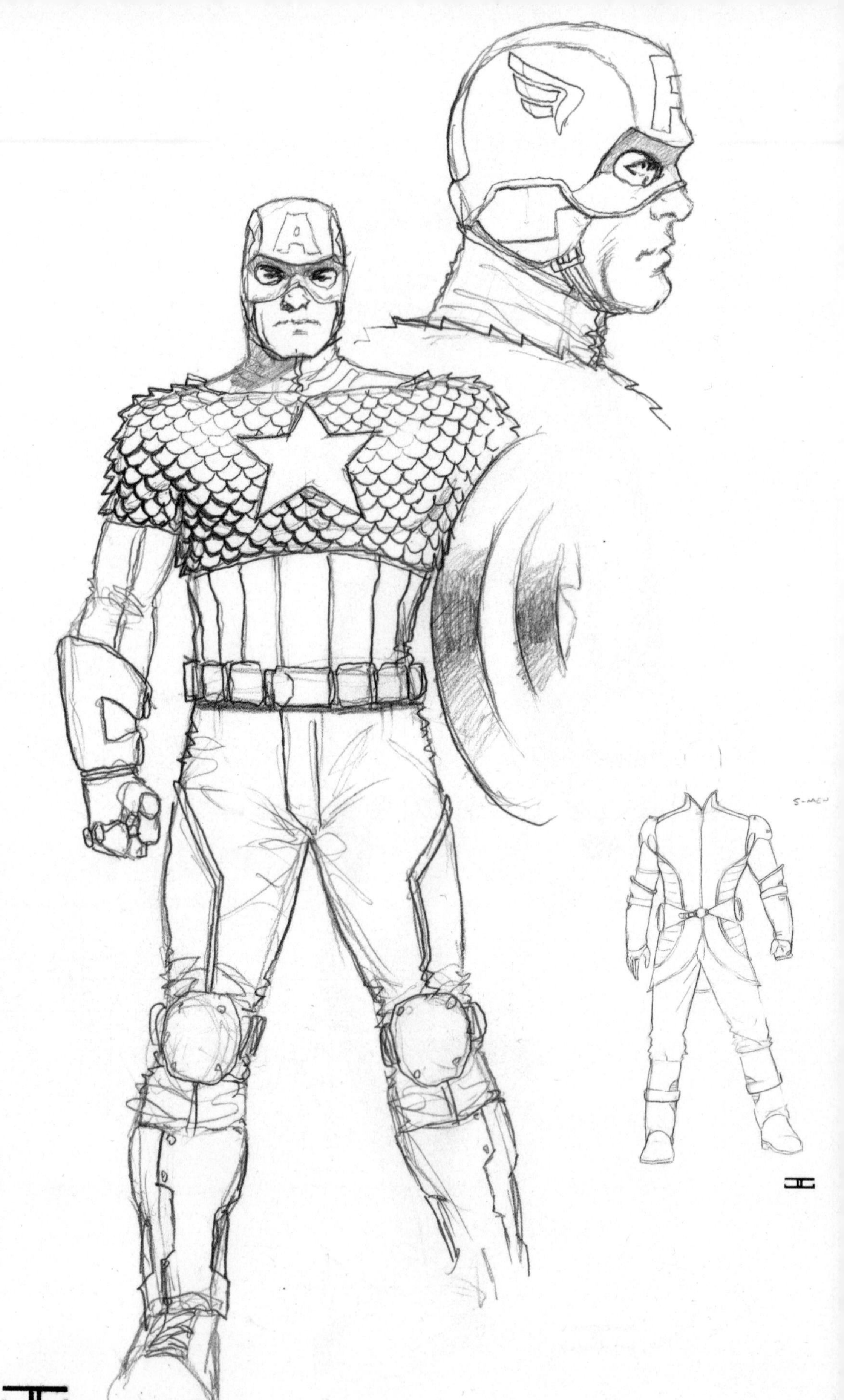
S-MEN

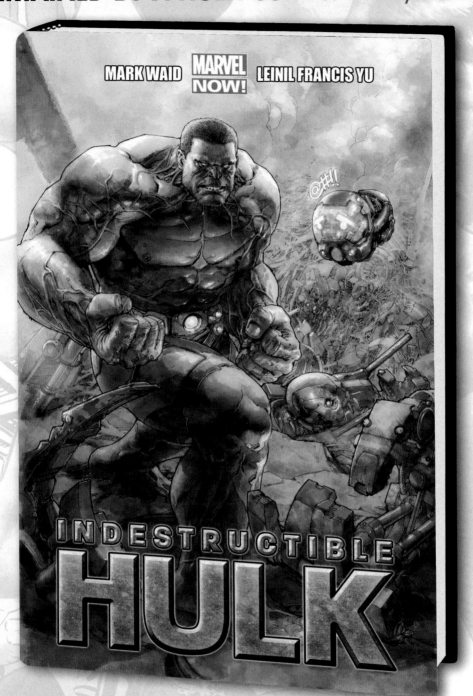

TO ACCESS THE FREE *MARVEL AUGMENTED REALITY APP* THAT ENHANCES AND CHANGES THE WAY YOU EXPERIENCE COMIC

1. Download the app for free via marvel.com/ARapp
2. Launch the app on your camera-enabled Apple iOS® or Android™ device*
3. Hold your mobile device's camera ov any cover or panel with the **AR** grap
4. Sit back and see the future of comics in action!

*Available on most camera-enabled Apple iOS® and Android™ devices. Content subject to change and availability.

UNCANNY AVENGERS AR INDEX